By most estimates, the average software engineering organization spends 60 to 70 percent of its overall resources correcting, adapting, enhancing, and reengineering existing programs—an activity that we call "software maintenance." Yet this extremely important subject receives relatively little attention in the technical literature.

With Practical Software Maintenance, *Thomas Pigoski has written one of the most detailed treatments of software maintenance currently in print. Unlike earlier authors who have addressed the subject, Pigoski considers software maintenance within the context of modern software process models. He exhibits a concern for disciplined software engineering—a prerequisite for effective software maintenance.*

This book is a worthwhile addition to the library of any software professional who works on the maintenance of existing computer programs—and that means most of us!

> —Roger S. Pressman, Ph.D.
> R.S. Pressman & Associates

. . . forceful, practical, direct and informative . . . unconventional wisdom on an activity that is vital to every organization that uses software.

> —Nicholas Zvegintzov
> President, Software Management Network
> Author of Software Management Technology Reference
> Guide and co-author of Tutorial on Software Maintenance

This book has a very comprehensive coverage of cases and real-world software maintenance experiences.

> —Dr. Norman F. Schneidewind
> Computer Research

Practical Software Maintenance

Best Practices for Managing Your Software Investment

Thomas M. Pigoski

WILEY COMPUTER PUBLISHING

John Wiley & Sons, Inc.
New York • Chichester • Brisbane
• Toronto • Singapore • Weinheim

To Joanne
my friend, my lover, my wife

Publisher: Katherine Schowalter
Senior Editor: Marjorie Spencer
Managing Editor: Angela Murphy
Text Design & Composition: Publishers' Design and Production Services, Inc.

Library of Congress Cataloging-in-Publication Data:

Pigoski, Thomas M.
    Practical software maintenance : best practices for managing your software investment / Thomas M. Pigoski.
        p.   cm.
    Includes bibliographical references.
    ISBN 0-471-17001-1 (cloth : alk. paper)
    1. Software maintenance.   I. Title.
QA76.76.S64P54   1996
005.1'6—dc20   96-25884

Printed in the United States of America
10 9 8 7 6 5 4 3 2 1

Preface

Software maintenance has been part of my life for over twenty years. I came up through the ranks and performed all the maintenance functions for large military software systems. I was fortunate enough to plan, establish, and direct a U.S. Navy software maintenance organization, participate at international conferences on software maintenance, be part of international standards efforts, and establish a company to provide maintenance services. Over the years I learned many valuable lessons as a software maintenance practitioner.

At the behest of the organizers of the IEEE Computer Society's *International Conference on Software Maintenance* (ICSM), I started delivering speeches and writing papers for ICSM. Later I began presenting workshops, seminars, and tutorials in which I discussed what I had learned over the years in software maintenance. Finally, after constant prodding by my peers to document the things that I had learned as a maintenance practitioner, I decided to document those practical experiences in a book.

My goals in writing the book are to share those practical experiences and help those performing the majority of the work in the software field today. I hope that this book assists software maintenance practitioners in their efforts and in some small way improves the overall posture of maintenance.

Acknowledgments

This book is dedicated to my wife Joanne for her constant and unfailing support of all my dreams and efforts.

Special thanks and appreciation are due my TECHSOFT colleagues, who all assisted in some manner. Christine Englert, who served as the editor for the book, deserves special recognition. She worked tirelessly on the manuscript, set up deadlines, and kept me on schedule. Without her assistance, the book would never have been finished. Thanks to Lew Schuchardt for all his administrative and research efforts. Robby O'Berry did a fantastic job of putting my thoughts into graphic form. Dave Gill provided needed critical reviews of the manuscript.

Thanks to Edd Burns for his contributions on the maintenance process and object-oriented technology. Thanks also to Frank Henry, Lynda King, Lauren Nelson, and Spike Henning for their assistance. A special thanks also to Dan Shanholtz and Mike Werner for taking care of business while I was writing.

About the Author

Thomas M. Pigoski is the President of Technical Software Services (TECHSOFT), Inc., located in Pensacola, Florida. TECHSOFT specializes in software maintenance. Mr. Pigoski started his career in software maintenance in 1969 with the U.S. Navy, and since that time has worked in every aspect of the maintenance field. He has served in positions from maintenance programmer to chief executive of a software maintenance organization that had worldwide maintenance responsibilities. He also planned and helped establish that organization.

Mr. Pigoski is an internationally recognized authority in the field of software maintenance. He was the General Chair of the IEEE Computer Society's *International Conference on Software Maintenance (ICSM)—1990* and currently serves as the General Chair of the Steering Committee for ICSM. He received the Software Maintenance Association's "1990 Newsmaker of the Year" award for his contributions to the field of maintenance. He is currently the project editor for the proposed ISO/IEC international standard for software maintenance.

Mr. Pigoski is a consultant on software maintenance, a speaker, a seminar leader, and an author. He is the author of numerous articles on maintenance. His practical efforts in the field of maintenance were chronicled in a 17-part series published by *Software Maintenance News*. His first book, *Life Cycle Strategy: Software Support on the Front Line* (Software Maintenance News 1995) described the transition of a strategic military software portfolio into a lean, mean, downsized, highly professional operation. His seminar on maintenance, *Practical Software Maintenance*, is routinely presented to the international software community.

Contents

1   Introduction   **1**

Experiment, Document, Tune and Retune   1

Software Practitioners, Developers, and Program
Managers   2

Students and Instructors   2

When Maintenance Starts   3

A Few Words About Words   3

Overview of the Book   4

Summary   5

2   Overview of Software Maintenance   **7**

Why Is There Confusion about Software Maintenance?   7

What Is Software Maintenance?   8

Why Is Maintenance Necessary?   12

Why Is Maintenance Hard?   19

Who Should Do Maintenance?   20

Summary   27

3	**Why Maintenance Is Expensive**	**29**
	Billions Spent Annually on Maintenance	29
	Maintenance Practitioners Are Paid Too Much!	31
	Where 80% of the Maintenance Dollar Goes	32
	Factors Influencing Maintenance Costs	35
	No Money for Maintenance	36
	Summary	36
4	**Evolution of Software Processes and Models**	**37**
	What Is the History of the Development Process?	37
	What Is the History of the Maintenance Process?	39
	Maintenance Begins When Development Begins	46
	What Is the ISO/IEC Model?	47
	Summary	50
5	**A Recommended Software Maintenance Process**	**51**
	The ISO/IEC 12207 Maintenance Process	53
	Process Implementation Activity	55
	Details of the ISO/IEC 12207 Maintenance Process	53
	Summary	80
6	**Pre-Delivery Software Maintenance Activities**	**81**
	What the Experts Say	82
	The Conflict	82
	How to Resolve the Conflict	84
	The Maintainer Must Influence the Logistics Organization	84
	Maintenance Begins with the Logistics Organization	85
	The Three Areas of Pre-Delivery Maintenance	86
	Summary	87
7	**Planning, Parts I & II: The Maintenance Concept and the Maintenance Plan**	**89**
	What Is Maintenance Planning?	89
	What Is the Maintenance Concept?	90
	What Is the Maintenance Plan?	96
	Summary	99

8   Planning, Part III: Resources   **101**

How Do You Determine Personnel Resources?   101

Two Approaches to Determining Personnel Resources   103

A Specific Personnel Resource Problem: A Case Study   106

The Lessons Learned from Estimating Personnel Resources   112

How Do You Determine Maintenance Environment
Resources?   113

How Do You Determine Financial Resources?   115

Summary   116

9   Transition   **117**

What Is Transition Planning?   118

What Is a Transition Plan?   123

The Lessons Learned from Transition Experiences   131

Transition Model and Process   135

Summary   138

10   Transition Experiences, Part I   **139**

When Maintainers Become "Comfortable"
with the System: A Case Study   139

Transition Training: A Case Study   146

The Lessons Learned from these Case Studies   153

Summary   155

11   Transition Experiences, Part II   **157**

How to Transition Systems: A Case Study   157

The Lessons Learned about Transition   162

Summary   162

12   Setting Up the Software Maintenance Organization   **165**

What Are the Roles and Responsibilities of Maintainers?   165

What Are the Functions of a Maintainer?   166

How Should a Maintenance Organization Be Organized?   176

How Should Personnel Resources Be Distributed?   182

A Sample Software Maintenance Charter   184

Summary   188

13   Tools and Environment   **189**

What Is CASE?   189

What Is ICASE?   190

What Is an Environment?   190

What Are Distributed Computing Environments?   198

Where Can You Get More Information?   200

How to Create an ICASE Environment: A Case Study   200

What Is the Outcome and What Are the Lessons Learned?   212

Summary   214

14   Software Maintenance Metrics   **215**

What Is a Software Metric?   215

Who Does Metrics Well?   217

Why Do You Want a Metrics Program?   217

How Do You Implement a Metrics Program?   218

How Does the Typical Practitioner Approach Metrics?   222

What Does the Software Engineering Institute (SEI)
Suggest?   223

A Set of Maintenance Metrics   228

What Are the Lessons Learned from Practitioners?   230

What Are Some Metrics Resources?   231

Summary   235

15   Software Maintenance Metrics Experiences   **237**

Evolution of a Metrics Program: A Case Study   237

Establishing the Initial Metrics Program   240

The Lessons Learned from the Initial Metrics Program   244

The Second Stage of the Metrics Program   246

Evolution of the Metrics Program   247

The Lessons Learned   249

Analysis of Software Maintenance Metrics: A Case Study   252

Insights and the Lessons Learned   268

Summary   270

16   Maintainability   **271**

What Is the Cost of Maintenance?   271

What Is Software Maintainability?   273

Are All Systems Equally Maintainable?   274

How Does a Maintainer Determine Maintainability?   274

Is Maintainability Possible?   275

Who Is Addressing Maintainability?   277

What Are Some Recommended Practices?   290

Summary   290

17   Software Maintenance Management   **293**

Who Are the Software Maintenance Professionals?   293

What Do You Think Are the Major Problems
in Maintenance?   294

What Are the Top Maintenance Problems?   294

Summary   304

18   Education and Training   **305**

Where Do Maintainers Traditionally Get Educated?   306

How Does Industry Train Its Software Professionals?   307

Who Is Teaching the Software Professionals?   307

How Do You Solve the Lack of Software Maintenance
Education Problem?   309

How Do You Start Training?   319

Summary   322

**19   Impact of Object Oriented Technology on Software
Maintenance**   **323**

What Are Some OOT Terms?   323

Why OOT Is Different   325

Why OOT is Being Used   331

What Maintenance Practitioners Are Saying   333

OO Maintainability   334

Related OO Issues   335

Metrics   336
Lessons Learned   338
Summary   339

20   Software Maintenance Resources   341
What Resources Are Available?   341
What Are Some Helpful Organizations?   341
What Are Some Conferences and Workshops?   342
What Periodicals Are Available?   342
What Are Some Internet Resources?   343
What Is the Latest Research Available?   343
Summary   345

21   The Future of Software Maintenance   347
Will Object-Oriented Technology (OOT) Stay?   347
What Will the Future Environments for Maintenance Be?   348
What Will Happen with Process Automation?   348
What Will the Software Development Methodologies Be?   348
What Will Happen with Commercial-off-the-Shelf (COTS)
Products?   349
What Will the Impact on Remote Software
Maintenance Be?   349
What Will Maintenance People Do?   350
What Will Happen to Outsourcing?   350
What Will Occur With Standards?   350
Summary   350

Glossary   351

Bibliography   359

Index   371

Introduction

The purpose of this book is to share practical, real-world software maintenance experiences with maintenance professionals (or those who need to know what is important in the field of maintenance). It gets to the heart of the matter and tells practitioners, program managers, and developers what is and is not important regarding life-cycle maintenance needs. This book fills the void between theory and practice, provides valuable lessons, and offers suggestions on how to improve the state of software maintenance.

EXPERIMENT, DOCUMENT, TUNE, AND RETUNE

In sharing my experiences, I will share what works—and what does not work. I was given the opportunity to establish a software maintenance organization from the planning stage to full operations (Pigoski 1995). With the help of numerous military software professionals, we were able to create and operate a cost-effective software maintenance operation. Granted autonomy by the headquarters of the project, together we were able to experiment, document, tune, retune, and learn along the way. We certainly did not do everything right the first time, but we started with nothing and attempted to improve continuously. Measurement data supported all our evaluation checkpoints. We had process improvement before it became the "in" thing—and we used it!

Since that time, my involvement with conferences on software maintenance, international standards work, teaching, and consulting all have provided additional practical experiences.

The lessons learned over many years are documented here, and are augmented by the best practices gained from the international software maintenance community. Hopefully, sharing these ideas and practices will help everyone save time and money. Budgets are decreasing, and the software maintenance practitioners need any edge they can get in these times of "rightsizing."

SOFTWARE PRACTITIONERS, DEVELOPERS, AND PROGRAM MANGERS

This book is written for anyone who is affected by software maintenance, including those folks in the trenches doing the unglamorous and sometimes unrewarding work of fixing bugs. It is written for those people dealing with increasing backlogs of maintenance requests and decreasing resources, as well as for those who are concerned about the escalating costs of maintenance—upper management, senior software managers, system engineers, and most importantly, program managers who are developing large software systems. People functioning in all areas of maintenance—managers, designers, programmers, testers, developers, technical writers, configuration managers, quality assur-

ance personnel, and students—all will find things of interest. This book also will aid practitioners and teachers in getting new students and employees onboard to the concepts and practical aspects of maintenance. There is no theory here—no mathematical formulas, no differential equations, no matrices—just down-to-earth, practical things that are easily understandable.

STUDENTS AND INSTRUCTORS

As there is not a current book with which to teach maintenance, this book can and should be used to teach maintenance either at the university or corporate level. It is not designed as a traditional textbook, but it can serve that function. Each chapter includes a summary and a set of review questions that follow the summary.

WHEN MAINTENANCE STARTS

This book's approach to maintenance is in stark contrast to what most of the literature tells us about maintenance and how it should be performed. Historically, maintenance starts when someone issues a Problem Report or Modification Request. Based on years of performing maintenance, this is not the proper approach, and I believe there is a better way. *Maintenance should begin coincident with the decision to develop a new system.*

Maintenance organizations can only be successful if they are involved totally throughout the development. Maintenance participation and budgeting should literally start with the agreement that a new system will be developed. Certainly, this participation should be well before the signing of any development contract, and before the initiation of any development effort. This approach is consistent with and extends Lehman's (1980) idea that maintenance is really evolutionary developments. The concept of maintenance put forth in this book starts maintenance very early in the life cycle, and the book provides rationale and case studies to document why starting maintenance early is necessary. If you are wondering what a maintenance organization will do during the development, keep reading; I'll tell you in Chapters 6 through 11.

Maintenance organizations must actively participate in the development phase of the software life cycle.

A FEW WORDS ABOUT WORDS

Many types of people are involved in the development of a software product and its maintenance. To simplify exactly who these people are,

I use the following definitions to identify the different groups of people. Please refer to these definitions throughout the book:

Customer:	"The person or persons for whom the product is intended, and usually (but not necessarily) who decides the requirements (IEEE 1219, 1993). ISO/IEC 12207 uses the term *acquirer*" and defines it as "An organization that acquires or procures a system or software products from a supplier" (ISO/IEC 12207, 1995). The acquirer can be the buyer, customer, owner, user or purchaser. I use *customer* and *acquirer* synonymously.
User:	"The person or persons operating or interacting directly with the system" (IEEE 1219, 1993). The user often states requirements to the customer, supplier, or maintainer.
Supplier:	"An organization that enters into a contract with the acquirer for the supply of a software product under the terms of the contract. [Synonymous with *contractor, producer, seller, vendor*]" (ISO/IEC 12207, 1995). *Supplier* can be synonymous with *developer*. A developer is "An organization that performs development activities (including requirements analysis, design, and testing through acceptance) during the software life cycle process" (ISO/IEC 12207, 1995). I use *supplier* and *developer* synonymously.
Maintainer:	"An organization that performs maintenance activities" (ISO/IEC 12207, 1995). Whether maintenance is performed internally or externally, I use the term *maintainer* and *maintenance organization* synonymously. Maintainers are people who work at the maintenance organization.

OVERVIEW OF THE BOOK

Chapters 1 through 4 discuss the traditional definitions and views of software maintenance. I include discussion regarding who should do maintenance. I break down the different categories of maintenance, and how much each of those categories take, from the maintenance budget. This discussion includes how maintenance fits into the traditional life cycle of software and its development.

The second part of the book, Chapters 5 through 8, discusses a new definition of maintenance, how this new definition fits into a new life cycle, and why accepting this new definition will change the way we do maintenance. This new maintenance definition affects quality, costs, and process. This section also discusses the different activities that must happen during the predelivery stage of the life cycle, and how to plan for maintenance.

Chapters 9 through 21 provide a path for applying the new definition of maintenance. In this part of the book, I provide case studies, details, and examples of how to embrace the new maintenance definition. There is discussion about transition, maintainability, management, training, the impact of new technologies on maintenance, and the future of maintenance.

SUMMARY

This chapter introduced the reason this book was written, the author's philosophy about maintenance, how this book uses words, and how this book is designed. The next chapter jumps right into an overview of software maintenance.

The following graphic indicates the end of the chapter and the start of the review questions. This graphic will appear in each chapter following the summary section. The purpose of the review questions is to stimulate discussion about topics presented in the chapter. They address areas such as maintenance concepts, practices, and major issues.

1. Who should be concerned about maintenance?

2. When should maintenance start?

3. What's the difference between a supplier and a developer?

Overview
of Software
Maintenance

2

This chapter provides an overview of software maintenance. It details why there's a misunderstanding about the definition of maintenance, how maintenance fits into the life cycle, why maintenance is performed, the different categories of maintenance, why maintenance is costly and time-consuming, and who should perform maintenance.

WHY IS THERE CONFUSION ABOUT SOFTWARE MAINTENANCE?

Software maintenance is a much-maligned and misunderstood area of software engineering. Although software has been maintained for years, relatively little is written about the topic of maintenance. Funding for research about software maintenance is essentially  nonexistent; thus, the academic community publishes very little on the subject. Practitioners publish even less because of the corporate fear of giving away the "competitive edge." There are a few textbooks on software maintenance (Martin and McClure 1983; Arthur 1988), but they are outdated. Periodicals address the topic infrequently. This lack of published information contributes to the misunderstanding and misconception, that people have about software maintenance.

WHAT IS SOFTWARE MAINTENANCE?

Part of the confusion about software maintenance relates to agreement regarding its definition; when it begins, when it ends, how it relates to development, and most importantly, what *really* happens during the maintenance phase of the life cycle.

What, then, is software maintenance? Where does it fit into the life cycle? How does it relate to software development? First, let's define some terms. ISO/IEC 12207 (1995) defines a system as "an integrated composite that consists of one or more of the processes, hardware, software, facilities and people, that provides a capability to satisfy a stated need or objective." Simply put, a system is many things. For the sake of discussion in this book, the software portion is the one that I'll concentrate on. Now let's look at some generally accepted traditional definitions of software maintenance.

1. "... changes that have to be made to computer programs after they have been delivered to the customer or user." (Martin and McClure 1983).
2. "... the performance of those activities required to keep a software system operational and responsive after it is accepted and placed into production." (FIPS 1984).
3. "Maintenance covers the life of a software system from the time it is installed until it is phased out."(von Mayrhauser 1990).
4. "Modification of a software product after delivery to correct faults, to improve performance or other attributes, or to adapt the product to a modified environment." (IEEE 1219 1993).
5. "... software product undergoes modification to code and associated documentation due to a problem or the need for improvement. The objective is to modify existing software product while preserving its integrity." (ISO/IEC 12207 1995).

The common theme of the above definitions is that maintenance is an "after-the-fact" activity. Based on these definitions, no maintenance activities occur during the software development effort (the predelivery stage of the life cycle of a software system). Maintenance occurs after the product is in operation (during the postdelivery stage).

What Is the System Life Cycle?

Maintenance is part of the System Life Cycle, and its use is consistent with the definitions presented above. Even the models that represent the life cycle (discussed in the next section) put maintenance as a post-

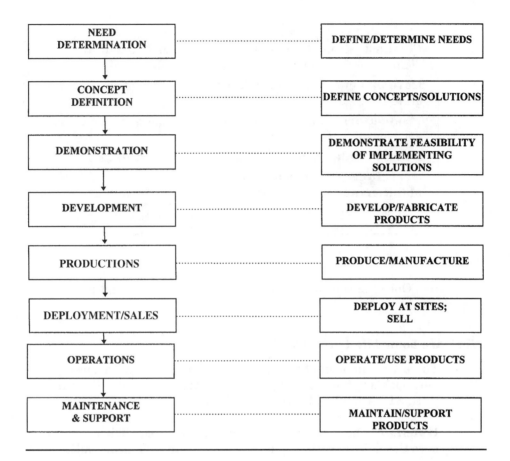

FIGURE 2.1 System life cycle.

delivery activity. Figure 2.1 shows one interpretation (Singh 1995) of the System Life Cycle with its phases and what should occur in each phase. The following describes how software would fit into the ISO/IEC 12207 System Life Cycle.

> **Need Determination.** The technical, operational, and economical feasibility is determined.
>
> **Concept Definition.** System requirements are drafted, prototypes are developed, and user feedback is analyzed to get proposed solutions.

> **Demonstration.** System requirements and architecture are defined, and software requirements are drafted.
>
> **Development.** The software is developed, built, tested, and integrated.
>
> **Productions.** This does not apply as no real manufacturing is done for software.
>
> **Delivery/Sales.** Software is installed and checked out.
>
> **Operations.** Operational services are provided.
>
> **Maintenance and Support.** After delivery maintenance and support services are provided.

Once the software is operational, Maintenance and Support are provided.

What Are Some Life-Cycle Models?

There are a number of life-cycle models in use today. The most prevalent ones are the Waterfall, the Incremental, and the Evolutionary (MIL-STD-498 1994; ISO/IEC 12207 1995).

Waterfall   The Waterfall model is the old classic. It is essentially a once-through, do-each-step-once approach. In this model, all requirements are defined first, there is essentially only one build, and the user does not get an interim product. Figure 2.2 from the draft technical report "Information Technology-Guide for ISO/IEC 12207 (Software Life Cycle Processes)" adapted the classic Waterfall model with system and hardware items so identified (Guide 12207 1995). As can be seen from the figure, Operations and Maintenance are performed once—at the end of the life cycle.

There are many problems with the Waterfall model. Critics cite the elaborate documentation requirements and the excessive amount of time required to deliver a product as the two main sources of irritation.

Incremental   Another model, the Incremental model, is also called the preplanned product improvement model. It starts with a given set of requirements, and performs development in a sequence of builds. All requirements are defined first, there are multiple builds, and there might be some interim product for use. If so, there is an Operations

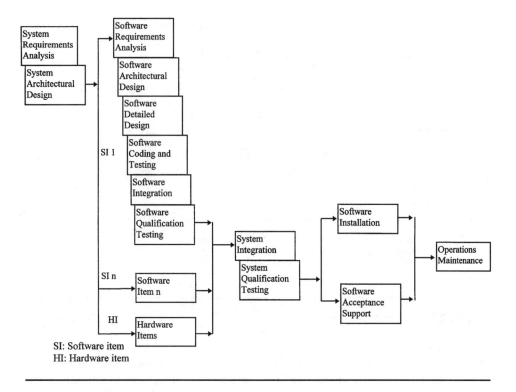

FIGURE 2.2 Waterfall model.

and Maintenance phase. The first build incorporates a part of the requirements, the next build adds more requirements, and so on until the system is complete. The activities within the model are employed repeatedly in the same sequence through all the builds. Figure 2.3 shows the Incremental model (Guide 1995).

In stark contrast to the Waterfall model, Operations and Maintenance can be employed while other builds are being developed. From a maintenance perspective this raises many issues, like "When does maintenance begin?" and "When does it end?" It is not as clean as the Waterfall model, but if you look at the definitions of maintenance, it would appear that maintenance starts after each build is delivered, and that maintenance is provided for each build.

Evolutionary The Evolutionary model also develops a system in builds, but differs from the Incremental model in that it acknowledges that the requirements are not fully understood and cannot be defined

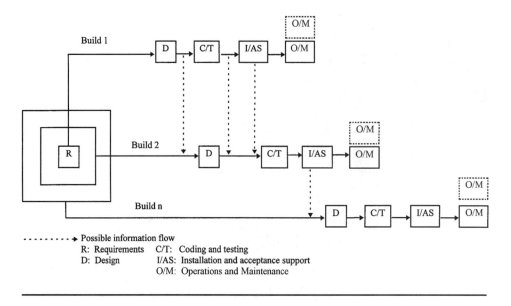

FIGURE 2.3 Incremental model.

initially. The requirements are partially defined up front and then are refined in each successive build. Interim products are available for use with the Evolutionary model, and thus there might be an Operations and Maintenance phase. The activities within the model are employed repeatedly in the same sequence through all the builds. Figure 2.4 shows the Evolutionary model (Guide 1995).

Operations and Maintenance can be employed in parallel with development efforts, and this too adds another dimension to the maintenance efforts.

Each of the models has a phase for Operations and Maintenance. All phases prior to the Operations and Maintenance are referred to as predelivery. What occurs in Operations and Maintenance is referred to as postdelivery.

Why is maintenance necessary? Why can't the life cycle just have operations without maintenance? The following section addresses that issue.

WHY IS MAINTENANCE NECESSARY?

Why do we need to perform software maintenance? If the software developer did a good job, is there a need for maintenance? If systems

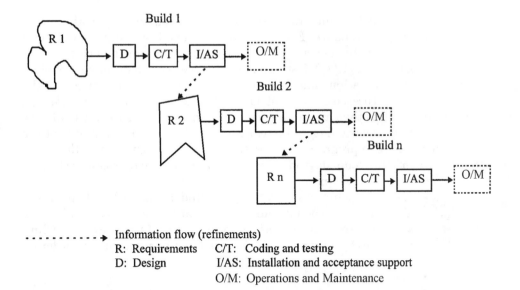

Information flow (refinements)
R: Requirements   C/T: Coding and testing
D: Design   I/AS: Installation and acceptance support
                  O/M: Operations and Maintenance

FIGURE 2.4 Evolutionary model.

are built using *computer-aided software engineering* (CASE) tools, or if they were developed solely using *commercial-off-the-shelf* (COTS) products, why do we need software maintenance? All of these questions are important to help explain why we perform maintenance. Let's first look at what occurs during maintenance.

During the Operation and Maintenance phase, users begin to operate the system. In some cases, users are going from manual systems to automated systems. In other cases, major overhauls of systems take place. In both cases, the users must be trained in the use of the new systems. During the course of operations, users find things wrong with the system, as well as things they would like to see added to the new system. They provide feedback to operational managers, who task the maintainer to correct or improve the system. The maintainer makes the approved corrections or improvements, installs the changes, and the users once again begin to learn the new system, thus perpetuating the loop of maintenance and extending the life of the product. Many times, the maintenance phase ends up being the longest process of the entire life cycle; using the Waterfall model to develop a system can take three to five years! However, systems developed with that model often have a life expectancy of 15–20 years. Even the Incremental or Evolutionary models, which field operational systems quickly, both quickly get into maintenance. Even for those models, the maintenance phase far outweighs the development phase in terms of time and cost.

Lehman's (1980) first two laws of software evolution help explain why the Operations and Maintenance phase can be the longest of the life-cycle processes. His first law is the *Law of Continuing Change*, which states that a system needs to change in order to be useful. The second law is the *Law of Increasing Complexity*, which states that the structure of a program deteriorates as it evolves. Over time, the structure of the code degrades until it becomes more cost-effective to rewrite the program.

Lehman's laws help us understand what happens to software when it is used, but what problems does performing maintenance solve? According to Martin and McClure (1983), software maintenance must be performed in order to:

- Correct errors.
- Correct design flaws.
- Interface with other systems.
- Make enhancements.
- Make necessary changes to the system.
- Make changes in files or databases.
- Improve the design.
- Convert programs so that different hardware, software, system features, and telecommunications facilities can be used.

Other reasons for performing maintenance might be to prevent problems or to improve performance. Remember, software evolves. Because software changes, maintenance must happen. So what makes software change? The best way to answer this question is to look at what happens during maintenance, and what types of changes are made.

What Are the Three Categories of Maintenance?

E.B. Swanson (1976) of UCLA was one of the first to examine what really happens in maintenance. He believed that by studying the maintenance phase a better understanding of maintenance would result. Swanson was able to create three different categories of the "fixes" that are performed in maintenance.

Swanson's three categories for maintenance (FIPS 1984) are:

- **Corrective:** Changes necessitated by actual errors (induced or residual "bugs" in a system).
- **Adaptive:** Any effort that is initiated as a result of changes in the environment in which a software system must operate.
- **Perfective:** All changes, insertions, deletions, modifications, extensions, and enhancements made to a system to meet the evolving and/or expanding needs of the user.

Corrective changes fix bugs. Bugs drive the users crazy; the system does not operate as it was designed or advertised. The trick here is to locate the original specifications in order to determine what the system was originally designed to do. If you wanted to make a corrective change to a car, for example, it might be fixing a flat tire.

Adaptive changes are those that must be made to keep pace with the changing environment. For example, the operating system might be upgraded and some modifications might be made to accommodate the new operating system. Unfortunately, the user does not see a direct change in the operation of the system, but the software maintainer must expend resources to effect the change. If you wanted to make an adaptive change to a car, it might be an upgrade of the engine to accommodate new anti-smog laws.

Perfective changes, or "enhancements," are all changes made to the system to accommodate the needs of the users. Simply put, if something was not in the original design or specification and the user wants it added to the system, it is classified as a perfective change. All the new user requirements are of this type. If the system performs in accordance with the specifications regarding performance and the user wants performance improved, that is a perfective change. If you wanted to make a perfective change to a car, it might be adding flames, a bigger tail fin, or a larger hood scoop.

IEEE Maintenance Categories

The categories of maintenance were further defined in the 1993 IEEE Standard on Software Maintenance (IEEE 1219 1993). Their definitions combine Swanson's adaptive and perfective definitions, and account for performance or maintainability changes in the perfective category. In addition, IEEE defines a fourth category called *preventive maintenance*, which is defined as "maintenance performed for the purpose of preventing problems before they occur" (IEEE 1219 1993). For safety-critical systems such as the space shuttle or aircraft systems, it is very important to prevent problems. Maintainers might want to use preventive maintenance as a fourth category when working on critical systems. Some maintainers chose to classify preventive maintenance under the corrective category. A preventive change in a car would be putting the top up on a convertible to avoid rain flooding the interior.

Finally, ISO/IEC 12207 does not define maintenance categories per se, but in discussing the maintenance process it does imply that there are the following types of maintenance: corrective, adaptive, improvement, or preventive. These match up rather nicely with the definitions discussed previously; improvement directly relates to perfective change. It is important to track the improvements of a software system, and organizations might want to use *improvement* instead of *perfective*. No matter which definitions you decide to use, it is imperative to discriminate between corrections and enhancements.

Join the adaptive and perfective categories together and call them Enhancements.

When categorizing the types of maintenance, an easy way to do it is to ask "Are we making a corrective change (fixing a problem or preventing one), or are we adapting or perfecting (improving) the system?" You'll soon see why these questions are important. Swanson's definitions allow the software maintenance practitioner to be able to tell the user that a certain portion of a maintenance organization's efforts is devoted to user-driven or environment-driven requirements. The user requirements should not be buried with other types of maintenance. The point here is that these types of updates are not corrective in nature—they are improvements.

These categories of maintenance help to answer the question, "Why must there be maintenance?" Regardless of which CASE tools are used (See Chapter 13), and regardless of which development model is used, maintenance is needed. The categories clearly indicate that maintenance is more than fixing bugs.

Is Maintenance More than Just Bugs?

Capers Jones (1991), president of Software Productivity Research, Inc., has been studying development and maintenance for years. He maintains extensive empirical databases, and has much to say about maintenance. He states that the work of enhancing an existing system

is much more costly than new development work if the base system is not well structured. Jones provides empirical data to substantiate his claims. Perhaps one of the most salient comments Jones makes is that *organizations lump enhancements and the fixing of bugs together.* He goes on to say that this distorts both activities, and leads to confusion and mistakes in estimating the time it takes to implement changes and budgets. Even worse, this "lumping" perpetuates the notion that maintenance is fixing bugs and mistakes. Because many maintainers do not use maintenance categories, there is confusion and misinformation about maintenance.

Practical Experiences

It is still important to understand that organizations do lump enhancements and bugs together. They do it in development and in maintenance. For one large development effort (over two million lines of source code), I was called in as the project approached acceptance testing. The program manager was concerned that the testing would not go well as there were still some 300 problem reports that had been generated during development and had not been implemented. The user had not yet had a chance to perform testing. I was called in to look at one aspect, the large volume of uncompleted problem reports, but my analysis quickly revealed another problem. I asked for the total amount of problems generated during development. The answer was 2,000 problem reports. I asked how many enhancement requests were generated. Then I was told that they were included in the problem report total. This organization had *no idea* how many of the 2,000 problems were corrections or enhancements. Similarly, they did not know how many of the unresolved 300 problem reports were really not problems and were, in fact, enhancements.

What if they all were enhancements? If there were 300 unfinished enhancement requests, do you think that the Program Manager would have had the same concern as they entered acceptance testing? I don't think so. Because they lumped corrections and enhancements together, they were concerned. The end of the story is that it was too hard and too costly to go back to find out which of the problem reports were corrections and which ones were enhancements. Thus, nothing was done. An informal polling of people involved in the project indicated that over 70% of the "problem reports" were, in actuality, enhancements. The statement that ". . . 2,000 problem reports were generated" was a disservice to the developer and certainly did nothing for the users' understanding of the development or maintenance process.

The above serves to illustrate the problems associated with lumping corrections and enhancements. In one case the developer's reputation was tarnished with "2,000 problems reports"; people viewed the developer as having done a poor job of developing the system.

Another experience, in this case relating to a number of operational systems, further illustrates the problems brought about by "lumping" corrections and enhancements.

Practical Experience

I was called in to assist with implementing a software metrics program at a large government agency. The organization maintained a large database that tracked all the incoming modification requests (MRs). The MRs were entered into the database and then analyzed by the group that was responsible for supporting the system against which the request was targeted. Their process called for deciding if the MR was a correction or an enhancement. As part of my analysis I looked at data from the database to determine what percentage of the MRs was for corrections and what percentage was for enhancements. My first cut was to look at the pure numbers, the number of MRs that became corrections and the number that became enhancements. Of the 450 MRs I reviewed, *all* of them were classified as corrective!

The results of this initial analysis were disseminated in a report to a large segment of the 400 people performing maintenance. The analysis report noted that all MRs were corrective, and this seemed strange because it was not consistent with experience within the industry. The fact that there were *no enhancements in the database* was rather striking. The report pointed out this dichotomy with industry data, and suggested that software maintenance at this large government agency was unique. One person even responded to say that it *was* unique! It was later determined that the process was flawed, and in-depth analysis revealed that over 50% of the MRs were in fact enhancements.

This case perpetuates the notion that maintenance is merely fixing bugs, because no other categories of maintenance were identified. Software maintainers must have good definitions for corrections and enhancements, and a process that forces proper classification.

WHY IS MAINTENANCE HARD?

 Schneidewind (1987) believes that maintenance is hard because of the myopic view that maintenance is a postdelivery activity. He states that:

1. We cannot trace the product nor the process that created the product.
2. Changes are not adequately documented.
3. It is difficult to track changes.
4. There is a ripple effect when making changes.

This lack of attention during development results in a loss of traceability. Thus, in tracing errors or adding enhancements, it is often impossible to trace back to design specifications and user requirements. As a result, maintenance is hard. In addition, the user's understanding of software maintenance also makes maintenance a very difficult thing to perform. How does the user of a software system view software maintenance? First is the notion that software maintenance is essentially a postdelivery activity. Second, the user compares software problems to hardware problems; if bugs occur or parts break, fix them. Yet, during hardware maintenance, deteriorating components are replaced, engineering changes that correct faults and make design enhancements are made, and mechanical parts are lubricated and cleaned. Hardware maintenance is about reliability. The user sees no real change!

For software maintenance, defects are corrected, and enhancements that change *how* the program behaves are made. When the user presses a key on the keyboard, the appearance of the screen changes. Software maintenance is primarily about addressing changing user requirements.

However, many users are under the impression that they can request any type of software change or enhancement because the change will be as easy as lubricating a part. They do not understand that most software maintenance actions require major structural changes. The users expect software maintenance to have the same mean time between failures as for hardware maintenance. They expect software maintainers to implement corrections for problems as quickly as hardware maintainers. They expect software to be like hardware, and this is the problem—software is not like hardware! Software maintenance practitioners must study what really happens in maintenance—corrections, enhancements and improvements—and let the users know. It is important to stress to users that maintenance is more than fixing bugs.

WHO SHOULD DO MAINTENANCE?

You now know what maintenance is and why it is difficult to do. But who should perform maintenance? Is it the supplier (developer), or should a different organization function as maintainer? Let's look at some advantages and disadvantages (Pigoski 1994) of the different approaches to answering the question of who should perform maintenance.

Developers Performing Maintenance

On the surface, leaving the maintenance responsibility with the developer (see Chapter 1 for a review of definitions) appears to have great merit. Ask any developer or the head of a large development effort, normally a program manager, who should provide maintenance responsibility. Usually, there is not much discussion. Give the software maintenance responsibility to some organization other than the developer? That thought is frightening for the program manager, and sometimes for the developer. Mostly it is easy to do nothing, and that is why very often maintenance responsibility remains with the developer. There are, however, distinct advantages to the developer maintaining the software:

- The developer has the best knowledge of the system.
- There is no need for elaborate documentation.
- There is no need to establish a formal communication system between the maintainers and the developers.
- The users of the software need only work with one software organization.
- Personnel at the developing organization are more personally satisfied because there is more diversity in the workload.

Surely the developers have the best knowledge of the system, but after a lengthy development for a large software system, will those same people be on the project? If the developers perform maintenance, somehow documentation is never really finished. The impetus to complete it goes away when the developers retain maintenance responsibility. After all—they don't need documentation because they developed the software, they know all about it, and they will be there *forever* supporting the system. (Yeah, right!!) There is no need for communications between the developer and the maintainer, because the software stays  within the developers' organization. The users, the operators of the system, are content when maintenance stays with the developing organization because they must deal only with one organization, the developer. Wouldn't it be nice if things were this easy?

Of course, there are disadvantages to the developer maintaining the software:

- Personnel might leave the developer organization if only maintenance is performed.
- New employees might be unhappy with the quantity of maintenance work.
- If the developer expert leaves, the people responsible for the maintenance might not be adequately trained.
- Developers often spend too much time perfecting the developed system.
- Often the original developers get reassigned to new, high-priority projects.

How often do people move around? Turnover of people in the 1960s and 1970s averaged 18 months before people changed jobs. Things aren't that bad now, but they haven't improved much either. Even if employees do not leave companies, how can managers guarantee growth of their people? Bill Curtis, who has studied software-related activities for many years, has often stated that it is better to have an individual perform three jobs over a ten year period than to have one person perform the same job over ten years; so even if people do not leave, it is good to rotate them around anyway. Thus, the likelihood of them staying with a development project is not great. (There are, of course, exceptions to this. For very specialized areas such as the space shuttle effort, people normally stay a long time.) Experts leave all the time; turnover in the maintenance field is a real problem (Deklava 1992).

Developers often spend too much time perfecting. Let's say the developers just spent three years developing a new system. They develop a "special" attachment to the system or some portion of it. Because of schedule and budget demands, the developer never gets the final tweaking done on a module. If the software stays with the developer during the maintenance phase, the developer gets another chance to perfect it!

Practical Experience

I had an experience that I believe will illustrate the above point perfectly. There was an open enhancement request from the development phase. As my team took over maintenance responsibility, this proposal stayed with the developer as we assumed software configuration management responsibility for all corrective actions. For about a year this proposal stayed active and was worked on. Finally, someone had the nerve to ask why that old enhancement proposal was still around and still being worked. We were told that the developer "never really got it to work the way he wanted and every so often he would go back and 'tweak it'." Needless to say, it was quickly deleted from the list of items to be worked on, so that no additional funds could be expended on it.

Separate Maintainers Performing Maintenance

Similarly, there are distinct advantages and disadvantages to transitioning a software system from a developer to a different organization to serve as maintainer. Having a different organization perform maintenance has distinct advantages:

- Better documentation is produced.
- Formal turnover procedures are created.
- Maintenance programmers get to know the strong and weak points of the system.
- Procedures for implementing changes are established.
- Morale is improved; people who like maintenance are likely to do a better job.

Before any system transitions to the maintainer, there must be some amount of documentation. If the developer did not complete or update the documentation during development, it should be updated prior to any transition. This ensures that there is some amount of documentation to support the system. Please don't believe that the documentation will be perfect or complete; but, because of the transition, there will be some!

To affect a transition or turnover, some formal mechanism is required. This too will help to ensure that all the things that are needed for a successful transition (See Chapter 9 for a detailed discussion about transition of software maintenance responsibility from the developer to the maintainer) are in place. Some of these items include software licenses, work backlog information, training, and documentation. The most important aspect of a formal turnover is that your boss, whoever he or she is, will understand the difference between what you *should* get to support the system and what you actually *receive*. Like the support documentation mentioned above, there is a good chance that the transition documents might also be incomplete.

Practical Experience

This was the case for two systems that transitioned to a U.S. Navy maintenance organization. A detailed transition plan was developed (by the maintenance organization). It had everything that was required, and everything that should be provided as part of the transfer of responsibility of software maintenance. However, owing to inadequate planning for maintenance by the Program Manager, many of these needed items—software training, transfer of backlog information, tools for maintenance—were not provided. The only solace for the maintainer was that at least people would see what was actually required and that the lack of some of these items would place an unnecessary burden on the maintainer.

Do maintainers have "special" attachment to the system? No. The maintenance software engineers or programmers take a more objective view of the system and the code, and they are not prone to perfecting certain modules or routines. They look at the system objectively, and get to know the strong and weak points of the systems.

What about getting people who *really* want to work on maintenance? One of the advantages of a different organization performing maintenance is that morale improves. Does it?

Practical Experience

If you are a maintenance organization performing software maintenance only, recruiting should be easy. You advertise that you are a maintenance organization, and that only those who want to do maintenance come to work with you. Morale should be better because your incoming employees will know ahead of time that they will not be doing original system development.

Think again.

All we did at a U. S. Navy software maintenance organization was software maintenance. When we recruited people it was very easy. We told them that they would be working in beautiful, sunny Pensacola, Florida, USA, near the whitest beaches in the whole world, three hours away from New Orleans, Louisiana. They would be working in a brand new facility, receive lots of formal vendor training, and have an opportunity to travel throughout the world. We even told them that all we did was maintenance. They still wanted to come, and did. However, within six months of their arrival, they invariably asked when they could do some development work. So much for the theory!

With these advantages of having a different organization perform maintenance, there are distinct disadvantages:

- Transition of the system may be slow.
- Morale can decrease if the wrong people are assigned.
- There is a significant training need.
- There might be funding problems.
- It takes time to learn the new system.
- It takes time to set up the maintenance organization and facilities.
- User support can suffer.
- The credibility of the support organization can suffer.

How long will it take to transition the system from the developer to the maintenance organization? If you were told at 5:00 P.M. on Friday that on Monday at 8:00 A.M. you will be expected to support a million lines of code system or a large system over 5000 function points, what would you think? Would you have wanted to know at least something about the system prior to Friday at 5:00 P.M.? It takes time to learn the new system. If the developer took three years to develop the one million

lines of source code, how long will it take the maintenance organization to set up shop or be "comfortable" to support the system? It takes time to transfer knowledge of the system from the developer to the maintenance organization, which causes an impact on the users and has a tremendous potential impact on the software maintenance organization.

Picture this scenario. The users worked with the developers for three years. Now the system is operational, and support is transitioning from the developer to the maintenance organization. The users are confused during the transition. To whom do they talk? What is going through the users' heads? Will they get the same level of support (or better) from the maintenance organization? Will they (the maintainers) be able to learn and understand the system quickly, and will they be able to implement all the changes? Will the maintenance organization respond as quickly as the developer? The point here is that there is great risk for the maintenance organization. There are more details about the transition process and how maintainers can control it in Chapter 9.

When the maintainers say that they are ready to provide support, they better be, or their credibility will suffer.

Large Organizations Need Separate Maintenance Organizations

Which is the better approach for software maintenance, to have the developer perform maintenance or to transition maintenance to a separate, different organization? As with so many things, it all depends. Clearly, each organization must weigh these advantages and disadvantages and apply them to their organizations, environment, and systems. What do the experts say about this topic? Martin and McClure (1983) state that large organizations should establish a separate maintenance staff to improve control and productivity. U.S. West Communications, one of the seven "Baby Bells" formed after the breakup of AT&T, is a good example. After the breakup, they looked ahead and split maintenance from development. U. S. West Communications was formally recognized for its outstanding performance in software maintenance when it won the Software Maintenance Association's Distinguished Performance in Software Maintenance Award for 1990. Swanson and Beath (1989), in their study of fourteen information systems organizations, state that separate maintenance organizations offer significant advantages.

For large software systems, transitioning to a separate maintenance organization is better over the life cycle than leaving the maintenance responsibility with the developer.

Practical Experiences

My own experience supports the notion of a separate software maintenance organization. While at headquarters in Washington, DC, I was one of the Information Systems Planners and was asked to study our future software maintenance needs. At the time we had only a few software-based systems, and these were supported by decentralized, fragmented software maintenance organizations (Pigoski 1990). Based on the number of new systems being developed, I needed to come up with a plan to provide software maintenance support. I was given the opportunity to visit government, industry, and academic institutions in my quest to come up with a good plan (Pigoski 1990a). I also was able to tap my peers from the software maintenance community for their views and experiences. What I learned was that those companies that had effective maintenance organizations separated maintenance from development. My research confirmed what Martin and Swanson had said. I found large U.S. companies developing software in Massachusetts and performing maintenance in Colorado. That kind of separation was the norm for many companies. Based on what I learned, the U. S. Navy established a separate software maintenance organization in Pensacola (Pigoski 1995). Defense contractors would develop all new systems, and all maintenance would be transferred to the organization in Pensacola.

SUMMARY

In this chapter, you learned the traditional software definition of maintenance and how it fits into the software life cycle. You have an understanding of how to categorize maintenance fixes, and why doing maintenance is difficult. You should understand that maintenance is more than fixing bugs, and that it is not going away. Maintenance is here to stay; even the new development models have a maintenance phase. You now know the advantages and disadvantages of the different entities performing maintenance. The next question you might want to ask yourself is "How much does maintenance cost?" Read on.

1. What is the traditional definition of maintenance, and what does it not take into account?

2. If you were designated to do maintenance on a software system, what are some things you would like to know beforehand so that you can prepare for it?

3. Why should a large company use a maintenance organization separate from development?

Why Maintenance Is Expensive

One of the primary views of users is that maintenance is expensive. It does not seem to matter if the Waterfall, Incremental, or Evolutionary model is used for development, nor does it seem to matter if maintenance is performed using a "cradle-to-grave" concept whereby the developer retains maintenance responsibility or if the maintenance responsibility transfers to a different organization. Still, the question remains, "Why is maintenance expensive?"

If a good product is developed, why is maintenance needed at all? This chapter will identify where the maintenance dollar goes and why. In addition, the chapter provides an analysis of the maintenance categories, which reveals that maintenance is much more than fixing bugs or mistakes. How much more? What percent of the maintenance effort is not fixing bugs?

BILLIONS SPENT ANNUALLY ON MAINTENANCE

What are the real costs of software maintenance? What portion of the overall software life-cycle dollars are consumed by software maintenance? If maintenance is merely fixing bugs or problems, then what are the maintainers doing with all their time?

Although there is no real agreement on the

TABLE 3.1 Maintenance Costs as a Percentage of Total Software Life-cycle Costs

Survey	Year	Maintenance (%)
Canning	1972	60
Boehm	1973	40–80
deRose/Nyman	1976	60–70
Mills	1976	75
Zelkowitz	1979	67
Cashman and Holt	1979	60–80

actual costs, sufficient data exist to indicate that maintenance does consume a large portion of overall software life-cycle costs. Arthur (1988) states that only one-fourth to one-third of all life-cycle costs are attributed to software development, and that some 67% of life-cycle costs are expended in the Operations and Maintenance phase of the life cycle. Jones (1994) states that maintenance will continue to grow and become the primary work of the software industry. As far back as 1981, Glass and Noiseux (1981) stated that essentially *everything* is maintenance. Table 3.1 (Arthur 1988) provides a sampling of data complied by various people and organizations regarding the percentage of life-cycle costs devoted to maintenance.

These data were collected in the late 1970s, prior to all the software engineering innovations, methods, and techniques that purport to decrease overall costs. What are the costs now?

Recent literature suggests that maintenance is gaining more notoriety because of its increasing costs. A research marketing firm, the Gartner Group, estimated that U.S. corporations alone spend over $30 billion annually on software maintenance, and that in the 1990s, 95% of life-cycle costs would go to maintenance (Moad 1990). See Figure 3.1. Clearly, maintenance is costly, and the costs are increasing. All the innovative software engineering efforts from the 1970s and 1980s have not reduced life-cycle costs.

Jones (1994) states that more than 60% of U.S. Fortune 500 enterprises have high software maintenance costs, and so do the federal and state governments and the military. High software maintenance costs are associated (Jones 1994) with large enterprises that maintain large amounts of software. Jones states that the average U.S. enterprise spends 45% of its total budget on software maintenance.

Do you know the costs of your software maintenance organization? What percent of life-cycle costs are devoted to maintenance? Surely

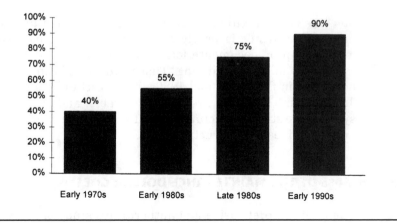

FIGURE 3.1 Software life-cycle costs devoted to maintenance.

your organization is different! Your maintenance costs are not at all like the numbers presented here—are they?

MAINTENANCE PRACTITIONERS ARE PAID TOO MUCH!

Recognizing that Operations and Maintenance consume the majority of software life-cycle resources, the question of why maintenance is expensive still remains. Schneidewind (1987) states that in the early days, programmers' salaries were an insignificant part of the data-processing budget. The programmers spent most of their time writing new programs, not fixing old code. Also, machine resources were inexpensive. Why then is software maintenance so expensive today? Why does software maintenance consume so many of the software life-cycle dollars?

The answer is that software maintenance practitioners get paid too much.

Today the programmers' salaries consume the majority of the software budget, and most of their time is spent on maintenance. Software maintenance is a labor-intensive activity. As a result, organizations have seen the Operations and Maintenance phase of the software life cycle consume more and more resources over time. Hardware is no longer the budget-grabber.

Others attribute rising maintenance costs to the age and lack of structure of the software. Osborne and Chikofsky (1990) state that much of today's software is ten to fifteen years old, and was created without benefit of the best design and coding techniques. The result is poorly designed structures, poor coding, poor logic, and poor documentation for the systems that must be maintained. You might be thinking "That might have been true for systems developed in the 1970s and 1980s, but it certainly is not true today." Think again! The costs are still comparable, and most of these older systems are still unstructured, because it is quite expensive to go back and re-engineer or restructure them.

WHERE 80% OF THE MAINTENANCE DOLLAR GOES

The most comprehensive and authoritative study of software maintenance was conducted by B.P. Lientz and E.B. Swanson (1980). Their study of 487 software organizations provides the best data regarding what actually occurs during the Operations and Maintenance phase of the software life cycle. The allocation of time for each maintenance category was determined during their study.

Figure 3.2 depicts the distribution of maintenance activities by category by percentage of time from the Lientz and Swanson study. Clearly, corrective maintenance (that is, fixing problems and routine debugging) is a small percentage of overall maintenance costs. Martin and McClure (1983) provide similar data. Over 80% of maintenance costs are for providing enhancements in the form of adaptive and perfective maintenance.

Times change. People change. Requirements change. Software changes. These changes are maintenance.

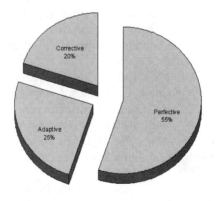

FIGURE 3.2 Distribution of maintenance by categories.

Earlier, I stated that *you*—the software maintenance practitioner— were getting paid too much, and that is why costs are so high. The real culprits are the *users*. They do not know what they want in systems, and over the Operations and Maintenance phase, they continue to bombard maintainers with change requests. Most of those are for enhancements. The users are the cause of the problem! They're the ones that make maintenance expensive.

Typically, users operate the system; as errors are found and new enhancements identified, they are forwarded to the users' management for action. Management, through a software configuration management process that will be discussed later, tasks the maintainer with providing a correction or enhancement. All of the efforts of the maintainer should be directed, and in most cases *paid for,* by the users. The maintainer is a service organization whose "customer" is the user.

The users are the ones who decide what gets worked on in maintenance. Historically, 80% of the effort for maintenance is for enhancements that are significantly more expensive to complete than corrections. Because of the user-driven enhancements, costs are high.

Well, it is not really all the users' fault. There are many factors that result in 80% of the costs being attributed to improvements. Software is designed to change, unlike hardware. It is designed and developed with change in mind, and change expected. Remember Lehman's (1980) Law of Continuing Change (See Chapter 2), which states that a system needs to change in order to be useful.

Often systems are developed for a particular purpose, and then through the passage of time things change, and what was once needed is no longer required. Military examples clearly illustrate this point. The Patriot missile system was designed as an antimissile defense system. During the Persian Gulf War the software that controls the system was changed to provide offensive capability. It worked.

Often requirements for systems are generated, and then the people who generated them are gone when the system is delivered. Different people with different views then operate the system. Thus, the new users generate new requirements (enhancements). These enhancements require major redesign work and considerably more coding than a corrective action. The result is that the enhancements (improvements) dominate the costs over the life cycle.

Swanson is still at the forefront of maintenance research and empirical studies. His efforts with C.N. Beath (1989) provide a detailed analysis of information systems maintenance for fourteen organizations, and reinforce his earlier findings that user-requested enhancements dominate the Operations and Maintenance phase. The systems used were a cross-section of the industry.

Several recent studies confirm that Lientz and Swanson's data from 1980 is still accurate. Zvegintzov (1991) compared the Lientz and Swanson data with data compiled by Ball in 1987 and Dekleva in 1990. Ball's and Deklava's data were compiled from participants at the Annual Meeting and Conference of the Software Maintenance Association and the IEEE Computer Society's Conference on Software Maintenance. Although there are some differences in definition of the categories, and in the interpretation of the Lientz/Swanson data, analysis shows that the preponderance of the maintenance effort is still noncorrective.

Abran and Nguyenkim (1991) present empirical data from a two-year measurement effort in the maintenance environment of a Canadian financial institution. Data were collected for the years 1989 and 1990. The findings are based on daily data collection on a process that included 2,152 work requests, which required 11,365 days to complete. Although their interpretation of the maintenance categories is a little different, their data indicates that 79% of the maintenance work was non-corrective. Abran and Nguyenkim's data compares favorably with all the other data points. Table 3.2 summarizes that data.

With noncorrective work ranging from 78% to 84% of the overall effort, it becomes clear where the maintenance dollars are being spent. Enhancements!

Maintenance is expensive because requirements and environments change. The majority of maintenance costs are driven by users.

All maintenance organizations need to know the distribution of these categories for all of their maintenance efforts.

TABLE 3.2 Summary of the Abran & Nguyenkim Study

Maintenance Category	Lientz & Swanson 1980	Ball 1987	Deklava 1990	Abran 1990
Corrective	22%	17%	16%	21%
Noncorrective	78%	83%	84%	79%

Practical Experiences

I, too, am a skeptic. I did my own study. At the U.S. Navy software maintenance organization that I set up and later managed, we collected data on two large systems for the full life cycle (six years) of the systems. We used Swanson's categories, and found out that the percentages of the maintenance dollars going to enhancements were 78% for one system and 82% for the other. Reliability problems are not the cause of high software maintenance costs. What necessitates software maintenance, and the attendant high costs, is changing user requirements.

FACTORS INFLUENCING MAINTENANCE COSTS

You know where the maintenance dollar goes based on Swanson's categories, but there are other factors influencing these costs. After all, users believe maintenance is just fixing bugs. If the customer can get the programmers to write bug-free code, maintenance costs will reduce. Within these categories, considerable time is spent trying to understand poorly documented code, its logic, and its design.

There is a whole subfield within the maintenance field called *program comprehension*. It is getting considerable attention, because maintainers spend 40% to 60% of their time reading the code and trying to comprehend its logic. This is a labor-intensive activity that increases costs.

Another factor influencing high maintenance costs is that needed items are often not included initially in the development phase, usually due to schedules or monetary constraints, but are deferred until the Operations and Maintenance phase. Therefore, maintainers end up spending a large amount of their time coding the functions that were delayed until maintenance. Development costs remain within budget, and maintenance costs increase. Why is this important? If you know that this is happening, you can allocate sufficient resources for the maintenance budget, plus you'll be able to explain to your enhancement-requesting users exactly where their maintenance budget gets spent. As can be seen from Table 3.2, the maintenance categories are particularly useful when trying to explain the real costs of maintenance. If organizations have this data, they will understand why maintenance is expensive and will be able to defend their time estimates to complete tasks and resource requirements.

NO MONEY FOR MAINTENANCE

Normally, after completing a lengthy and costly software development effort, organizations do not want to devote significant resources to postdelivery activities. What is a significant amount? 10% of the development cost per year for maintenance? 15%? If a system cost $1M to develop, is $100K per year for maintenance a good number, or is it $150K? The reluctance to devote significant resources to maintenance is human nature. In their hearts, developers do not believe that maintenance for the new system will consume a significant portion of life-cycle costs. Their system will be the exception. They used all the modern software engineering techniques and methods, and therefore the software maintenance phase of the life cycle will not, by definition, consume large amounts of money. Accordingly, sufficient amounts of money often are not allocated for maintenance. With limited resources, maintainers can only provide limited maintenance. The lack of allocating sufficient money resources for maintenance is due in large part to the lack of recognition by users that "maintenance" is primarily enhancing delivered systems.

Allocate 10%-15% of development costs, on an annual basis, for maintenance.

SUMMARY

You know the software maintenance categories and how much each category of maintenance affects the software maintenance budget. Additionally, you realize that often all enhancements are not in the original development effort. Sometimes enhancements intended for the development effort get moved to the maintenance phase due to time and budget constraints. How has maintenance evolved over time? Chapter 4 will tell you.

1. Search the literature and describe the current costs of maintenance.

2. Where do 80% of maintenance funds go? Why?

3. Why is studying where your maintenance dollars are spent important?

Evolution of Software Maintenance Models

4

As you learned from Chapter 2, the System Life Cycle model has eight processes. As a software product is produced as part of system development, it moves through each process in the life cycle.

The two processes to focus on here are the development process and the maintenance (and support) process. Most people in software development are familiar with the different types of models used during development. Previously, the Waterfall, Incremental, and Evolutionary development models were discussed. Many people are not aware that there are also models used during the maintenance process, too. Is there a maintenance model? Is it similar to the development models? Are they the same? How have they evolved? A discussion of the types of models and how they evolved will help answer these questions.

WHAT IS THE HISTORY OF THE DEVELOPMENT PROCESS?

 The development process includes many processes of the life cycle. Before the concept of a life cycle existed, there was not much done formally regarding how to develop a software product. Eventually the first model appeared, followed by more advanced models. The following is a brief discussion of the history of development models.

The Code and Fix Development Model

One of the early software development models was the Code and Fix. It consisted of two steps: Code, and then fix the code.

There were many difficulties with this approach. After a time, because of enhancements, updates, and a lack of formal change standards, the code structure deteriorated. It became apparent that a *design phase* was needed. Often the software did not match the users' needs. Thus, the need for a *requirements phase* surfaced. Eventually, quality became a concern, and a *testing phase* was developed.

Over the next few decades, the models evolved as the development process became more sophisticated. One of the more popular models in the 1950s was the Stagewise software development model; it broke down the process into successive stages. Eventually this model evolved into the Waterfall software development model.

The Waterfall Development Model

1970 brought perhaps the most widely known model for the software development process, the Waterfall model (See Chapter 2). The Waterfall model refined the Stagewise model and added two primary enhancements.

The first new enhancement concerns the need to create a system of feedback between stages. Guidelines were established to confine feedback loops to successive stages to minimize the expensive rework involved in feedback across many stages.

The second enhancement was the initial incorporation of prototyping in the software life cycle. Boehm (1988) states that the Waterfall was the basis for most software development in the U.S. government and industry. Today there are many difficulties that have been recognized with the Waterfall model. Bill Curtis (1985) documents this model's difficulties.

- It requires fully elaborated documentation.
- It does not work well for end-user application.
- It reflects a manufacturing orientation.
- It fails to treat software development as a problem-solving process.

These difficulties resulted in the development of more recent models, such as the Incremental and Evolutionary (See Chapter 2), to represent the software development process. The Spiral model (Boehm 1988) also evolved from the Waterfall model. The Spiral model was developed to encompass the best features of the classic life cycle (Waterfall) and prototyping. It adds a new element: risk analysis. As the Spiral model is evolutionary in nature, some organizations, such as ISO/IEC (ISO/IEC 12207 1995) and the U.S. Department of Defense (MIL-STD-498 1995), do not use the term Spiral model but instead use the term Evolutionary model.

It is important to note that the discipline of software engineering is still relatively new. Models and processes for software engineering are evolving and will continue to evolve.

WHAT IS THE HISTORY OF THE MAINTENANCE PROCESS?

You now know how the software development models evolved. What about the software *maintenance* models? How have they evolved? Why do we need software maintenance models? The last phase of the life cycle is Operations and Maintenance. This last phase occurs after product delivery. Schneidewind (1987) states "The traditional view of the software life cycle has done a disservice to maintenance by depicting it solely as a single step at the end of the cycle." He states that maintenance would be more accurately portrayed as additional development stages. Because there is so much disagreement about what occurs during maintenance and when maintenance occurs, it is easy to think of maintenance as the murky, ill-remembered area of the life-cycle process.

Chapin (1988) states that the common view of the software maintenance life cycle is to regard it as essentially the same as the software development life cycle. However, Chapin states that the two life cycles are different, and that this has a major impact on tool selection and the management of software maintenance. The following describes some historical models that apply to the maintenance process, and provides the details for one of the models.

Maintenance Models of the Late 1970s and Early 1980s

Several software maintenance models have been proposed since the 1970s. Many are very similar. In general, each model has three stages: Understand the software, modify the software, and revalidate the software. Sharpley (1977) proposed a model that focused on the corrective maintenance activities through problem verification, problem diagnosis, reprogramming, and baseline reverification. A more specific software maintenance model was proposed by Yau and Collofello (1980). Their model consisted of several phases:

- Determine the maintenance objective.
- Understand the program.
- Generate a maintenance change.
- Account for the ripple effect.
- Conduct regression testing.

Later Maintenance Models

The 1980s brought about a classification of software maintenance models. There are two families of maintenance models: process-oriented, and organizational- or business-oriented models (Calliss and Calliss 1992). Each model provides a different view of the maintenance effort.

Process-oriented models view the maintenance process in terms of (1) The activities that are performed, and (2) The order in which these activities are performed. Published process models include Boehm (1976), Yau and Collofello (1980), and Chapin (1987). Process modeling tries to determine the "who, what, where, when, how, and why" (Kellner and Hansen 1988) of the process. These models are useful for sharing knowledge and expertise, and foster an enhanced understanding of the process.

Extensive research into process modeling is conducted at the Software Engineering Institute (SEI). The SEI, a U.S. DoD software engineering organization at Carnegie-Mellon University, has championed process modeling and improvement with its *Capability Maturity model* (CMM) for software (Humphrey 1989; Paulk 1993). Five levels of process maturity (see Figure 4.1) are now used to foster software process improvement for software development organizations. These levels can (and should) be applied to maintenance organizations as well.

Very little is written regarding the organizational or business models. These models view the maintenance effort in terms of (1) The activities that are performed, and (2) The flow of information between the activities. Additionally, these models show the organizations or people involved at the various stages of the software maintenance process, and the communication channels between them. Pressman (1992) and Gamalel-Din and Osterweil (1988) provide additional details regarding these models.

Every successful maintenance organization must have and use a model that reflects its maintenance process.

These models help define and improve the maintenance process. The following provides an example of one model that captures the essence of the software maintenance process.

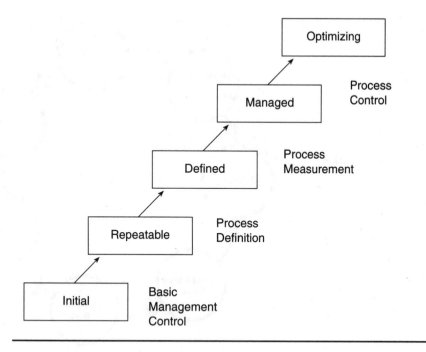

FIGURE 4.1 Process maturity levels.

The IEEE Maintenance Model

You now have an overview of the history of the various software maintenance models. But what has happened recently?

Schneidewind (1989) stressed the need for standardization in software maintenance and, as a result, the IEEE Computer Society Software Engineering Standards Subcommittee published the "IEEE Standard for Software Maintenance" (IEEE 1219 1993). The standard detailed an iterative process for managing and executing software maintenance activities. The process model includes input, process, control, and output for software maintenance. The standard states that maintenance planning should begin when planning for software development begins. However, the suggestions for planning maintenance are just suggestions—they are not part of the standard. They are included in the standard's annex for information only.

If you were setting up a software maintenance organization and needed to implement a process model for maintenance, you would first ask, "Is there a standard, or do we have to invent one?" The IEEE standard does exist, and if you needed to establish a maintenance process you might look into implementing the IEEE model, which is discussed

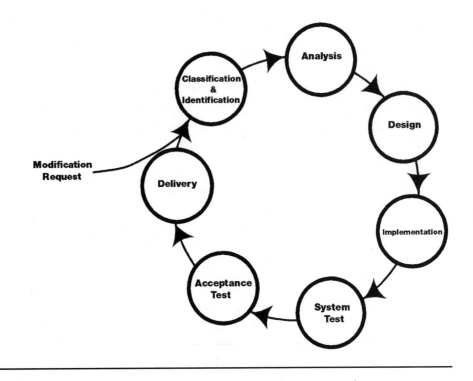

FIGURE 4.2 The IEEE Maintenance process.

below (see Figure 4.2). The standard starts the software maintenance effort during the post-delivery stage, as do all the other maintenance models. It does not take into account the predelivery activities that are critical to cost-effective support of a software system.

The following describes the phases of the IEEE Maintenance model.

Problem/Modification Identification, Classification, and Prioritization

A request for change to the software (normally from a user, programmer, or manager) starts the maintenance process. This request for change is submitted in the form of a modification request (MR). The MR might be for a correction or for an enhancement (see Chapter 2). The maintenance organization determines what type of request it is, the appropriate maintenance category (corrective, perfective, or adaptive), and its handling priority. A unique number is assigned to the request and the data are entered into an automated database (a repository), which tracks the requests. The process of collecting and reviewing measurements and metrics begins during this phase.

Analysis During this phase, a feasibility analysis and then a detailed analysis are conducted. The feasibility analysis looks at items such as the impact of the modification, alternative solutions, and costs. The detailed analysis provides firm requirements for the modification, identifies the elements of modification, devises a test strategy, and develops an implementation plan. The Configuration Control Board (CCB) reviews the information and determines if work should commence.

For many organizations, the maintenance organization is authorized to implement solutions to corrective requests and merely informs the CCB after the fact. Each maintenance organization must fully understand what it is authorized to modify, and what it is not authorized to modify.

For enhancements, which take over 80% of maintenance resources, the CCB must approve the work first.

The CCB really should prioritize all enhancements for the maintainer, and the maintainer should not start any work on an enhancement until the CCB authorizes the work. This practice should be followed even if the enhancement is characterized as "easy" or "small." Once this analysis phase is complete, the change should be planned for a scheduled release.

One of the most important practices for a maintenance organization is to have regularly scheduled releases.

Successful maintainers attribute much of their success to scheduled releases. Approved changes can be aggregated and decisions made to include some in the next scheduled release. A determination is made as to which corrections and enhancements will be worked on, when they will be finished, and when the new software version (a release) will be fielded. Emergency problems are accommodated as expeditiously as possible. To ensure that the structure of the code remains sound, and that a formal process is followed, scheduled releases are recommended.

Design During the Design phase, all of the information that has been gathered up to this point is now reviewed and is used to design the modification. That information includes system/project documentation, the output from the analysis phase, source code, and repository information. This phase provides an updated design baseline, updated test plans, a revised detailed analysis, and verified requirements.

Implementation During the Implementation phase, a plan is developed to put the modification into effect. The Implementation phase includes the following processes: coding and unit testing, integration, risk analysis, and test readiness review. All documentation, including the software, design, test, user, and training information is updated.

All production software should be under the control of an automated software configuration management system. Programming personnel should check out a copy of the production software and work on code that is separate from the production version. *Software Maintenance Technology—Reference Guide* (Zvegintzov 1994) provides some details on the automated software configuration management systems that are integral to the software maintenance process. Risk analysis is done at the end of this phase, rather than at the beginning.

System Test   System testing tests the interfaces between programs to ensure that the system meets all of the original requirements plus the added changes. Regression testing is part of system testing and validates that no new faults have been introduced. Testing is one of the most important phases, and (unfortunately) is not always given its due. Testing should ensure that the new production system will function properly, that the original requirements are still satisfied, and that the new changes are implemented properly. Beizer (1992), a noted testing authority, states that testing theory and techniques are theory and techniques for new-code production rather than for maintenance. He also asserts that maintenance testing is in its infancy. The focus of maintenance testing should not be the traditional (Myers 1979) approach, such as finding errors, but should ensure that the system runs. Beizer states that a system can run with errors.

Arthur (1988) discusses two types of testing: human and computer. Under human testing, he lists activities such as code walk-throughs or inspections for requirements, and design. These are very valuable; however, many organizations do not enforce their use.

To be successful, maintainers need to use code walk-throughs or inspections.

Of significance is that many organizations still do not use separate testing groups for maintenance. Whether small or large, many still leave integration and system testing to the maintenance software engineers or programmers who designed and coded the maintenance changes. This is a very risky practice. Successful maintenance testing also requires a current test database.

If a test database does not exist for maintenance, create one.

A test database is imperative for regression testing. Excellent work has been accomplished in the maintenance testing area at the University of Naples, Italy. A three-part series by A. Cimitile and U. De Carlini (1989a, 1989b, 1989c) describes a recommended test database as well as valuable maintenance testing techniques. Although dated, Myers (1979) is a classic in the testing field and is valuable, although it says little about maintenance specifically. Beizer (1992) also addresses maintenance testing and is a recommended resource.

Acceptance Test   Acceptance testing is done on a fully integrated system, and is performed by either the customer, the user, or a third party. During acceptance testing, the tester should do the following: report the test results, conduct a functional configuration audit (determine if the system functions in accordance with requirements), and establish a new software version (or baseline.)

In addition, the final versions of the documentation are prepared. Historically, documentation was in the form of paper—and lots of it. Now CASE tools and other automated repositories permit the accessing of system documentation on-line. With the ever-increasing use of tools, and concomitant improvements in telecommunications, the majority of documentation can now be stored and accessed electronically.

Maintainers require system and user documentation. System documentation helps the programmers learn the system and its components. As a minimum, this documentation includes high-level system flows, system functional description, source listings, and documentation describing data flows. This documentation should be under full software configuration management control. User documentation is composed of user manuals, error lists, training materials, and functional descriptions for the use of the system.

All documentation related to the software change must be updated after testing and prior to delivery.

The level of documentation varies from system to system, from programmer to programmer, and from maintainer to maintainer. Who performs the documentation function also varies. Programmers do not like to document, and thus some organizations have a documentation specialist assigned to the programming group. How the maintenance group is organized to do documentation functions is a local choice. What is important is that the documentation is updated concurrently with the systems. Once the documentation and acceptance testing phase are completed, the system is ready for the delivery phase.

Delivery   During this phase, the supplier delivers the new system to the user for installation and operation. The supplier must conduct a *physical configuration audit* (determine if all items of the configuration are delivered), notify all the users, develop an archival version for backup, and perform installation and training. After delivery, operation of the system begins.

MAINTENANCE BEGINS WHEN DEVELOPMENT BEGINS

You now have an understanding about development and maintenance processes and the models you might choose to use. Like all things, models continue to evolve, and so do definitions. Do you remember the example of getting a call on Friday afternoon and being asked to start supporting a one-million-line-of-code system on Monday morning?

After some thought, there should be *some things* that you might like to do in order to ensure that software maintenance is provided in a timely, cost-effective manner; but, based on the old life cycles, processes, models, and definitions, you are not allowed to think about maintenance of a product until after it is delivered to you. The problem with this process is that you, the maintenance organization, end up ill-prepared for the delivery of the product, and the customer and its users suffer greatly. But what if we changed the definition of maintenance and incorporated this new definition into a new life cycle and a new maintenance model?

Let's consider a new definition:

> Software maintenance is the totality of activities required to provide cost-effective support to a software system. Activities are performed during the predelivery stage as well as the postdelivery stage. Predelivery activities include planning for postdelivery operations, supportability, and logistics determination. Postdelivery activities include software modification, training, and operating a help desk.

Why is this definition new? Previous definitions (See Chapter 2) focused on maintenance as an after-delivery activity. As a result, needed predelivery actions, such as planning for maintenance, are often overlooked (if not totally avoided). Even worse, maintainers have been hamstrung by the traditional definitions, which seem to say that maintainers need not be involved until the Operations and Maintenance phase.

Clearly, some modification of the traditional definitions is required, as software maintenance is now a mainstream activity consuming considerable corporate resources.

What does the new definition do for us? It recognizes that predelivery involvement is part of the maintenance process. It also highlights items such as training and a help desk as vital parts of postdelivery.

Why is predelivery involvement by a maintainer so important? Please consider again the question about getting called on Friday at 5:00 P.M. and being asked to provide maintenance for a million-lines-of-code system or a large system with over 5,000 function points by 8:00 A.M. on the following Monday. Intuitively, it seems obvious that if there was some early involvement by the maintainer, something *good* would happen!

People like Martin and McClure (1983), Swanson and Beath (1989), and organizations like the U.S. DoD are not hesitant to note that life-cycle costs can be reduced by predelivery involvement of the maintainer (Chapter 6 discusses this topic in more detail).

A new definition will permit maintainers' involvement early-on during development.

Models continue to evolve. The international community now has a maintenance model of its own. The model is provided under the maintenance process of the recently published international standard ISO/IEC 12207 (1995). Of note is that the new definition of maintenance, provided earlier in this chapter, is consistent with the maintenance process of ISO/IEC 12207.

The following section discusses ISO/IEC 12207 and how maintenance fits in with the other software life-cycle processes.

WHAT IS THE ISO/IEC MODEL?

In 1989 the Joint Technical Committee 1 (JTC1) of the International Organization for Standardization (ISO) and the International Electrotechnical Commission (IEC) sponsored the development of ISO/IEC 12207, the International Standard for Information Technology Software—Life Cycle Processes. Dr. Raghu Singh of the United States was the project editor, and the International Standard was published in 1995.

The objectives of the International Standard (IS) are: (1) To provide a stable architecture for the software life cycle, and (2) To provide a common framework for world trade in software. The IS establishes a top-level architecture of the software life cycle with the life cycle beginning at concept and ending with retirement of the software. The IS groups the activities that are performed during the life cycle into five primary processes, eight supporting processes, and four organization processes. Each life-cycle process is divided into a list of activities, and each activity is further divided into a list of tasks. These life-cycle processes are depicted in Figure 4.3 (Singh, 1995).

The primary processes provide for conducting major functions during the life cycle. As a practical matter, the *acquisition process* causes the initiation of the software life cycle. The *supply process* responds by performing the *development, operation*, and/or *maintenance process*. A primary party (the acquirer, the supplier, the developer, the operator, and the maintainer of software products), initiates or performs the development, operation, or maintenance of software products.

The supporting processes may be used, as needed, by other processes, and they can support other processes with a specific purpose. These processes contribute to the success and quality of the software project.

The organizational processes may be employed by an organization to establish, implement, and improve a life-cycle process. These processes are normally outside specific contracts and projects, but the lessons learned while doing these processes help to improve the overall organization. A description of each process follows.

Acquisition Process

 The acquisition process provides guidance for the acquirer of software. It defines the activities of the acquirer and the organization that acquires a system, software product, or software service. It begins with the need to acquire software, continues with requests-for-proposals, selection of suppliers, acquisition-project management, and supplier monitoring and interface. This process ends with acceptance of products and services.

Supply Process

The supply process provides guidance for the provider of development products, maintenance service, and operation service. It defines activities for the supplier. It begins with a proposal and agreement, and continues with project management. It ends with delivery of products and services. This process extends to training and assistance to the acquirer.

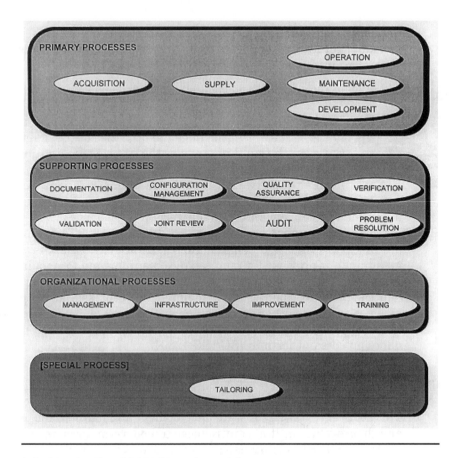

FIGURE 4.3 The ISO/IEC life-cycle model.

Development Process

The development process provides guidance for the developer of software. It defines the activities of the developer, the organization that defines and develops the software product. It begins with analysis of requirements and continues with design, coding, testing, and integration. This process ends with product completion and installation.

Operation Process

The operation process provides guidance for the operation of software. It defines the activities of the operator, the organization that provides the service of operating a computer system for users. This process includes operational support to users and depends on the maintenance process for modifications.

Maintenance Process

The maintenance process provides guidance for the maintenance of software. It defines the activities of the maintainer, the organization that provides the service of maintaining the software product. It is used to plan for maintenance and to modify the software due to the need for corrections, enhancements, or preventive actions. This process also includes the migration and retirement of the software.

The maintenance process is one of ISO/IEC 12207's five primary processes (See Figure 4.3), and it guides the activities and tasks of the maintainer. It provides for maintenance planning and for modification to code and associated documentation. The activities of the maintenance process are specific to the maintenance process, but the process may use or invoke other processes, such as the development process of ISO/IEC 12207. The next chapter goes into detail about the maintenance process put forth in ISO/IEC 12207.

SUMMARY

This chapter reviewed software development and maintenance models and their evolution. It also introduced a modern maintenance process model, the IEEE maintenance model. This chapter then redefined maintenance, put this new definition into the ISO/IEC 12207 life cycle, and introduced the ISO/IEC 12207 maintenance process. Now that you have all of this new information, you should be asking yourself, "If maintenance starts at the beginning of the life cycle, how exactly do we do maintenance, and what do these activities involve?" The next chapter answers these questions by providing details about the ISO/IEC 12207 maintenance process.

1. Adapt the historic maintenance models to include predelivery activities.

2. Review the ISO/IEC 12207 life cycle and determine how it will affect maintenance at your organization.

3. Think about what the ISO/IEC 12207 maintenance process might include, and how it will differ from the IEEE maintenance model.

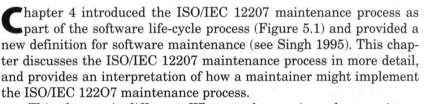

A Recommended Software Maintenance Process

5

Chapter 4 introduced the ISO/IEC 12207 maintenance process as part of the software life-cycle process (Figure 5.1) and provided a new definition for software maintenance (see Singh 1995). This chapter discusses the ISO/IEC 12207 maintenance process in more detail, and provides an interpretation of how a maintainer might implement the ISO/IEC 122O7 maintenance process.

This chapter is different. Whereas the previous chapters introduced important background information for maintenance, and chapters that follow Chapter 5 give lots of practical experience and case study data, Chapter 5 is dry. It details the ISO/IEC 12207 Maintenance process. The key word is *details*. If you are not interested in learning more about the ISO/IEC 12207 maintenance process—skip this chapter. For those who are going to implement ISO/IEC 12207, the chapter is valuable. It provides some amplification of the ISO/IEC 12207 maintenance process in case organizations are trying to implement it.

The ISO/IEC 12207 maintenance process defines the activities of the maintainer and encompasses all maintenance activities (See Figure 5.2). This process starts whenever a requirement exists to maintain a software product, and ends when the software product is eventually retired. According to the new maintenance definition, the maintainer should be involved in the maintenance process before the product is delivered. This is necessary to establish a support infrastructure for accepting and resolving modification requests once the

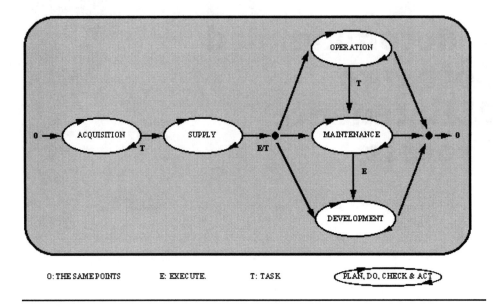

FIGURE 5.1   The ISO/IEC 12207 software life cycle.

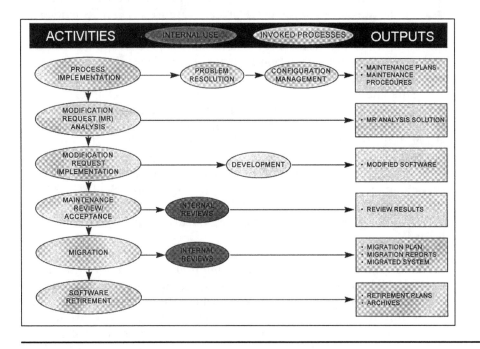

FIGURE 5.2   The ISO/IEC 12207 maintenance process.

software has been delivered. The ultimate goals of the maintenance process are:

1. To fix problems.
2. To adapt the software to new environments.
3. To implement enhancements while preserving the integrity of the system.

THE ISO/IEC 12207 MAINTENANCE PROCESS

The ISO/IEC 12207 maintenance process contains activities and tasks that are applied during the supply, development, operation, and maintenance of software products and the software portion of firmware. The maintenance process discussed in this chapter defines, controls, and improves the overall maintenance effort.

It is important to understand that software maintenance is a controllable and normal part of the life of a system. If properly implemented, the maintenance process helps to reduce the effort and cost of maintenance. A good software maintenance process also reinforces the idea that software maintenance is an integral part of the complete software engineering discipline. In order to implement an effective maintenance process, the process must be well defined and take advantage of the tools and techniques that are unique to maintenance.

The maintenance process requires that an agreement between the customer and the maintainer be established (perhaps in a maintenance plan, as discussed in Chapter 7). This agreement can range from an informal agreement up to a legally binding contract, and identifies the responsibilities of both parties. It is also possible to implement a maintenance process within a single organization. In this instance, the maintainer is also the customer and the user.

DETAILS OF THE ISO/IEC 12207 MAINTENANCE PROCESS

A process describes how to do something. The basic structure of an ISO/IEC 12207 process is made up of activities. An activity is made up of tasks (Figure 5.3). Each task describes a specific action with inputs and outputs. A task specifies *what* to do, not *how* to do it.

The maintenance process must be tailored according to the type and scope of software changes required. The maintainer is responsible for the activities and tasks identified in the maintenance process, and ensures that the maintenance process is in existence and functional. This section

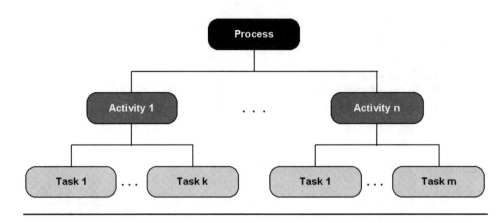

FIGURE 5.3 Process hierarchy.

describes the six maintenance activities identified in ISO/IEC 12207, on which the maintenance process is based (See Figure 5.4).

Figure 5.5 is a sample of the notation used in this chapter to depict a maintenance activity. The box at the center would list the maintenance activity (e.g., process implementation). The following defines the remaining terms used in the sample.

- *Input* refers to the items that are required as input to the activity
- *Output* refers to the items that are output from the activity
- *Control* refers to those items that provide control over the activity
- *Support* refers to the items that support the activity. Specifically, there are the supporting and organizational processes defined in ISO/IEC 12207.

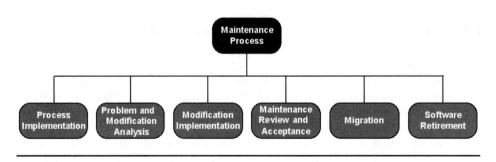

FIGURE 5.4 Maintenance process activities.

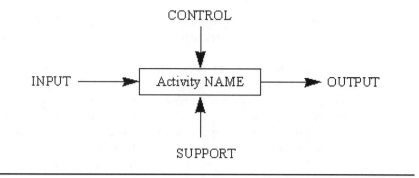

FIGURE 5.5 Conventions.

The supporting processes can also include any metrics (See Chapter 14) collected during the activity. When each activity is described, the tasks from ISO/IEC 12207 needed to perform each activity are identified. In this chapter, I divide the tasks further into task-steps to provide the detail needed to implement the software maintenance process.

PROCESS IMPLEMENTATION ACTIVITY

During this activity (which occurs early in the software product life cycle) the maintainer establishes the plans and procedures that are used during the maintenance process. In fact, the maintenance plan is prepared in parallel with the development plan (See Chapter 7). The maintainer also establishes needed organizational interfaces during this activity. Figure 5.6 shows the tasks associated with the process implementation activity. For the process implementation activity there is a maintenance planning task, a modification requests task, and a CM task.

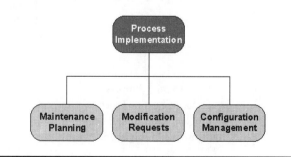

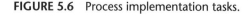

FIGURE 5.6 Process implementation tasks.

Figure 5.7 graphically depicts the Process Implementation Activity with the appropriate input, output, control, and support items shown.

Maintenance Planning In order to implement an effective software maintenance process, proper planning is required. The planning should be documented in the form of a comprehensive maintenance plan. Procedures, other plans, and reports will result as by-product, of the plan. The first step in developing the maintenance plan is to acquire a complete understanding of the software product by analyzing all available project and system documentation. Quite often this information is incomplete and sometimes it is contradictory, therefore it is very important that any problems be identified as early as possible, so that they can be resolved before plan preparation begins. The details for developing a maintenance plan are addressed in Chapter 7. The following task-steps are needed for process implementation:

1. Develop the maintenance concept.
2. Determine the scope of maintenance.
3. Analyze maintenance organization alternatives.
4. Identify the maintainer.
5. Conduct resource analyses.

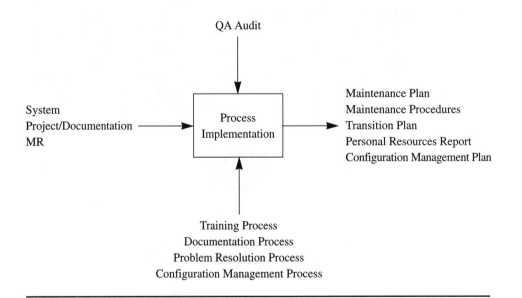

FIGURE 5.7 Process implementation activity.

6. Estimate life-cycle costs.
7. Perform a maintainability assessment of the system.
8. Determine transition requirements.
9. Determine transition milestones.
10. Identify the maintenance process which will be used.
11. Document the maintenance process in the form of operating procedures.

The importance of establishing the plan early cannot be over emphasized. If you wait too long to perform some of the steps, decisions will be made without the appropriate maintainer input. As a result, there will be a significant impact on the maintenance effort. Remember—Chapter 6 discusses the virtues of predelivery involvement. The maintenance planning task is where predelivery actions take place.

Modification Requests   The ISO/IEC 12207 problem resolution process is initiated whenever a modification request is generated. Users submit modification requests, which are further classified by the maintainer as either problem reports or enhancement requests (See Figure 5.8). The term *modification request (MR)* identifies *all* requests to modify the software product, regardless of whether the change is corrective, adaptive, or perfective (See Chapter 2). The term *problem report (PR)* is used if the request is corrective only; and the term *enhancement request (ER)* is used if the request is perfective or adaptive. Even though users submit only one type of request—modification requests—maintainers, who have the responsibility to identify the type of request, use the terms problem report and enhancement request in order to document maintenance activities and costs properly.

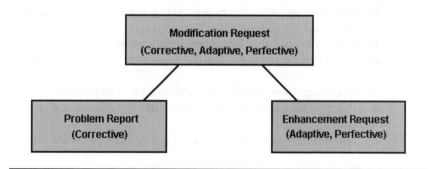

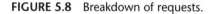

FIGURE 5.8   Breakdown of requests.

Do you remember the discussion in Chapter 2 regarding the maintenance categories, corrective, adaptive, and perfective? Do you also recall the discussion of how "lumping" corrections and enhancements together as "problem reports" caused grief for everyone? If not, please take another look at Chapter 2.

These are important points. If a maintainer establishes procedures whereby problem reports are the sole initiation of the process, the notion that maintenance is merely fixing bugs is perpetuated. MRs should start the process, the maintainer should classify the MRs as problems or enhancements, and the maintainer should advise the initiator of the MR whether the MR was in fact a problem or enhancement. (Another approach to classification is to have the initiator of the MR state whether it is a problem or enhancement.)

The maintenance process must track these requests individually as different types of maintenance. Proper implementation of the problem resolution process and the software configuration management process (discussed below) enables proper tracking to occur.

Modification requests are the most important vehicle for the user or customer to communicate with the maintainer. They identify a problem or an enhancement that the user has in a manner that provides the maintainers with the information they need to perform analysis and develop a solution. In order to make this task work effectively, the maintainer must establish procedures for receiving, recording, and tracking modification requests from the users and for providing feedback to the users. The feedback is important, because it shows customers that their concerns are being addressed. As part of the modification requests task, the maintainer performs the following task-steps:

1. Develop an identification numbering scheme for modification requests.
2. Develop a scheme for categorizing and prioritizing modification requests.
3. Develop procedures for determining trend analysis.
4. Determine the procedures for a user to submit a modification request.
5. Determine how initial feedback will be provided to the users.
6. Determine how data are entered into the status accounting database.
7. Determine what follow-up feedback will be provided to the users.

The above task-steps ensure that the tracking system for maintenance meets the needs of the customers and the maintainers.

Software Configuration Management It is not sufficient to simply track the modification requests; the software product and any changes made to it must be controlled. This control is established by implementing and enforcing an approved *software configuration management (SCM)* process. For the process to work, management must support the concept of software configuration management. The SCM process is implemented by developing and following a *configuration management plan (CMP)* and operating procedures. This plan should not be limited to just the software developed, but it should also include all system documentation, test plans, and procedures. Additionally, the configuration manager for the software product must establish a database that contains all the information needed to generate all configuration status accounting reports. As part of the software configuration management task, the maintainer performs the following task-steps:

1. Develop the configuration management plan (CMP) for maintenance.
2. Baseline the code and associated documents.
3. Analyze and report on the results of configuration control.
4. Develop the reports that provide configuration status information.
5. Develop release procedures.
6. Perform configuration control activities such as identification and recording of the request.
7. Update the configuration status accounting database.

Problem and Modification Analysis Activity

The problem and modification analysis activity is the most critical step in the modification request resolution process. The maintainer evaluates the modification request to understand the problem, develop a solution, and obtain approval for implementing a specific solution. This activity is comprised of the tasks identified in Figure 5.9. Figure 5.10 graphically depicts the modification analysis activity.

Verification When a modification request is received, it is logged by the maintainer. Logging a modification request includes creating a *software development folder (SDF)* and creating a record in the database that contains the history of all modification requests for the software product. The SDF is designed to contain all the information generated from the time the modification request is received until it is resolved, either by implementing it or canceling it. The modification request database contains the following information:

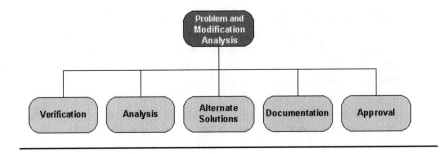

FIGURE 5.9 Modification analysis tasks.

- Statement of the problem or new requirement.
- Problem or requirement evaluation.
- Classification of the type of maintenance required.
- Initial priority.
- Verification data (for corrective modifications).
- Initial estimate of resources required to modify the existing system.

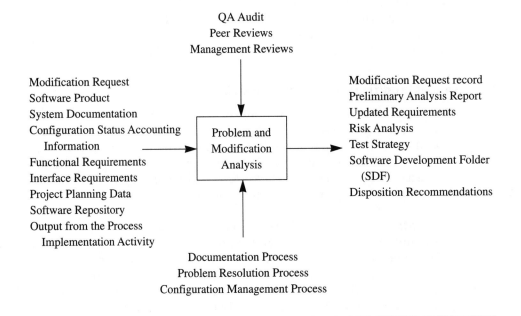

FIGURE 5.10 Problem and modification analysis activity.

After the modification request has been logged, the first task to be performed as part of modification analysis is to verify that the request is valid. In order to determine the validity of the request, the maintainer must either replicate the problem if the request is corrective, or verify that the request is reasonable and feasible if the request is adaptive or perfective. As part of this task, the maintainer performs the following task-steps as appropriate for the type of request:

1. Classify the type of maintenance: corrective, adaptive, or perfective.
2. Check out the affected software version from SCM.
3. Install the affected version.
4. Develop a test strategy to verify or replicate the problem.
5. Run tests to verify or replicate problem.
6. Determine if the proposed change is feasible.
7. Document verification results.

Analysis The maintainer analyzes the modification request to determine the impact on the organization, the existing system, and the interfacing systems. This analysis includes the following task-steps:

1. Determine if the maintainer is adequately staffed to implement the proposed change.
2. Determine if the program is adequately budgeted to implement the proposed change.
3. Determine if sufficient resources are available and whether this modification will affect ongoing or projected projects.
4. Determine the operational issues to be considered. For example, what are the anticipated changes to system interface requirements, the expected useful life of the system, and the operational priorities? What will be the safety and security impacts if it is not implemented?
5. Determine safety and security implications.
6. Determine short-term and long-term costs.
7. Determine the value of the benefit of making the modification.
8. Determine the impact on existing schedules.
9. Determine the level of test and evaluation required.
10. Determine the estimated management cost to implement the change.

Alternate Solutions Based on the analysis performed, the maintainer must outline two or three different solutions to the modification request. The alternate solutions report must include the cost, the level of effort, and the projected schedule for implementing each of the solutions. To identify alternate solutions, the maintainer performs the following task-steps:

1. Assign a work priority to the modification request.
2. Determine if a work-around exists.
3. Define firm requirements for the modification.
4. Estimate the size and magnitude of the modification.
5. Determine if the problem correction impacts hardware.
6. Perform a risk analysis for each of the options identified.

Documentation   Once the analysis is complete and alternate solutions are identified, the maintainer must document the modification request, the analysis results, and implementation options in a preliminary (or *impact*) analysis report. To write this report, the maintainer performs the following task-steps:

1. Verify that all appropriate analysis and project documentation have been updated.
2. Review the proposed test strategy and schedule for accuracy.
3. Review resource estimates for accuracy.
4. Update the status accounting database.
5. Include a disposition recommendation to indicate whether the modification request should be approved or disapproved.

Approval   The last task for the problem and modification analysis activity is the approval task. The maintainer submits the analysis report to the appropriate approval authority, usually the *configuration control board (CCB)*, to obtain approval for the selected modification option. The maintainer performs the following task-steps:

1. Provide analysis results for software CCB approval.
2. Participate at CCB discussions regarding the modification.
3. Upon approval, update the status of the modification request.
4. Upon approval, update the requirements if the request is perfective.

Modification Implementation Activity

Once a decision is made by the CCB to implement the change, the maintainer begins the real work of updating the software product. The ISO/IEC 12207 modification implementation activity encompasses all the design, implementation, testing, and delivery actions needed to resolve maintenance requests. Essentially, the inputs to this activity include all the analysis work performed in previous activities, and the

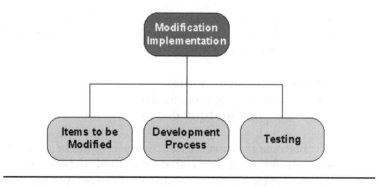

FIGURE 5.11 Modification implementation tasks.

output is a new software baseline. Figure 5.11 shows the tasks that are a part of the modification implementation activity.

Figure 5.12 graphically depicts the modification implementation activity. For this activity, the development process task is further subdivided to reflect the invocation of the ISO/IEC 12207 development

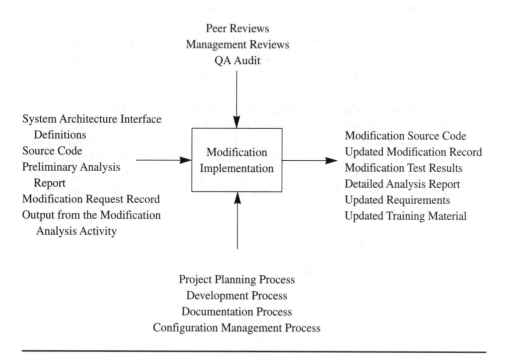

FIGURE 5.12 Modification implementation activity.

process. While the development process becomes a part of the modification activity, it is tailored to eliminate the activities that do not apply to a maintenance effort:

- Process implementation.
- System requirements analysis.
- System architectural design.

Because the development process is made up of its own activities, separate figures are provided for each of its tasks. Each of these development process tasks is a subtask of the Maintenance Implementation Activity.

Items to Be Modified An implementation plan is developed to actually make the approved change. A test strategy is developed to be used to test the change once it has been implemented. The maintainer needs to review the analysis performed earlier and determine which documentation, software units, and versions must be modified to implement the modification request. This information must be documented. This task includes the following task-steps:

1. Identify the elements to be modified in the existing system.
2. Identify the interface elements impacted by the modification.
3. Identify the documentation to be updated.

Development Process Once all the preliminary analysis is accomplished, the maintainer invokes the ISO/IEC 12207 development process to actually implement the modifications. Where the term *development* appears in ISO/IEC 12207, the term *maintenance* should be understood to apply. The ISO/IEC 12207 development process is comprised of the following tasks, which are subtasks for the modification implementation activity:

1. Software analysis.
2. Software architectural design.
3. Software detailed design.
4. Coding and testing.
5. Software integration.
6. Software qualification testing.
7. Software installation.

The following sections discuss these subtasks.

Software Analysis The software analysis subtask builds on the analysis performed earlier, and identifies the following quality characteristics as they relate to the modification request:

- Functional and capability specifications.
- External interfaces.
- Qualification requirements.
- Safety specifications.
- Security specifications.
- Ergonomic specifications.
- Data definition and database requirements.
- Installation and acceptance requirements of the software product.
- User documentation.
- User operational requirements.
- User maintenance requirements.

Not all of the above characteristics apply to all modification requests. Some might not be addressed at all. The analysis determines which of the characteristics are relevant and should be included in the design.

Figure 5.13 graphically depicts the software analysis subtask.

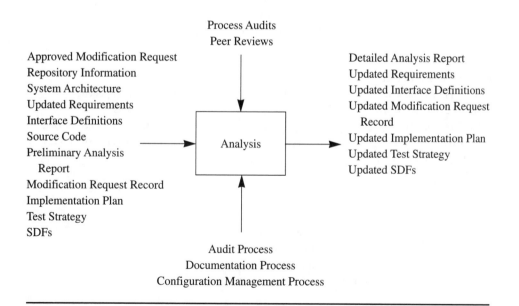

FIGURE 5.13 Analysis subtask.

Software Architectural Design For the software architectural design subtask, the maintainer uses the requirements to modify the software architecture in a way that describes the top-level structure and identifies the software components to be modified. The key aspect of this task is to document, document, document. The maintainer must document:

- The changes to the design.
- The changes to the database.
- The changes to the user documentation.
- The test requirements.
- The schedule for software integration.

Once the architectural design has been finished, it must be reviewed in accordance with the ISO/IEC 12207 joint review process and included in the SDF.

Figure 5.14 graphically depicts the software architectural design subtask.

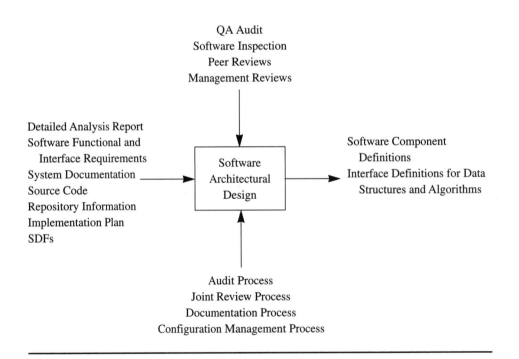

FIGURE 5.14   Software architectural design subtask.

Software Detailed Design The software detailed design subtask refines the design developed in the previous task. This level of design might require the design of interfaces, algorithms, and data. All the system documentation must be updated to reflect any detailed design changes. Once the detailed design has been finished, it must be reviewed in accordance with the joint review process and included in the SDF.

Figure 5.15 graphically depicts the software detailed design subtask.

Coding And Testing The coding portion of this task modifies the software product to implement the solution developed during the design tasks. The coding performed by the software engineer and programmers should be consistent and should comply with the appropriate standards and guidelines. In addition to writing the code, the program should collect metrics that measure complexity and productivity. The testing portion of this task addresses the testing of the actual software

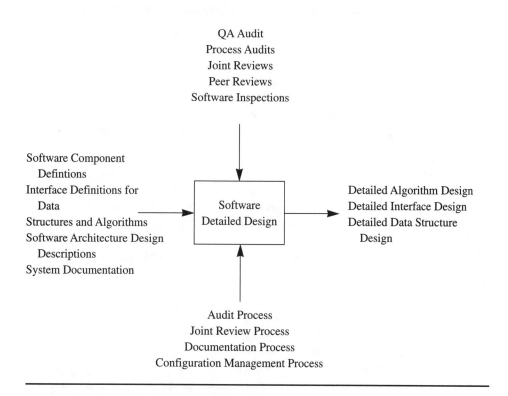

FIGURE 5.15 Software detailed design subtask.

units that were modified. The programmer should update the unit test procedures associated with the modified code and use them to conduct the unit-level testing. This testing includes a determination of whether the modifications actually satisfy the requirements contained in the modification request. This testing may be accomplished in the host or target environment. Throughout coding and testing, the programmer is also responsible for updating the status accounting (tracking) database to ensure that both new and old request are tracked and resolved. All of the information related to the implementation of the solution should be entered into the SDF for the modification request.

Figure 5.16 graphically depicts the coding and testing subtask.

Software Integration After software units are coded and tested, they are integrated into system components or configuration items. These components or configuration items are tested by individuals other than the programmers who actually developed the code. The goal of these testers is to verify the performance of the components, including interfaces to other components or configuration items. All areas within

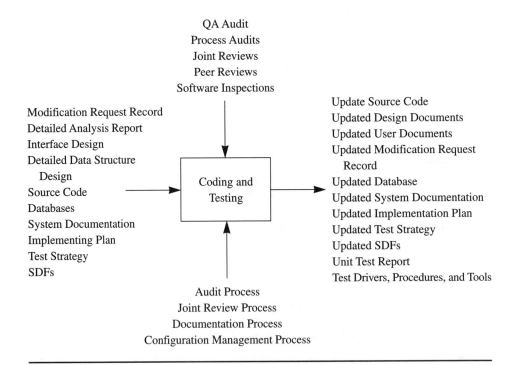

FIGURE 5.16 Coding and testing subtask.

a program that could be affected by the modification must be evaluated through a comprehensive integration test plan. This testing may be accomplished in the host or target environment. As each software item is tested to verify that it satisfies the new requirements, it must also undergo regression testing to ensure that the changes do not have any unwanted side effects. The maintainer integrates the software units and components as they become available, to ensure that each aggregate satisfies the requirements of the modification request. As each software item becomes available, the maintainer modifies the tests, test cases, and test procedures to reflect the modifications to the software. All of this information is added to the SDF.

Ensure that the units are integrated one at a time. Do not try to integrate several units simultaneously!

Once a configuration item has been fully integrated, the maintainer conducts a review in accordance with the joint review process.

Figure 5.17 graphically depicts the software integration subtask.

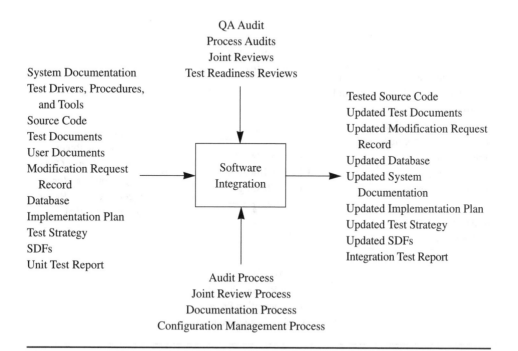

FIGURE 5.17   Software integration subtask.

Software Qualification Testing Software qualification testing is performed to ensure that the requirements of the modification requests are tested for compliance. As part of qualification testing, the maintainer evaluates the design, code, tests, test results, and documentation. The maintainer is then responsible for auditing the software product in accordance with the audit process. If the audit is successful, the maintainer updates and prepares the software product for software acceptance support or software installation, as appropriate. Joint reviews are also conducted.

Figure 5.18 graphically depicts the software qualification testing subtask.

Software Installation The software installation subtask requires the maintainer to develop a plan to install the software product in the target environment. If the product is replacing an existing system, the plan must address operating the old and the new systems in parallel. The installation schedule should be promulgated to the user community to make it clear when the systems become available. If the soft-

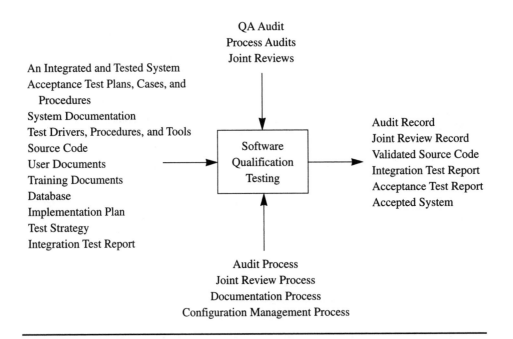

FIGURE 5.18 Software qualification testing subtask.

ware product is simply an upgrade, the old product should be backed up to prevent any loss of data. The installation team should also provide user training as needed.

Figure 5.19 graphically depicts the software installation subtask.

The ISO/IEC 12207 modification implementation activity is finally over. The ISO/IEC 12207 development process is concluded, and the maintenance process continues with the fourth activity—maintenance review and acceptance.

Maintenance Review and Acceptance Activity

The maintenance review and acceptance activity is used to ensure that the software product is correct. This activity invokes the quality assurance, verification, and validation processes. The maintenance plan should have documented how these supporting processes were tailored to address the characteristics of the specific software product. While most of the work can be completed after the change has been implemented, portions of the supporting processes should be in force throughout the implementation activity. Figure 5.20 depicts the tasks that make up the maintenance review and acceptance activity.

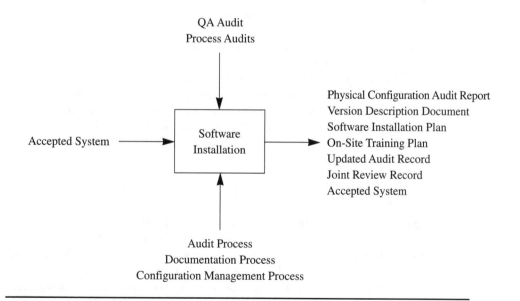

FIGURE 5.19   Software installation subtask.

FIGURE 5.20   Maintenance review and acceptance tasks.

Figure 5.21 graphically depicts the maintenance review and acceptance activity.

Review   In order to ensure that the modified system retains its integrity and that the software product is modified as requested, the maintainer reviews the modification work with the organization authorizing the modification. The code, integration, and documentation are verified. Acceptance and test reports are reviewed. Finally, approval is granted by the acquirer or customer.

The following task-steps are required for the review task:

1. Trace the MR from requirements, to design, to code.
2. Verify testability of the code.
3. Verify that coding standards were met.
4. Verify that only necessary software components were modified.
5. Verify that the new software components were integrated properly.
6. Check documentation to ensure that it was updated.
7. Perform testing.
8. Develop a test report.

Once the review is completed, the approval task is exercised.

Approval   The maintainer obtains approval for the satisfactory completion of the modification as specified in the contract. This approval is obtained by invoking the quality assurance process and coordinating it with the verification, validation, joint review, and audit processes. These processes culminate in a final approval by conducting *functional* and *physical configuration audits* (*FCA* and *PCA*). An FCA assures the customer and the acquirer that the software product and its related docu-

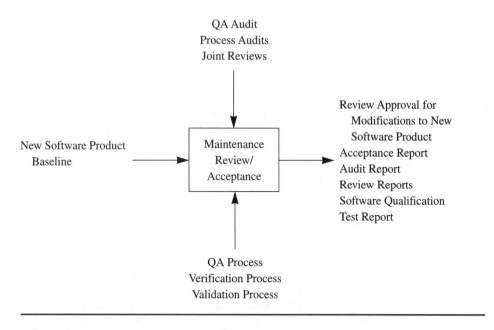

FIGURE 5.21 Maintenance review and acceptance activity.

mentation comply with the contract, and that it satisfies the functional requirements requested in the modification request. The PCA assures the customer and the acquirer that all the software, documentation, and hardware have been delivered. In a maintenance environment, these audits are not usually performed on individual modification requests, but are usually performed for each new release, which may include one or more modification requests.

As part of the approval task, the maintainer obtains approval by executing the following task-steps:

1. Obtain quality assurance approval.
2. Verify that the process has been followed.
3. Conduct an FCA, as appropriate.
4. Conduct a PCA, as appropriate.

Software Migration Activity

Over time, computer systems tend to evolve; a new version of the operating system might provide a new capability, the computer might be upgraded or replaced, or the system might become part of a larger net-

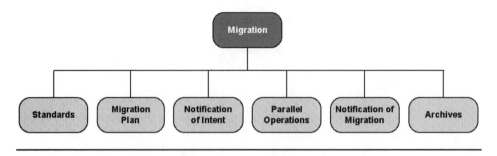

FIGURE 5.22 Software migration tasks.

work. All of these changes could require that the existing software product be adapted to the new environment. If the change involves moving the software product to a new processor, ISO/IEC 12207 calls this type of change a migration from "an old to a new operational environment." There are six tasks associated with migration as depicted in Figure 5.22.

Figure 5.23 graphically depicts the software migration activity.

The following section discusses the tasks associated with the software migration activity.

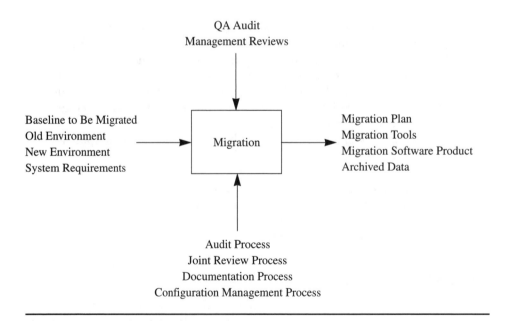

FIGURE 5.23 Software migration activity.

Migration Standards In the process of migrating a software product to a new operational environment, the maintainer must ensure that any additional software products or data produced or modified adhere to ISO/IEC 12207.

As part of the standards task, the maintainer must:

1. Identify all software products or data that were added or modified.
2. Verify that they adhere to ISO/IEC 12207.

Migration Plan In order to ensure a successful migration, a migration plan must be developed, documented, and executed. This plan must be developed in concert with the users and must address the following:

- Requirements analysis and definition of migration.
- Development of migration tools.
- Conversion of software product and data.
- Migration execution.
- Migration verification.
- Support for the old environment in the future.

As part of the migration plan task, the maintainer must execute the following task-steps:

1. Analyze the migration requirements.
2. Determine the impact of migrating the software product.
3. Establish a schedule for performing the migration.
4. Define and document the migration effort.

Notification of Intent As soon as the customer agrees that the software product must be migrated to a new environment, the users should be notified to allow them as much time as possible to prepare for the attending changes. This notification also allows them time to identify site specific issues which may be related to the migration effort.

As part of the notification of intent task, the maintainer notifies the users by executing the following task-steps:

1. Identify all the locations that will be affected.
2. Identify site-specific issues.
3. Promulgate the schedule.
4. Process site feedback.

Parallel Operations Once the software product has been modified and tested in a maintenance environment, it should be installed in an operational environment to run in parallel with the old system. Running the new and old systems in parallel should make the migration smoother by allowing the users an opportunity to become familiar with the new hardware. It also allows the maintainers to observe the system in an operational environment so that they can compare the new system output with that of the old system to ensure that inputs to the systems generate the appropriate outputs. During this period, training should also be provided.

As part of the parallel operations task, the maintainer validates the software product by executing the following task-steps:

1. Perform a site survey.
2. Install the equipment.
3. Install the software.
4. Perform preliminary tests to ensure a successful installation of the hardware and software.
5. Run the software under an operational load in parallel with the old system.
6. Collect data from the new and old products.
7. Perform data reduction and analysis.

Notification of Implementation   After the system has been running in parallel long enough to demonstrate proper operation and allow training to be performed for an appropriate amount of time, the maintainers should notify all sites that the new system will become operational, and that the old system can be shut down and uninstalled. Once the old system has been shut down, all the documentation, logs, and code associated with the old system should be placed in archives.

As part of the notification of implementation task, the maintainer notifies the users of the impending change by executing the following task-steps:

1. Promulgate changes to the migration schedule.
2. Document site specific issues and how they will be resolved.
3. Archive the old software and data.
4. Remove the old equipment.

Impact Analysis   A post-operation review shall be performed to assess the impact of changing to the new environment. The results of the review shall be sent to the appropriate authorities for information, guidance, and action. As part of the impact analysis task, the maintainer reviews the activity by executing the following task-steps:

1. Review the results of operating the systems in parallel.
2. Identify potential risk areas.
3. Identify site-specific issues.
4. Document any lessons learned.
5. Generate and forward an impact analysis report.

Archives Data used by or associated with the old environment need to be accessible in accordance with the contract requirements for data protection and audit applicable to the data. As part of the archives task, the maintainer makes arrangements to preserve old data by executing the following task-steps:

1. Store the old software and data obtained during the notification of implementation task.
2. Make copies of the old software and data obtained during the notification of implementation task.
3. Store the media in a safe place.

Software Retirement Activity

 Eventually a software product outlives its usefulness and must be retired. Sometimes the work performed by the product is no longer needed; in other cases, a new system has been developed to replace the current system. In either case, the software product must be removed from service in an orderly manner. The tasks associated with software retirement are depicted in Figure 5.24.

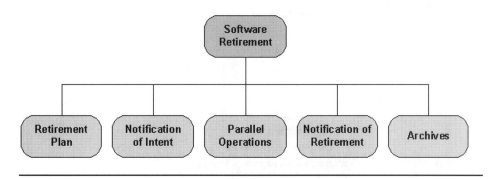

FIGURE 5.24 Software retirement tasks.

Figure 5.25 graphically depicts the software retirement activity.

Retirement Plan In order to ensure a successful retirement, a retirement plan must be developed, documented, and executed. This plan must be developed in concert with the users and must address the following:

■ Cessation of full or partial support after a certain period of time.
■ Archiving of the software product and its associated documentation.
■ Responsibility for any future residual support issues.
■ Transition to the new software product, if applicable.
■ Accessibility of archived copies of the data.

As part of the retirement plan task, the maintainer must execute the following task-steps:

1. Analyze the retirement requirements.
2. Determine the impact of retiring the software product.
3. Establish a schedule for retiring the software product.
4. Define and document the retirement effort.

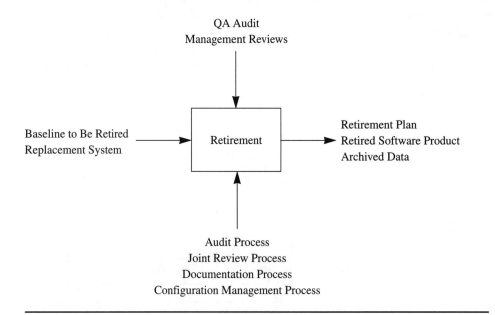

FIGURE 5.25 Software retirement activity.

Notification of Intent As soon as the customer agrees that the software product must be retired, the users should be notified to allow them as much time as possible to prepare for the attending changes. This notification also allows them time to identify site-specific issues that might be related to the retirement effort. The notice of intent should include the following:

- Description of the replacement or upgrade with its date of availability.
- Statement of why the software product is no longer to be supported.
- Description of other support options available, once support has been terminated.

As part of the notification of intent task, the maintainer notifies the users by executing the following task-steps:

1. Identify all the locations that will be affected.
2. Identify site-specific issues.
3. Promulgate the schedule.
4. Process site feedback.

Parallel Operations If there is a replacement system for the software product to be retired, it should be installed in the operational environment to run in parallel with the old system. Running the new and old systems in parallel should make the transition smoother by allowing the users an opportunity to become familiar the new product. During this period, necessary training should also be provided. As part of the parallel operations task, the maintainer validates the software product by executing the following task-steps:

1. Perform a site survey.
2. Install the equipment.
3. Install the software.
4. Perform preliminary tests to ensure a successful installation of the hardware and software.
5. Run the software under an operational load in parallel with the old system.
6. Collect data from the new and old products.
7. Perform data reduction and analysis.

Notification of Retirement After the system has been running in parallel for an appropriate amount of time, the maintainers should notify all sites that the new system will become operational, and that the old system can be shut down and uninstalled. Once the system has been shut down, all the documentation, logs, and code associated with the old system should be placed in archives. If there is no replacement system, the users should be notified when they can shut down and uninstall the old system. As part of the notification of implementation task, the maintainer notifies the users of the impending change by executing the following task-steps:

1. Promulgate changes to the retirement schedule.
2. Document site specific issues and how they will be resolved.
3. Archive the old software and data.
4. Remove the old equipment.

Archives   Data used by or associated with the retired software product needs to be accessible in accordance with the contract requirements for data protection and audit applicable to the data. As part of the archives task, the maintainer makes arrangements to preserve old data by executing the following task-steps:

1. Store the old software and data obtained during the notification of implementation task.
2. Make copies of the old software and data obtained during the notification of implementation task.
3. Store the media in a safe place.

SUMMARY

For those of you who read this chapter—Congratulations! It was dry, but hopefully it will help you implement a correct process. The following chapters are easier to read.

1. How could you use the ISO/IEC maintenance process in your organization?

2. What is not represented in the ISO/IEC maintenance process?

3. Does following the ISO/IEC maintenance process enable better planning for the maintainer? Why?

4. Model the maintenance process.

Predelivery Software Maintenance Activities

The previous chapter provided details of the ISO/IEC 12207 maintenance process. Recognizing that ISO/IEC 12207 is designed primarily for contractual arrangements (it can be used for in-house maintenance), the verbiage is very structured and discusses *what* the software life-cycle processes should be. The implementation, or *how*, is left to the maintainer.

The remaining chapters in the book provide some of the *how* information that maintainers need. These chapters include several case studies to reinforce concepts and to provide additional practical experiences. From there, maintainers can select approaches they deem appropriate for their maintenance organization, and include them in an implementation of ISO/IEC 12207. Topics run the gamut from predelivery planning to education and training. First of all, however, there is discussion of predelivery activities, why this topic is important for maintainers, and what maintainers should do as predelivery activities.

The role of software maintenance changes throughout the predelivery and postdelivery stages. There is a need for software maintenance involvement, whether the development organization will maintain the system or a separate maintainer will maintain it. The fact remains that certain activities should be performed during the predelivery stage. In the context of ISO/IEC 12207, predelivery is during the process implementation activity. Postdelivery begins in process implementation and runs all the way to the retirement activity.

If the developer is to retain maintenance responsibility, the developer needs to plan and provide for its cost-effectiveness. Regrettably, most developers do not focus on such issues as supportability and overall life-cycle costs, because they are so busy trying to get a product out the door that they cannot focus on these important issues. What if there was a separate organization whose sole purpose during development was to prepare for the life-cycle support of the system? Maybe it could be the maintainer? Well—that seems like a neat idea, but is it practical? This chapter provides an introduction to predelivery activities. Stay tuned.

WHAT THE EXPERTS SAY

Martin, Swanson, and Capers Jones emphatically state that the cost of software maintenance and the software maintainer's capability to conduct software maintenance is greatly influenced by what occurs or does not occur during the predelivery stage. Norm Schneidewind (1987) states that many of the problems in maintenance are because maintenance is viewed as a postdelivery activity. These ideas are absolutely accurate. If the software maintainer is not involved in the predelivery activities, the cost of maintenance will increase over the life cycle, and the ability of the maintainer to perform software maintenance will be hampered.

The cost of software maintenance and the ability of software maintainers to perform software maintenance functions are directly related to their level of involvement during the predelivery stage.

THE CONFLICT

Early involvement of the software maintainer during predelivery is a nice concept, but how does it work in practice? Many corporate and government directives state that software maintainers should be involved during the predelivery stage, but what really happens? Is it that easy? Is there general consensus that it is a good idea to have the software maintainers involved early? What would they do? Is it really cost-effective? Does early involvement really enhance the capability of the software maintainer to perform maintenance?

Answers to the above depend upon a number of factors. First you must understand the roles and responsibilities of all the parties involved and the politics that relate to the software development effort. Having the maintainer involved early during predelivery causes a potential conflict. The parties involved in the conflict include the customer, user, supplier (developer) and maintainer. (Please review the definitions of these parties in Chapter 1.)

- The customer (or acquirer) acquires the system, and wants it built quickly and inexpensively.
- The developer (or supplier) must develop the system, and wants to deliver on time and within budget.
- The user will ultimately operate the system, and will want the system *yesterday*!
- The maintainer must live with the results of the development, and must maintain it for some extended period (far longer than the development).

Each has a different focus. Whereas the first three (customer, developer, and user) are primarily interested in getting a new system fielded, the maintainer should be more concerned with ensuring that the new system is supportable and can be maintained in a cost-effective manner. Therein lies the conflict. Can you imagine the maintainer being inserted in the development organization and trying to infuse supportability or maintainability issues *during the development?* What would be the result? Schedule slippage? Cost overruns?

Fearing the answers (or not wanting to ask the questions) often tips the decision in favor of getting the new system fielded. Therefore, many times the maintainer is not involved during predelivery and merely comes in late (when the system is completed) and must assume maintenance responsibility.

HOW TO RESOLVE THE CONFLICT

What can be done to resolve this conflict? What is in the best interest of all concerned? The facts are very clear—*early involvement reduces life-cycle costs*. The maintainer must strive to accommodate all the other parties, but must be successful in reducing life-cycle costs. Maintainers must find a way to "work within the system" and be involved early. What is the best approach?

In comes the logistics organization: that element of an organization responsible for procuring, maintaining, and transporting material, personnel, and facilities. For many organizations, the IS or DP Department performs logistic functions. In the context of the parties discussed thus far (customer, developer, user, maintainer), the customer (or acquirer) typically makes provisions for logistics support. Some organizational element within the customer organization is responsible for logistics support for hardware, software, and systems.

Logistics organizations have been around for a long time, and their expertise lies in systems and hardware—not software. Until recently, logistics planning efforts have not applied to software, and planning for maintenance has not been accomplished by logistics organizations. Often the developer plans maintenance. The maintainers have tried to force supportability and maintainability issues on customers, developers, and users, and in many cases have not been successful.

This is where the logistics people can help. Logistics organizations are well-established. They do an outstanding job of planning system and hardware life-cycle (or maintenance) support. However, they have done very little in the area of software life-cycle support.

Based on the backgrounds of the logistics people, the traditional logistics organizations have deferred the software life-cycle support planning to the developer or the maintainer. Thus, you could have the developer, who may or may not perform maintenance, deciding what the software maintenance organization will have in terms of resources. Historically, this has not worked. Developers are concerned with developing, and when saddled with the responsibility of planning maintenance support, they pay very little attention to maintenance. More importantly, the developer's viewpoint will not be the same as the viewpoint from the software maintenance organization.

THE MAINTAINER MUST INFLUENCE THE LOGISTICS ORGANIZATION

Often when the software maintenance organization plans maintenance support, it is viewed as self-serving by the customer and users. Very often customers and users state that maintainers want (or demand) too much: too many resources, too much time, too much maintainability. This goes back to the customer and user perceptions that maintenance is merely fixing bugs. On one hand, customers and users have a hard time agreeing to devote significant resources to maintenance and often use the recommendations of the developer for maintenance planning. If you were a developer and wanted to continue performing maintenance, would your cost and resource estimates be colored by your desire to get the work? After all, once you have the work, the user really decides (through the software configuration management process) what the maintainer actually works on! However, the software maintenance organization is the organization that will have to live with the maintenance support decisions, and had better be very active during predelivery. The maintainer must live with the product of the predelivery stage for a long time. The best way for the maintainer to get the proper support is by influencing the logistics organization and the support documentation.

The maintainer must influence the logistics organization.

MAINTENANCE BEGINS WITH THE LOGISTICS ORGANIZATION

When should involvement by the customer's (acquirer) logistics organization commence? The customer's logistics organization should be involved during the preparation of specifications, and prior to any decision to either contract out the development or assign the development to an in-house development organization. During that time, the logistics organization must also discuss maintenance. The logistics organization should:

- Develop a support strategy for maintenance.
- Designate the maintainer.
- Investigate alternative support concepts.
- Assist in defining the scope of maintenance.
- Help define the maintenance support system (hardware and software).

The maintainer should work through the logistics organization to get the resources it needs for maintenance.

When should involvement by the maintainer commence? Involvement by the maintainer, whether it be an organization separate from the developer (which is recommended) or the developer who retains the responsibility, begins early-on in the predelivery stage. What does that mean? For example, say a software development effort is to be undertaken by means of a contract. The software maintenance organization should be designated and involved before the signing of the contract. The software maintenance organization should even participate in the development of the contract specifications!

Practical Experiences

The software maintenance organization must be involved in the predelivery stage. But when? How early in the development effort? How early is early? When should the software maintenance organization get involved? At the IEEE Computer Society's Conference on Software Maintenance—1990 in San Diego, CA, Tom Vollman (1990) stated that maintainers should be involved in excess of two years before the system is due to transition. My experience indicates that it can be up to three years in advance of delivery of a large system. If a system is under development and the software maintenance organization has not been formally designated in writing and is not participating in the predelivery activities, life-cycle costs will increase. Quite often the software maintenance organization is not designated early-on because the delivery of the product will not occur for two to three years. The developers don't want to think about maintenance, and neither do the customers or users. I submit that at the two-year mark, the software maintenance organization is getting involved too late. On the other hand, software maintenance organizations normally know which systems may come to them for support. They too have a responsibility to "force the issue" regarding designation of the software maintenance organization. The maintainer needs to get designated and involved early. It's in everyone's best interest.

THE THREE AREAS OF PREDELIVERY MAINTENANCE

What does the software maintenance organization do during the predelivery stage? The activities of the software maintenance organization during the predelivery stage can be grouped into three major areas:

1. Plan for the logistics of supporting the system.
2. Ensure the supportability of the system.
3. Plan for transition of the system.

The next few chapters discuss each of these areas in more detail and provide some practical experiences.

SUMMARY

This chapter discussed the conflict among the different people involved in developing the maintenance strategy and supplying maintenance. Making maintenance a predelivery activity disrupts the traditional flow of how to supply maintenance, but moving maintenance planning to the beginning of the life cycle, designating what activities should occur, and determining who will be responsible for these activities produces a better product. This chapter also introduced the three things a maintenance organization should do in the predelivery stage: Plan for the logistics of supporting the system, ensure the supportability of the system, and plan for transition of the system. These activities will be discussed in greater detail in the upcoming chapters.

1. Why is there a conflict between the different organizations that are involved in maintenance when maintenance becomes a predelivery activity?

2. What is the difference between the activities the logistics organization is responsible for and the activities the maintenance organization is responsible for during predelivery?

3. Discuss the activities you think the maintainer should do during predelivery.

Planning, Parts I and II: The Maintenance Concept and the Maintenance Plan

7

It is sometimes not clear who has the responsibility for software maintenance. For federal government-developed systems, program managers (who are part of the customer organization) have the ultimate responsibility. They receive assistance from the developer and the software maintenance organization. Developers know the system best, so they are the ones best suited to determine the maintenance needs—or so the story goes. Remember, however, the roles, responsibilities, and goals of the various parties involved. The customer and developer want the system on time and within budget; the maintainer's focus is on the supportability of the system. One way to help alleviate the conflict is good planning. This chapter discusses the first two parts of planning, the *maintenance concept* (which is accomplished very early in planning) and the *maintenance plan*, which follows later.

WHAT IS MAINTENANCE PLANNING?

Maintenance planning prepares for the human and material resources required to provide software maintenance for delivered systems. With proper planning and logistical support, maintainers can reduce life-cycle costs. Proper planning for software maintenance consists of the following elements:

- Maintenance concept.
- Maintenance plan.
- Resource analysis.

The following sections discuss the maintenance concept and maintenance plan, while resource analysis is addressed in Chapter 8.

WHAT IS THE MAINTENANCE CONCEPT?

The maintenance concept addresses:

- The scope of software maintenance.
- The tailoring of the postdelivery process.
- The designation of who will provide maintenance.
- An estimate of life-cycle costs.

The maintenance concept should be developed early in the development effort by the customer with help from the maintainer. The following discusses each element of the maintenance concept.

The Scope of Software Maintenance

Defining the scope of maintenance helps determine exactly how much support the maintainer will give the customer. Scope relates to how responsive the maintainer will be to the users (MIL-HDBK-347 1990). There are many ways to define scope, but the following provides what I have seen in use:

Level 1 Full maintenance: includes improvements, training, help desk, full documentation, and delivery support. For example, the maintainer performs all the functions of software maintenance, and implements all problem reports and enhancement requests.

Level 2 Corrective maintenance: provides for full maintenance, but no improvements. Only corrective maintenance will be performed. The system will not evolve, and no new user requirements will be implemented. For example, the customers might decide that they only want corrections fixed, as there is not sufficient funding to implement enhancement requests.

Level 3 Limited corrective maintenance: provides for reduced maintenance. Only the highest priority problem reports are worked. For example, the customer might experience a problem that causes the system to fail. Level 3 provides for correction of the problem.

Level 4 Limited software configuration management: provides no money for maintenance. Only limited SCM functions are performed. For example, the customer might designate one of its employees to perform the software configuration management functions of tracking problem reports and doing system configuration. This might be performed until future funding becomes available to increase the level of support.

Budgetary constraints often dictate the scope of maintenance. If you are the software maintenance organization, you can be a hero. Just tell your boss that you can cut maintenance costs by 80%. Then tell her that only corrective actions will be performed; there will be *no new enhancements*. If some capability was not designed in, but is now a requirement, it will never get included in the system because no money exists for improvements. Tell the news to the customers, acquirers, and users who are very concerned about the high cost of maintenance, too; they probably will not be happy with having to settle for a stagnant system. The point here is that *you can control the costs by controlling the scope*. However, everyone involved (particularly the users) must understand what they will or will not get.

The users must understand the scope of maintenance for their system.

The Tailoring of the Postdelivery Process

The maintenance concept also addresses the activities of postdelivery software maintenance. Different organizations often perform different activities in the postdelivery process. An early attempt should be made to identify these organizations and to document them in the maintenance concept. Take the example of distributing a large software manufacturer's commercial word-processing product: The developer might not be the maintainer; the maintenance activity could be given to another organization. The maintainer might be in Oregon, a regional

group might perform training, and a subcontractor in Utah might operate the help desk. The maintenance concept should address the fact that maintenance involves many activities, and there might be different entities performing each activity.

The maintenance concept must determine which activities of maintenance will be performed and by whom. For example, the customer could decide not to have the maintainer provide training and a help desk. The maintenance concept must reflect the customer's wishes. It must be recognized that the concept is developed very early in the development phase. Many decisions will change by the time the product is delivered. A maintenance concept is just that—a concept. As further information develops, the concept is modified as it is implemented.

The maintenance concept reflects the maintenance process that will be employed. If the new definition of maintenance and ISO/IEC 12207's maintenance process is used, the maintenance concept will define who does which activities prior to delivery and who is responsible for postdelivery activities. It might be the same people; the maintenance concept must reflect this.

The Designation of Who Will Provide Maintenance

 Figuring out exactly who or which maintenance organization should perform maintenance for a particular system involves many factors. If the system only has a lifespan of two years, perhaps the developer should maintain it. Large multinational corporations might decide to have a separate maintenance organization perform the maintenance functions. These are only two of many factors impacting the decision process.

Each maintenance organization alternative needs to be evaluated against a set of evaluation factors. The evaluation factors are those items that are considered important in the selection of an organization, such as cost and past performance. The following text delineates the actions needed to select a maintenance organization.

The first step is to look at alternatives for performing maintenance. Should one organization provide all maintenance activities, or would multiple organizations perform maintenance? Next, the candidate organizations are identified, and then an evaluation to determine the appropriate one to perform maintenance activities is performed.

In theory there is an unlimited number of organizations who can potentially support the software products. To keep the number of candidates manageable, it is best to do some prescreening and narrow the list to only realistic candidates. The next step is to develop criteria for evaluating the candidates. Finally, a weighting factor is applied to each evaluation factor.

Evaluation Factors for Organization Alternatives The following is the set of evaluation factors that can be used to evaluate each candidate organization:

- Long-term costs.
- Start-up costs.
- Space.
- Qualifications.
- Past performance.

- Availability.
- Schedule.
- Domain knowledge.

Each evaluation factor can be assigned a rating (e.g., from 1 to 3), with 1 being the lowest and 3 the highest rating. The ratings are applied to each evaluation factor for each organization alternative. As each evaluation factor is considered more important or less important in the selection process, a weighting factor is also applied to each evaluation factor. The following provides more details concerning evaluation factors that are often used.

Long-Term Costs. The relative cost of each organization to provide the needed support is determined. The cost factor is a subjective measure of the cost to provide the needed support for the full life-cycle of the software products.

Start-Up Costs. The relative cost to procure and install requisite software maintenance requirements, develop processes, and fully train personnel in order to provide the needed services is determined.

Space. The space required to house a maintainer is determined. An assessment of each organization's capability to accommodate its requirements must be made.

Qualifications. The maintainer must be qualified and geared to provide the needed support. Each organization is evaluated to see if it is performing similar maintenance activities and if it is qualified to assume the role of the maintainer.

Past Performance. Each organization's past performance as a maintainer is evaluated.

Availability. Each organization is evaluated regarding its availability to take on additional responsibility as a maintainer.

Schedule. Each organization is evaluated regarding its ability to start the maintenance effort in the near term and build up to a fully operational maintainer.

Domain Knowledge. The selected organization should possess domain knowledge. Possession of domain knowledge would accelerate the establishment of the maintainer and aid in providing quality support. Each organization is evaluated regarding its domain knowledge and specific knowledge.

TABLE 7.1 Evaluation Factors/Organization Alternatives

Evaluation Factors	Organization						
	A	B	C	D	E	F	G
Long-term Costs	1	1	3	3	2	1	2
Start-up Costs	1	3	3	1	2	1	1
Space	3	3	3	3	3	3	1
Qualifications	1	3	3	3	2	2	3
Past Performance	1	2	3	2	2	2	3
Availability	3	3	1	3	3	3	1
Schedule	1	3	1	3	2	3	1
Domain Knowledge	2	2	1	3	3	3	1
TOTALS	13	20	18	21	19	18	13

Analysis of Evaluation Factors for Organization Alternatives: A Case Study The eight evaluation factors discussed above are used to determine a recommended organization alternative. Based on the relative advantages and disadvantages of each concept alternative, ratings are applied to each organization alternative. For example, a rating of "3" for cost indicates that the cost relative to that organization is better (in this case lower) than for the other alternatives. Table 7.1 shows actual data from a case study for seven organizations. They are referred to as Organizations A through G, respectively.

Weighting Factors. The evaluation factors discussed above are not equally weighted. Based on stated requirements, the weighting factors shown in Table 7.2 are used to provide a more accurate assessment of the various organization alternatives.

Analysis of Weighting Factors. The results of applying the weighting factors to the evaluation factors are depicted in Table 7.3.

Recommendation As can be seen from Table 7.3, the optimal organization to provide maintenance activities is the organization noted by the letter *D*. Thus, "D" would be the organization recommended to provide the support.

Conclusion of Case Study Now you have an idea of how to select an organization to serve as maintainer. Once you know who will perform maintenance, the next step in finalizing the maintenance concept is to determine the costs associated with the maintenance effort.

TABLE 7.2 Weighting Factors

Factor	Percentage
Long-term Costs	30%
Start-up Costs	10%
Space	15%
Qualifications	10%
Past Performance	10%
Availability	5%
Schedule	10%
Domain Knowledge	10%

An Estimate of Life-Cycle Costs

An estimate of life-cycle costs needs to be prepared. The costs are purely a function of the scope of software maintenance. Level 1, or full maintenance, is considerably more expensive than Level 4, limited software configuration management. Additional factors to include are:

- Travel to user locations.
- Training for the software maintenance staff as well as for the users.
- Cost and annual maintenance of the hardware and software environment.
- Personnel costs such as salaries and benefits.

TABLE 7.3 Weighted Results of Organization Alternatives

Evaluation Factors	Organization						
	A	B	C	D	E	F	G
Long-term Costs	0.30	0.30	0.90	0.90	0.60	0.30	0.60
Start-up Costs	0.20	0.30	0.10	0.10	0.10	0.20	0.10
Space	0.45	0.45	0.45	0.45	0.45	0.45	0.15
Qualifications	0.10	0.30	0.30	0.20	0.20	0.20	0.30
Past Performance	0.10	0.20	0.30	0.20	0.20	0.20	0.30
Availability	0.15	0.15	0.05	0.15	0.15	0.15	0.05
Schedule	0.10	0.30	0.30	0.30	0.20	0.30	0.10
Domain Knowledge	0.20	0.20	0.10	0.30	0.20	0.30	0.10
TOTALS	1.60	2.20	2.50	2.60	2.10	2.10	1.7

Initially, it is very difficult to estimate all the above. The estimates must be determined based on the limited data available at the time. These will be refined as the system takes shape. A good rule of for annual maintenance costs for full maintenance is between 10% and 15% of the development costs. Thus, if a system cost $1M to develop, between $100K and $150K *per year* for *each year* in the life of the system should be budgeted for software maintenance.

Allocate 10% to 15% of total development costs to annual maintenance costs.

WHAT IS THE MAINTENANCE PLAN?

Once the maintenance concept is determined, the next step is to develop the maintenance plan. The maintenance plan should be prepared during software development and should specify how users will request modifications or report problems. It should also define all quality assurance and test activities, including how users are involved in acceptance testing. The *IEEE Standard on Software Maintenance* (IEEE 1219 1993) suggests an overall maintenance plan but does not state who is responsible for the planning.

A typical maintenance plan should cover:

- Why support will be needed.
- Who will do what work.
- What the roles and responsibilities of everyone involved will be.
- What the estimated size of the staff for the project will be.
- How the work will be performed.
- What resources will be available for support (See Chapter 8).
- Where support will be performed.
- When support will commence.

For some organizations, like the U. S. DoD, the maintenance plan is part of a *computer resources life cycle management plan (CRLCMP)*. For other organizations, the maintenance plan can be part of a life cycle plan or a stand-alone maintenance plan. It is not critical what form the plan takes, or if it is part of another document. What is important is that it is developed!

The following provides a sample of an outline of a maintenance plan.

Example of a Maintenance Plan

1. Introduction
   Describe the system to be supported.
   Identify the initial status of the software.
   Describe why support is needed.
   Identify the maintainer.
   Describe any contractual protocols between customer and supplier.
2. Maintenance concept
   Describe the concept.
   Describe the level of support for the system.
   Describe the support period from predelivery to postdelivery support.
   Tailor the maintenance process by referring to the maintainer's process manual.
3. Organization and maintenance activities
   Define the predelivery roles and responsibilities of the maintainer.
      Quality Assurance.
      Testing.
      Independent Verification and Validation (IV&V).
   Define the postdelivery roles and responsibilities of the maintainer.
   Software Modification.
      Quality Assurance.
      Software Configuration Modification.
      Training of the maintainer.
      Training of the user.
      Help desk.
      Documentation.
      Installation.
   Define the role of the user.
      Acceptance Testing.
   Interface with other organizations.
4. Specify resources
   Determine personnel requirements.
      Size of staff for the project.
   Identify software needed to support the system, plus software maintenance tools requirements.
   Identify hardware needed to support the system, plus software maintenance testing requirements.

> Identify facilities requirements.
> Identify documentation units.
>> Software quality plan.
>> Project management plan.
>> Development documents.
>> Maintenance manuals.
> Identify data requirements.
> Identify other resource requirements (if needed).
> 5. Identify the process and how the work will be performed
> Give an overview of the maintainer's process.
> Tailor the process.
> 6. Identify training requirements
> Identify training needs of the maintainer.
> Identify training needs of the user.
> 7. Identify maintenance records and reports.
> Determine what is needed to produce accurate records
> Lists of requests for assistance or problem reports.
>> Status of requests.
>> Priorities of requests.
> Metric data on maintenance activities.

The maintenance plan should be developed early in the development phase. Although all the data might not be available at that time, as much detail as possible should be included in the plan. Updates will be necessary and common. For large, multi-year projects the plan should be updated annually. For contractual efforts between a customer and supplier, it should have sufficient detail to ensure that both parties understand and agree to the scope and level of the maintenance effort.

When to Address Supportability   One aspect of the maintenance plan needs further attention. During the predelivery stage, the maintainer should endeavor to ensure that the software is supportable. However, supportability is often not given much consideration during this time. The program manager for a system needs to field that system on time and within budget, and is not necessarily concerned with supportability. Mosemann (1992) tells us that supportability is not a goal in system acquisition.

The maintainer has an interest in supportability. After the program manager receives a promotion and bonus for fielding the system on time and within budget, the maintainer now has the problem of supporting the system with an environment, resources, and quality provided by the program manager during the development. How can the maintainer help to ensure the supportability of the system? The maintainer should look at the characteristics of the software. How about the maintainer performing a maintainability assessment of the system? How about identifying error-prone modules? The maintainer should evaluate the software engineering environment and the status of maintainer resources. Opportunities for the maintainer to evaluate the software supportability occur during reviews, IV&V activities, testing, and so forth. For a discussion of maintainability, see Chapter 16. For now, it is important to note that the maintenance plan needs to allow the maintainer to get involved in the maintainability aspects of the system under development.

When to Address Metrics

The other aspect of the maintenance plan that needs attention is the statistical or metric data for outstanding modification requests. As a minimum the maintainer must evaluate metrics (see Chapter 16) to determine the maintainability of the software. These metrics must be applied to the software and documentation throughout predelivery and postdelivery of the software. The maintainer must have access to the outstanding requests and their status in order to estimate maintenance efforts. This is particularly important in maintenance outsourcing.

SUMMARY

You now know how to do the first two parts of maintenance planning, the maintenance concept and the maintenance plan. The maintenance plan will include the maintenance concept and details about resource analysis. So how do you do resource analysis? Often, because the details of the system take so long to become established, resource analysis ends up being the last part of the planning process. So how do you determine resources? The next chapter will tell you.

1. What are the four levels of the scope of maintenance?

2. Why is it important to add weighting factors to determine which maintenance organization you should pick?

3. Create your own maintenance concept and outline a maintenance plan.

8

Planning, Part III: Resources

Once you determine the scope of maintenance and which organization will perform maintenance, you can concentrate on how to determine your personnel, maintenance environment, and financial resource requirements. Who's responsible for determining the resource requirements for software maintenance? For the U. S. DoD, it is the customer (acquirer) with assistance from the supplier (developer) and the maintainer. In the commercial sector, it is usually the developing organization with assistance from the maintainer. In either case, good communications are necessary in order to obtain the needed resources. Outsourced maintainers will have to estimate resources competitively to win contracts. What kind of resources are we talking about? There are personnel, environment resources and financial resources. First is a discussion of the personnel resources.

HOW DO YOU DETERMINE PERSONNEL RESOURCES?

One of the major issues in planning for software maintenance is the issue of software maintenance resource requirements planning. Personnel requirements are a major cost factor, and, at the same time, the most difficult to accurately estimate. Remember the example of a million-lines-of-code system or a large system with over 5,000 function points coming to the maintainer for support. Earlier you were asked to consider some of the things that the maintainer could do during the pre-

delivery stage. Certainly one of those things is to help with estimating the required personnel resources. How many people would it take to support a system of one million lines of code or 5000 function points? How do you determine that number? Even better—who determines that number? Who has to live with the results of that number?

Perhaps, the most important issue here is who determines the software maintenance personnel resource requirements. As previously stated, the customers or developers normally make that decision, but hopefully with input from the maintainers. What if the maintainer is not identified, not designated, and thus not participating in predelivery activities? If the program manager for the effort determines that, say 10 people can support 1M LOC, and uses that number for life-cycle resource profiles, that is all that the maintainer will get. Certainly, if the maintainer is not designated early nor involved early, the maintainer will have to live by someone else's estimates.

Another question persists: Is it in the best interest of the program manager to come up with a realistic number of people to perform software maintenance functions? Of course not. This can be the case even if the developer will also have maintenance responsibility under a "cradle-to-grave" concept of support. In this case, the PM is still involved throughout the life cycle. He or she must deal with the delicate issue of convincing everyone concerned about the large quantity of maintenance resources needed. The acquirer has just paid millions of dollars to develop a system, and now the program manager drops the bomb that it will take a large number of people per year to perform routine maintenance functions. The acquirer's (customer's) reaction is that

they want the program manager to build a system that requires *virtually no maintenance*, and therefore little or no maintenance resources. Have you ever heard a user or customer state that if the system were built better, there would be no need for maintenance? I have!

Why do they say that? It all goes back to how users view maintenance. You need to recognize that the majority of users still classify maintenance as merely fixing problems or mistakes. Thus, they believe that if the system were built better, it would not require maintenance. That is one reason why they are willing to accept new technology, such as object-oriented technology (OOT), without any analysis; they believe that maintenance will be decreased.

For many government or industry organizations, there might be joint planning efforts to determine the level of personnel required to provide software maintenance for a software system. In these efforts, the maintainer must clarify exactly what happens in the maintenance phase, and the scope of the maintenance effort, so that the program manager understands. If the program manager realizes that maintenance is more than just fixing bugs, determining how many people need to be designated for maintenance will be much easier. In any event, it is important to address this area very early in the predelivery stage, get agreement on what that number of personnel is, and to document the agreement.

You now know *who* is responsible for estimating software maintenance personnel resources. The next questions are: How do you estimate them at your organization? Do you have a methodology or process for estimating?

Is it difficult to estimate software maintenance resources? Is it different from development? Do the same approaches work? When do you determine them? How do you verify the accuracy of the estimates? Finally, if you had to estimate resources and live with those estimates, how would you do it? How do you determine maintenance personnel resources at your organization?

TWO APPROACHES TO DETERMINING PERSONNEL RESOURCES

The two most popular approaches for estimating resources for software maintenance are use of parametric models and use of experience. Both have mixed reviews, and there are pluses and minuses for each approach.

Use of Parametric Models

The most significant and authoritative work in the area of software estimating is *Software Engineering Economics* by Dr. Barry W. Boehm (1981). His book discusses a model that puts the software life cycle and the quantitative life-cycle relationships into a hierarchy of software cost-estimation models bearing the generic name *COCOMO* (derived from COnstructive COst MOdel). Surprisingly, many do not realize that COCOMO can be used to estimate staffing for software maintenance. Seemingly all the other available models, both in the private sector and DoD, are by their own admission derivatives of COCOMO.

There are numerous other estimating tools, and at least one new one enters the market every month (Jones 1994). Some of the other popular estimating tools are:

- GECOMO
- REVIC
- SLIM
- CHECKPOINT
- SOFTCOST

Some of these models use lines of code, and the new models use function points. For details on cost estimating, including models and tools, the Software Technology Center (STC 1994) regularly provides details about estimating tools. Jones (1994) provides an entire chapter on inaccurate cost estimating. Putnam and W. Meyers (1996) state that the key estimate for cost is size, and they provide more informa- 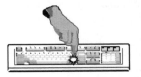 tion regarding estimating. For all of these models, historical data is needed. As an example, for COCOMO, you must input annual change traffic (ACT). Boehm defines ACT as the number of source lines of code modified or the number of lines "touched" during the year. If you add, subtract, or modify lines of code, you count them. ACT is expressed as a percentage of the total size of the system in lines of code and is computed on an annual basis. If system size is 100K LOC and you "touched" 10K LOC during the year, the ACT would be 10%. Without good ACT data, you really cannot use the models.

Models need historical empirical data.

These models are discussed later in the chapter in the form of a case study.

Boehm (1981) also provides a cost-of-effort estimating model based on a ratio of maintenance to development effort. Using a subjective industry ratio that says that the life cycle is 40% development and 60% maintenance, we get a maintenance-to-development ratio of 1:1.5. This ratio is applied and maintenance estimates are calculated.

Use of Experience

What about experience? If a parametric model is not used to determine maintenance staffing, you must use experience. What are the elements of experience? You could use sound judgment, reason, a work breakdown structure, a wild guess, an educated wild guess, or a scientific wild guess. Those are about the only options. Do you use this approach? Has it been successful? Try to convince your boss that you need personnel resources for software maintenance using one of those approaches!

Empirical Data The best approach in using experience is to have empirical, historical data. Ideally, organizations should have this as part of a metrics program (Chapters 14–16 provide details on metrics). If not, organizations can canvass the literature for data collected, compiled, and analyzed by other organizations. Software Productivity Research (SPR) has extensive data relating to maintenance. Jones' books (1986, 1991, 1994) all provide empirical data. Howard Rubin, now editor of "IT Metrics Strategies (ITMS)," continues to publish measurement results, including maintenance data. Both of these sources are good for empirical maintenance data. The International Workshop on Empirical Studies of Software Maintenance, held in conjunction with the International Conference on Software Maintenance, provides maintenance data from real-world sources.

Call Your Peers Another approach, albeit very informal and not very scientific, is to call your software maintenance practitioner peers and find out if they have empirical data. Also find out what "methodology" they use to estimate personnel resources for maintenance.

Practical Experience

A peer of mine in the field of software maintenance worked for a large government agency and was called upon to determine personnel resources for a large system transitioning to his maintenance organization. The good news was that he was a maintainer and was asked to determine the resources. The supplier, a sister organization at the government agency, did not address the personnel needs. Once given the task, he developed his estimates based on experience. He had been in the software business for 25 years and in maintenance for about 15. He presented his numbers and his case to his boss, who promptly dismissed him with, "You don't have an algorithm! You don't have any empirical data! How did you determine the estimate?" Unfortunately, his extensive experience was not sufficient.

Experience, without empirical data and methodology, is often not sufficient to obtain needed maintenance resources!

Summary of Approaches

What are maintainers using as approaches or methodologies for estimating resources for maintenance? Most of the literature recommends the use of models. In practice, maintainers use models colored by lots of experience and black magic.

The *Military Handbook on Mission-Critical Computer Resources Software Support* (MIL-HDBK-347 1990) devotes an entire appendix to a general methodology for performing postdelivery resource analysis and projecting maintenance resource requirements. Among other things, the *Handbook* states that personnel requirements are a major postdelivery cost component, and, at the same time, the most difficult to accurately estimate. It also states that estimating postdelivery personnel resource requirements is often a "best-guess" endeavor. It finally states that, although there are many models available, they do not consider all postdelivery phases and activities, and they are not intended to replace sound judgment or experience. Sound judgment and experience often do not work. Without historical data, they never will work.

There are real issues when determining software maintenance staffing requirements. Unfortunately, there is not a standard methodology. Most organizations do not have an approved approach and do not "trust" parametric models. Everyone does it differently. However, the only other approach—use of experience and "sound judgment"—usually has no substance, and, therefore, is not accepted at the upper-management level. More importantly, everyone's experience is different. Thus, how can experience be used effectively to estimate resources? Worst of all, most organizations do not have *any* empirical data from systems that were supported in the past upon which to base future estimates. Based on these issues, it might be fair to say that estimating maintenance personnel is an art and not a science. Most organizations have a basic mistrust of models.

A SPECIFIC PERSONNEL RESOURCE PROBLEM: A CASE STUDY

The above illustrates the approaches that can be used to estimate maintenance personnel resources. The following case study (Pigoski 1992) provides an example of what was used as a methodology for estimating maintenance resources. In this case study, a Navy software maintenance organization (the maintainer) maintained large intelligence-related systems. As the software maintenance organization was a brand-new organization, obtaining resources was not difficult initially. Included in the resource allocation was staffing to maintain two large software systems. No real methodology was used to determine the staffing. The program manager of the Navy development effort never did provide an estimate. The maintainers did not exist, so they could not "assist" in the estimating. In the end, the staffing for the two systems was buried in the overall staffing for the new organization.

Details of the Problem

As expected, additional systems were destined to come to the Navy software maintenance organization. On one of the many trips to Head-

quarters in Washington, DC, maintenance personnel were asked informally how many people it would take to support a new system under development. The new system was very complex, estimated at over 700K lines of code, used a language that the maintainer did not currently support or have experience with (Ada), and was a very high-visibility project. Based on experience and an "old rule of thumb" that each programmer could maintain 20K LOC, the estimate came in at about 35 people. The number 35 was totally unacceptable. Headquarters advised that only 17 people were supporting the existing system (the one that the new one would replace) and that 17 was all that would be available.

Experience indicated that 17 people could not provide Full support—Level 1. It would not have been so bad if the scope of software maintenance was limited in some fashion to say a Level 2 or 3, whereby some activities were not performed—but that was not the case. This system was so important and so complex that it required full maintenance support.

The problem was that a standard methodology for estimating maintenance resources did not exist. No methodology was used. Particularly

irritating was that the program manager at the Navy systems command stated that if the true maintenance number was 35, he would be fired for building a system that was so complex and that required so many people to maintain it.

The real problem here was that the system was the first of many new ones to come to the Navy maintenance organization for support. If the proper number of resources were not provided for this system, this problem would occur every time a new system came for maintenance. For a brief second or two, the maintainers wondered if their estimate of 35 was way off base. Maybe 17 was a better number!

The real problem was that an agreed-upon staffing methodology did not exist. Obviously, some standard methodology for estimating the software maintenance staffing was required. It was also apparent that empirical data needed to be collected in order to support estimates.

A Practical Approach

The stark reality was that experience was not acceptable as the method to determine staffing. Parametric models were also viewed as suspect. Further, no corporate-wide empirical data regarding its software maintenance operations had been collected, and thus no data were available to use as a "sanity check" or to input to models.

To solve this problem, the maintainer decided to use many models to estimate staffing. The maintainer contacted peers from the international software maintenance community to see how they estimated staffing for maintenance. The maintainer solicited their experience, methodologies, thoughts, and recommendations. As there were no empirical data available from Navy databases, the maintainer found other empirical data and learned from it. The maintainer developed a range of values and compared them to the estimates of 17 and 35. The goal was to ensure that a reasonable staffing level for the new 700K LOC system would be sufficient to properly perform the software maintenance activities.

If you believe that staffing estimation is a science, then certainly this approach would not appeal to you. If, however, you believe it to be an art, and perhaps a black art, then perhaps you might like this approach. In any case, the maintainer wanted to do *something* and wanted to ensure that this kind of battle over resources was not fought all the time!

Using Parametric Models

The first step was to use parametric models, and the maintainer decided to just use COCOMO. The COCOMO model has two different models: the basic and intermediate. In addition to these two models, there are three modes: organic, semidetached, and embedded. In keeping with the "brute force" approach, the maintainer used both levels and all three modes. First is a discussion of the basic model.

The Basic COCOMO Model Initially, the basic COCOMO model was applied to the 700K LOC software system in question. Of note is that the basic COCOMO applies to small and medium-sized software products that are developed in a familiar in-house environment. Additionally, the basic COCOMO model is only useful for quick, order-of-magnitude estimates. This did not seem to apply to the system in question, but it was interesting to see how the resulting staffing levels related to the offer of 17 and the informal estimate of 35.

The real problem was that annual change traffic (ACT) is required for the COCOMO model. Well—no empirical data existed and, therefore, there was no basis for ACT. How then could the models be used? What would or could be used for ACT?

What was the maintainer paying in annual fees for software licenses? Recognizing that there might not be a direct correlation to

ACT, it was nevertheless a start. What are you paying in the way of annual fees for software licenses? 15% or so? The first thought was to see what commercial vendors were charging. One vendor was charging about 12% as the annual maintenance fee, and another 15% for commercial software products and operating systems. Further research indicated that Lientz and Swanson collected ACT during their large data processing survey (Lientz and Swanson 1980). Albeit the information was a little outdated and it applied to COBOL systems, nonetheless

{1,2,3.......15,16,17}   is was a number. They indicated that the range of ACT was about 10% to 17%. So the first range of values—a range of ACT values—was determined.

Thus, ACT values of 10%, 12%, and 17% with the basic COCOMO model were used. The output of the model is the number of full-time support people (FSP) required to provide maintenance for the system. FSP includes all the people involved in maintenance, such as programmers, testers, quality assurance people, and configuration managers. The results of this analysis are shown in Table 8.1.

The range of full-time support personnel (FSP) was from 19.43 to 132.34 annually. What is significant is that the basic COCOMO model (organic mode) is not at all appropriate for systems in the 700K LOC range. It should only be used for systems up to 50K LOC. However, even using this worst case still yielded 19.43 FSP per year. Certainly this confirmed that the staffing would have to be in excess of 17 people.

The Intermediate COCOMO Model   Next, the more advanced intermediate COCOMO model was used. Again all three modes were applied using arbitrary ACT data (10%, 12%, and 17%). Table 8.2 sum-

TABLE 8.1 Staffing Estimates for 700K LOC System (Basic COCOMO)

MODE	ACT	FSP
Organic	10%	19.43
	12%	23.31
	17%	33.02
Semidetached	10%	38.41
	12%	46.09
	17%	65.30
Embedded	10%	77.85
	12%	93.42
	17%	132.34

TABLE 8.2 Staffing Estimates for 700 K LOC System zx (Intermediate COCOMO)

MODE	ACT	FSP
Organic	10%	29.53
	12%	35.43
	17%	50.20
Semidetached	10%	43.79
	12%	52.55
	17%	74.44
Embedded	10%	69.02
	12%	82.83
	17%	117.34

marizes the data for the three different modes of Intermediate CO-COMO. The range was 29.53 to 117.34 FSP. This model was more appropriate for the type of system to be supported, and with a range of 29.53–117.34, the informal, experienced-based estimate of 35 started looking better.

Empirical Studies The next step was to try to find some empirical data to see what other practitioners had learned from maintaining software systems. Bennet P. Lientz and E. Burton Swanson of UCLA conducted the most comprehensive data collection and analysis effort. Their book, *Software Maintenance Management* (Lientz and Swanson 1980), provides the results of software maintenance of 487 data-processing organizations.

While these statistics provided by Lientz and Swanson do not give the number of LOC per person, with some extrapolation it was determined that an average programmer could maintain about 18.6K LOC. Further extrapolation indicated that for the 700K LOC system in question, some 37.63 FSP were required using Lientz and Swanson's data.

Informal Methodology A large government agency had been developing and maintaining systems for over ten years: They use a 7-to-1 ratio to determine annual staffing for software maintenance. Simply put, if it took seven person-years to develop a system, they would allocate one person-year per year for the life of the system. Isn't 1/7 about 14.3%? Very interesting. Using our 700K LOC example, and knowing how many person-months it took to

7:1

TABLE 8.3 Summary of Staffing for 700-K LOC System

Methodology	FSP Range
Basic COCOMO (Semi-detached)	38.41–65.30
Intermediate COCOMO (Semi-detached)	43.79–74.44
Maintenance/Development	57.62
Lientz/Swanson	37.63
Government Agency	54.87

develop (under the intermediate COCOMO model, organic mode), it was determined that 37 full-time support personnel were required to maintain the system. For the semi-detached mode, 54.87 would be required.

Results of Study All of the ranges collected are summarized in Table 8.3. What was learned from this "brute force," although very practical, approach? Using multiple models, experience, empirical data—all indicated that 17 people was a totally unacceptable number to support the system, and that no less than 37 FSP should be provided for support of the 700K LOC system.

Reaction to the Results All of the above data was published in a neatly bound, 45-page, blue-covered technical study. The immediate reaction  of the various organizations involved, including the customer and the acquirer, was as expected. Nothing happened! No formal action. No response. *Nothing.* However, as time passed, it was difficult not to acknowledge that 45-page technical study that detailed the basis for the software maintenance organization's estimate of 37 people. It might not have been a very scientific approach, but it sure provided insight into the possible range of values. Most importantly, no other approach was documented.

Conclusion

 So what happened? The software maintenance organization got 37 people! What happened next? The Navy software maintenance organization was advised that it was going to get a total of five people to support the next system (109K LOC) that was going to transfer for software maintenance. The Navy software maintenance organization quickly responded that there was now a methodology for estimating software maintenance personnel resources (the methodology was proposed in the 45-page technical study) and that the methodology would be used to estimate the resources. Another very similar analysis for a new system was performed, and another study was developed. The methodology in the study yielded the number six for the new system, and the maintenance organization was given six people for that software maintenance effort.

What was the next action? Metrics were collected for the two older systems (see Chapter 15) that were being supported, so that later the estimates for the two new systems could be validated. Even with a methodology, obtaining the needed personnel resources for other systems might be a problem if no historical data were available. The next time estimates were required, empirical data would exist to help validate estimates.

THE LESSONS LEARNED FROM ESTIMATING PERSONNEL RESOURCES

What can be learned from this case study? First, a standard, agreed-upon methodology for estimating personnel resources is needed. You cannot fight the battle each time using different rules. The maintainer must force the issue and come up with the methodology. For each new system, the maintainer must estimate the personnel resources. The maintainer is the one "stuck" with the results of the estimates, and the maintainer better participate and provide the estimates.

A standard, agreed-upon methodology for estimating maintenance personnel resources is needed.

Second, a separate "maintenance staffing study" should be developed and published to address the methodology for determining personnel resources and the results. The summary results can be placed in other documents, like logistics plans, life-cycle plans, or maintenance plans.

A separate maintenance staffing study should be developed and published which addresses the methodology for determining personnel resources and the results.

Third, citing personal experience as the rationale for staffing does not work, and decision-makers are skeptical of non-algorithm- or non-methodology-based estimates. Use models and empirical data.

HOW DO YOU DETERMINE MAINTENANCE ENVIRONMENT RESOURCES?

Now you know how to plan for personnel resources and who should estimate them. What else do you need to plan for? The next areas concern hardware and software resources, often referred to as the environment. As defined by Sommerville (1989), "The term environment is used to encompass all of the automated facilities that the software engineer has available to assist with the task of software development." This definition also applies to maintenance.

Software development and maintenance are specialized activities, and need separate systems dedicated to them. Software engineering environments are designed to support all phases of the software process. Every environment has a tool set to aid the software engineers. Sommerville (1989) stresses the need for separate environments for all the detailed software engineering work, and a separate test environment (target machine).

The following are considered essential for a maintenance environment:

1. Automated software configuration management tools to provide for source code control and software library functions.
2. An automated problem report/enhancement request tracking database. If the process is to be improved, there must be a database to track the efforts of the maintenance organization.
3. Automated test tools to assist in regression testing.
4. Auditing tools.
5. Performance monitors.
6. Code analyzers.

Chapter 13 provides more details on environments. The focus here is on the planning effort and not the details of the environment.

Normally the maintainers would have an existing environment. It is one they are familiar with, and they have already resolved the risks and training issues. If the maintainer is in a position to influence the development effort, it might lead to life-cycle costs savings. For example, the maintainer might already be using a set of tools and languages that are appropriate for the new development. If the developer suggests the maintainer should use new tools and languages, life-cycle costs could go up and inherent risks result. This does not mean that no new technology, nor new tools, nor new ideas are to be used. However, in cases where there is no clear-cut advantage, or cost saving, or great technological advance associated with the change, perhaps the tools in use are appropriate.

The maintainer must assist with the plan for the maintenance environment. It is critical to get the maintenance environment included in early planning efforts when funds are allocated and a budget is developed for the development and maintenance of the system. Sometimes the acquirer and developer do not have the same perspective as the maintainer. The maintainers must let them know what they themselves need, rather than have their needs dictated to them by the acquirer or developer. Maintainer assistance in the planning of the maintenance environment result in life-cycle cost savings.

The maintainer must assist in early planning of the maintenance environment.

Practical Experience

The first system that came to a Navy maintenance facility for maintenance was developed in FORTRAN. Formal Navy training was developed for FORTRAN, one of the Navy's predominant programming languages. When the second system was under development, the Navy Systems Command (the acquirer) proposed that the system be developed in Pascal. The Navy had no systems developed in Pascal, and there was no formal training. In spite of strong objections, the system was developed in Pascal. The maintainer fought the good battle, but lost. Guess who was stuck with the training problem for Pascal? The maintainer! There was no technological advantage in using Pascal for a large operational system, and the maintainer had the problem of training people and supporting the system. Of note, the system was the only one ever developed in Pascal of the 15 or so systems that went to the maintainer for software maintenance.

A similar experience occurred with the large 700K LOC system, a large database application that I discussed under Personnel Resources. Early on the developer proposed that the system be developed using SYBASE. The two systems we were supporting were developed using ORACLE. Formal Navy training was in place for all aspects of ORACLE. However, the developers wanted to use the new toy on the block, SYBASE, even though it did not have any clear technical advantage. The maintainer fought the battle and lost again. The system was developed using SYBASE. One small system was subsequently also developed using SYBASE and transitioned for support.

What about training? The U.S. Navy scrapped the ORACLE training and developed a whole new course that addressed SYBASE. Guess what database management system (DBMS) the next two large systems were developed with? Naturally, ORACLE. The maintainer had no formal training for ORACLE, and guess who got stuck with the results of those wonderful decisions? You guessed it right! The poor maintainer! Now they will support systems with two similar but different DBMSs, and for one there is no formal training. Gee—do you think that their operation budget will get increased significantly over the entire life cycle for the system so that the maintainer gets proper DBMS training?

HOW DO YOU DETERMINE FINANCIAL RESOURCES?

The third and final aspect of resources are the monetary ones. To provide effective maintenance support, the maintainer must have a budget. That budget needs to be approved early in the planning. If you wait until the system is half way through development and then start addressing the need for a maintenance budget, you will be faced with many problems. It gets increasingly harder to get any resources for a project once it is underway. If you have not gotten funding for the maintenance environment, approved personnel resources, and an approved budget, your chances of getting them are small.

What are the elements of the maintainer's financial plan for a system? The maintainer must address:

■ Salaries for the maintenance staff (the largest cost driver).
■ Training (2–3 weeks per year per person).
■ Annual maintenance costs for software licenses for commercial products (about 15% of the cost of the product).
■ Travel (if appropriate) to user locations.
■ Attendance at conferences.
■ Technical publications and other related support material.
■ Overhead expenses per day.
■ Hardware and software for the engineering and test environments.
■ Upgrades to the hardware and software for the engineering and test environments.

It would be nice to be able to estimate these accurately. A good rule of thumb is to use 10% to 15% of the total development cost per year as a good estimate for needed financial resources (See Chapter 7). Naturally, if good ACT data existed and could be predicted, better estimates would be possible. How do outsource maintainers estimate financial costs? They must be competitive but also cover costs (and make a profit)! These estimated financial resources (costs in this case) may be driven by the cost of each Modification Request or Problem Report. In any event, outsource maintainers must consider all the elements listed above.

SUMMARY

This chapter discussed the second part of planning; resources. It provided a case study on how to determine maintenance personnel resource requirements. Also discussed were the requirements for a maintenance environment and the fact that the maintenance budget must be determined as early as possible to enable proper maintenance planning.

1. What are the three things you must consider regarding staffing resources?

2. Why should you use models to determine your resource requirements?

3. Why should the maintenance planning budget be developed early?

Transition

9

Chapter 6 began the discussion of predelivery activities, and this chapter concludes the predelivery discussion. This chapter provides an introduction to transition, the two parts of transition, a sample transition plan, and an introduction of the major issues that are encountered during transition. The end of the chapter includes some solutions for those issues and a transition model that maintainers can use.

Software transition, the transfer of the software product from the developer to the maintainer, is a critical element in the life cycle of a software system. It does not matter which development model is used (Waterfall, Incremental, or Evolutionary). At some point, maintenance is required and different people might be performing maintenance. Even with a "cradle-to-grave" philosophy where the developer retains responsibility for the entire life of the product including its maintenance, some transfer of responsibility is necessary. Thus, the topic of transitioning responsibility is germane to all approaches.

Historically, very little attention is paid to transition and even less is written about it. John Foster (1989) of British Telecomm authored an article titled "An Overview of Software Maintenance," and discussed the "handover" problem. Foster wrote two very short paragraphs that stated that the transfer process can become expensive and protracted. He further stated that better planning would help to alleviate the problem, but that the steps to be taken must be published. Foster concluded by stating that the "handover" problem is a topic for further study. Regrettably, the issue of transition still needs more research.

WHAT IS TRANSITION PLANNING?

The most detailed reference on the transitioning of software responsibility for large software systems is the *Military Handbook for Mission Critical Computer Resources Support* of May 1990 (MIL-HDBK-347 1990). A review of that very useful document was conducted shortly after it was published (Pigoski 1991). Although tailored for the U.S. DoD, it provides information useful for all organizations. The *Handbook* defines software transition as, "A controlled and coordinated sequence of actions wherein software development passes from the organization performing initial software development to the organization performing Post Deployment [Delivery] Software Support." As also stated in the *Handbook*, the capability of the maintenance organization to conduct sound maintenance and the eventual cost of maintenance closely depends on what occurs or *fails to occur* during the transition stage. However, there might even be some relationship to the success of the development effort. Practitioners state that early involvement in the development effort is mandatory for the maintenance organization to be successful.

What is needed for a successful transition? What really will transition? Development of a transition plan and a checklist are good starting points. However, these are sometimes clouded by the roles and responsibilities of the parties involved in the transition.

What Are the Complications That Can Occur During Transition?

Assuming the decision is made to transition the maintenance responsibility (for large software systems) from the developer to a different organization for maintenance, additional complications occur. The following major issues normally arise:

1. When should the maintainer be designated?
2. When should the maintainer get involved during the development process?
3. What should the maintainer do during development?

Hopefully, earlier chapters responded to these questions with the answers centered around early involvement by the maintainer. One of the things that the maintainer can and should do during the development is to prepare to assume responsibility for maintaining the newly developed software. Part of that responsibility is to prepare for the transition and transfer of responsibility from the developer to the maintainer.

The issue of transitioning software maintenance responsibility from a developer to a maintainer for large software systems is one that  is often very dissatisfying for the maintainer. Without proper planning, the credibility of the maintainer can suffer and, more importantly, the support to the customer can suffer. This is true in many cases because the software developer produces software, and *later* a determination is made as to which organization will perform the software maintenance for the rest of the life cycle of the system.

What about outsourcing? What if your company or organization is going to get an outsourced maintenance contract? The company that will function as the maintainer might not get an opportunity to get involved in the predelivery activities, but it still must address the transition problem. This section provides insight into what outsource companies will face as they assume maintenance responsibilities. It also provides a transition process that outsource maintainers can adapt. The successful outsource maintainer will develop a transition process even though the time frames might be shortened considerably.

The Conflict That Makes Transition Difficult

Remember the conflict discussed in Chapter 6 regarding making maintenance a predelivery activity? The same situation applies here. Transition is often a painful experience due to the different roles and responsibilities of the parties involved. The developers are chartered to deliver a system on time and within budget. They are driven to produce an operational system. The maintainers, however, are more concerned with the maintainability and supportability of the system and its transition. Thus, they are more interested in mundane items like documentation and procedures. They too want to be involved early to plan transition, and that causes friction. The developers have a schedule to meet, and any time or attention paid to the transition process or the maintenance organization is, in their view, not a productive activity. Normally time for the transition activities is not included in the schedule. Thus, there is often a standoff.

What if the maintainer is successful in getting involved early—and  then the development effort schedule slips significantly? Can the maintainer keep resources on the development project and continue to plan transition, all the while still having a day-to-day maintenance responsibility for other software? The longer the development schedule slips, the harder it is for the maintainer to keep resources on the transition effort.

The Two Parts of Transition

Software transition is divided into two parts: software development transition and maintainer transition. The following describes the differences between the two events.

The First Part of Transition: Software Development Transition

Software development transition is the sum of the activities to successfully transition all the software development responsibilities from the developer to the maintainer. This involves the transfer of hardware, software, data, and experience from the developer to the maintainer. Transfer of hardware, software, and data are routine activities that can be effected without any consternation. However, what about transferring experience? How would you transfer experience? How do you ensure that experience is transferred? The best ways of transferring experience are:

■ Conduct system- and software-specific training.
■ Review configuration status.
■ Review software development folders (SDFs).
■ Use maintenance escorts.
■ Spend time with the developer.

Many development contracts call for the developer to provide some form of software-specific training to the maintainer. Typically, this is in the form of a short (three-day) lecture series in which the developer provides an overview of the software, its structure, and its capabilities. It is usually put forth by the technical developers and is typically a verbal presentation of a maintenance manual. This short training session is normally provided one time. A maintenance manual, sometimes called a programmer's maintenance manual, provides details regarding the software to be maintained. It addresses code structure, conventions, etc. Maintainers use this material and keep it for training as the staff turns over. Often this type of training is not provided to the maintainer because it is not specified in the development contract. The maintainer should try to get it included or added in later.

During development, the developer must have a software configuration management plan (SCMP) and must keep track of problems encountered and modifications requested and made to the software product. The maintainer can learn a lot by analyzing the configuration accounting status database. The analysis will reveal what problems exist, which subsystems or modules the problems relate to, and what the users are asking for in terms of enhancements. Reading the SCMP helps to create a smooth transition.

The developer also uses *software development folders (SDFs)*; these are files that contain modification requests, the appropriate 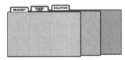 source code to enable the fix, and solutions to the request. If the maintainer has access to these folders, the maintainer can get very specific information about particular segments of code. This analysis by the maintainer and subsequent discussions with the developer will significantly aid in the transfer of experience.

By far the best approach to a smooth transition is to have some of the development team transfer to the maintenance organization. This practice is often referred to as using "maintenance escorts." In many cases this is not possible. Try to have people from San Diego move to the maintenance location in Nebraska! If the developer does not come to the maintainer—the maintainer must go to the developer. Go work with them for some period of time. You must recognize that the developer still has a schedule to meet, and every time the maintainer comes to visit to get some "experience transfer," it can impact the developer. These events need to be planned, and there must be money to account for travel, if needed.

 One last thought: How long does it take for the maintainer to be comfortable in supporting the new software? Think about the one-million-lines-of-code example. How long would it take for the maintainer to provide solid, adequate support? How long would you take? If you got called at 5:00 P.M. on Friday, would you be ready at 8:00 A.M. on Monday to provide maintenance?

There are really two answers. First, take the example of a transition where the maintainer is identified and involved early. The maintainer might be looking at code and performing all the predelivery activities. Still, how long does it take? A case study later in this chapter addresses that issue.

Second, take the example of an outsourced maintainer. The prospective maintainer would not be involved in the development, and is bidding on a contract to provide the support. How much time does the outsourced maintainer have to get ready? Not much! Instantaneously, the heroic outsource maintainer will know all there is to know (or so it is expected). Certainly, that is not realistic. The point here is that it does take time, and all parties involved—the acquirer, the maintainer, and the user—must recognize that it does take time to become knowledgeable on the new software product.

The Second Part of Transition: Maintainer Transition Maintainer transition includes all the activities needed for the maintainer to implement the software Maintenance Concept discussed in Chapter 7.

Maintainer transition includes activities intended to provide for a smooth transition from development to postdelivery maintenance. This effort needs to be planned.

Some of the important activities include:

- Staffing.
- Training.
- Developing software configuration management plans and procedures.
- Conducting turnover, installation, and checkout of hardware and software.
- Implementing all maintenance activities.
- Replicating maintenance problems.
- Generating software builds.

The maintainer might have to augment the staff or reassign people to accommodate the new software. Part of the transition is to plan for the needed staffing. In Chapter 8, the methodology to determine the number of people needed for maintenance was discussed. For the transition, an orderly assignment of people is necessary. Are all the staff needed at once? The answer is *no*. High-level (particularly SCM) people come first, then testers, then software engineers and programmers.

The maintainer transition training here is very similar to the training in the software transition. There the developer provides specific software training for the software being developed. The focus is to transfer the experience of the developer. The maintainer transition training augments the specific software training the developer provides. As the new software might well use new methodologies, tools, and techniques, part of the maintainer transition is to ensure that the maintainer has training for the new tools. For example, if the new software is developed using object-oriented design, the maintainer needs that type of training. If the programming language is C++, training is needed in this language. These training requirements should be documented in the transition plan, discussed later.

Software configuration management plans and procedures might have to be developed or at least updated. The maintainer must update them to reflect the new software and to ensure that the new software is managed with the same process as other software that is maintained.

Once people are in place and trained, the hardware and software (for the engineering and test environments) need to be turned over, installed and checked out. Finally, the maintenance process needs to be exercised. The maintainer must ensure that it can replicate problems and generate new software versions. At the end of transition, the maintainer reports that the transfer is completed and will have assumed responsibility for maintenance of the software product.

Transferring Experience Is Possible

 Transition can be lengthy and expensive. There are those who say experience cannot be transferred. It is difficult, but not impossible. Program managers and many developers believe that because they spent three to four years building a software product that no one else could possibly maintain it. Surely only the developer can maintain the software!

These statements are simply not true. However, sometimes the developer convinces everyone that no one else can perform maintenance. The acquirer is kept hostage by the developer and usually pays an inflated price for support.

WHAT IS A TRANSITION PLAN?

A comprehensive transition plan is needed if the transition is to be successful. Who should develop it? If time permits, and the maintainer is involved early, the maintainer should. In the U.S. DoD arena, the developer is normally required to develop the plan. Picture this: The developer (who wants to do the maintenance) is charged with setting up a smooth orderly transition to some other organization so that the other group can perform the maintenance!

The organization that is in the best position to develop the transition plan is the maintainer. The maintainer should have some expertise in transitioning systems. If you are a maintainer, once you receive a few systems, you quickly find out what is important and necessary to you.

The Difference Between the Transition Plan and the Maintenance Plan

A transition plan should cover both elements of software transition: software development transition and maintainer transition. It should delineate time frames for the transition, and should use some elements from the maintenance plan. However, it is separate and distinct from the maintenance plan.

■ The maintenance plan addresses the higher level issues of who will perform maintenance, where it will be done, and what level of support will be provided.

■ The transition plan clearly focuses on the actual transfer of responsibility from the developer to the maintainer, and includes detailed milestones and plans of action. It formalizes the agreements regarding the use of a maintenance escort, the maintainer visiting the developer, the funding needed to effect the transition, and the authorization to look at SDFs.

The maintainer should develop the Transition Plan.

Solid transition planning is critical for the maintainer, and a good plan is imperative. The following is an outline of a transition plan (Werner 1995). It might be useful for other maintainers.

Sample Transition Plan

1. General
   Purpose of the Plan
   Overview of the Plan
   Software Transition Process
   Designation of the Maintainer
   Transition Planning
   Transition Objective and Phases
   Software Transition Responsibilities
   Maintenance Responsibility
   Maintenance Funding
2. Requirements
   Software Documentation Requirements
      Development Documentation
      Test Documentation
      User Documentation
      Quality Assurance and Software Configuration Management Documentation
   System Software
   Support Software
   Software Packages
      Developer Written Software Tools
      Other Software Tools
      Special Devices
      Software Licenses

Software Support Hardware Requirements
Equipment Description (On board/Order)
Equipment Description (Option)
System Firmware
Maintenance Contractor Support (if required)
3. Installation and Testing
Installation Schedule
Software Testing
Developmental Testing
Operational Testing
Testing Capability
Test Programs and Test Data Files
4. Training
Training Planning for Maintenance Personnel
Factory/Vendor Training
System Specific Training
Software Training Funding
5. Other Transition Requirements
Facilities
Personnel
Other Resources
6. Milestones
Master Schedule and Milestones
7. References
8. Appendix
A. Software Transition Checklist
B. Listing of Software Modules

Why a Smooth, Orderly Transition Is Important

Why is a smooth, orderly transition important? To maintain user support. With the initial fielding of a newly developed system, the users have high expectations. The first few years result in a flood of modification requests. Figure 9.1 shows a typical influx of requests, with them leveling out after 3 years.

The first three years of operation results in a large influx of Modification Requests. After three years, it levels out.

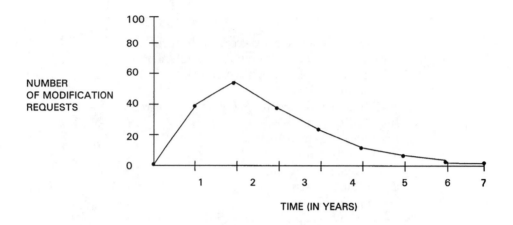

FIGURE 9.1 Typical influx of modification requests.

If there was a large backlog of modification requests held over from the development effort, and there usually is, the graph may look even worse. Figure 9.2 is typical of what you might expect.

Based on what happens during the first few years of fielding the software product, it is imperative that the maintainer be in place to provide the needed support and that a smooth transition take place. Resources must be in place at turnover time to accommodate the influx

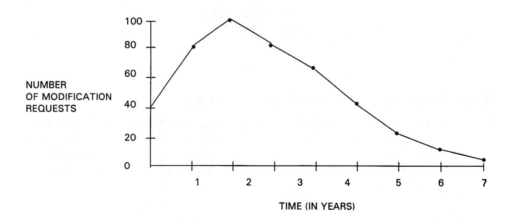

FIGURE 9.2 Typical startup with outstanding modification requests.

of modification requests. Can you imagine a scenario with a large backlog (Figure 9.2) and only limited initial staffing? For those systems with a large backlog, full staffing early on is imperative. When can staffing be reduced? Normally, after two to three years of full operations, the MR number decreases and then staffing can be reduced. The reduction is typically 50%.

After three years ,the maintenance staff can normally be reduced by 50%.

In the case where development is complete, and at some later date a decision is made to transition the maintenance to another organization, the flurry of modification requests slows down. Even still, there needs to be a smooth transition in order to provide proper support for the users.

The first few years are very critical to the maintainer. The user might have worked with the developer, and must get used to working with a new organization which has not spent three to four years with the system. This is a very critical, vulnerable period for the maintainer. Total credibility with the users can be lost if the transition is not smooth and orderly (Pigoski 1991a). More importantly, if it appears that the maintainer cannot perform the functions, the users lose confidence in the maintainer. That's bad for business.

A checklist is a very important element of transition planning. The following is an example of a transition checklist:

Sample Software Transition Checklist

The following list contains items that should be considered in the transition schedule and verified or resolved before the maintainer assumes maintenance responsibility:

1. Have the engineering environment and test environment software been delivered, installed, and evaluated?
2. Have licensing agreements been properly transferred for commercial software?
3. Have documents, notebooks, and manuals used in the software development process been identified and turned over to the maintainer?

4. Have all modification requests and problem reports been delivered?
5. Have formal configuration audits been completed?
6. Have identified discrepancies been accounted for and properly documented in the corrective action system?
7. Has the current configuration been delivered to the maintainer?
8. Are sufficient personnel with the skills and experience necessary available to sustain the projected maintenance level of effort?
9. Have functional area and system specific training identified in the transition plan been completed?
10. Have adequate office, work, and storage space been identified to support maintenance?
11. Are adequate utilities available (e.g., electrical power, air conditioning, and heat) to support maintenance?
12. Has computer cabling been properly laid, connected, and tested?
13. Has network wiring been properly laid, connected, and tested?
14. Has the maintainer's complete software-generation process been exercised, and the maintainer's ability to generate and support the software in accordance with the maintenance concept been demonstrated?
15. Has each software modification request and problem report been classified by category and priority, and accounted for in the maintainer's status accounting system?
16. Have the computer system operator's manual and software user's manual been accepted, and are they available for issue?
17. Have system fielding plans, which include provisions for software distribution, been approved and promulgated?
18. Has the maintenance budget been approved, and is it adequate to support maintenance operations at the projected level of effort?
19. Has the software replication facility (equipment, media, etc.) been installed?
20. Have hardware and software maintenance responsibilities been properly identified for customers and users?

What Are Some of the Issues Regarding Transition?

What are some of the issues that arise when transition from the developer to the maintainer is to occur? The following are major issues (Pigoski and Cowden 1992) that were encountered during the actual transitioning of systems from a developer to a maintainer, and they must be addressed during the transition process.

- Transfer of knowledge.
- Documentation.
- Communications with developer.
- Communications with user.
- Formal turnover process.
- Training.
- Speed of transition.
- Who performs the transition.
- The cost of transition.

 ***Transfer of Knowledge*** How is detailed knowledge, which only the software developers possess, transferred to the maintainers? When does the process start? How long will it take? When will the maintainer be ready to support the system? How long will it take the maintainer to feel "comfortable" in supporting the system?

Documentation What level of documentation is needed? When will it be ready? When will the maintainer be able to look at it? Will the maintainer be able to comment on and review documentation as it is produced? Will the transition get held up until all the documentation is current and approved? In theory, more and updated documentation is needed as transition occurs. Is all that documentation necessary?

Communications with Developer When does the maintainer start talking with the developer? At design reviews? At system testing? At formal acceptance testing? When the system is declared operational? The developer has a job to do: deliver a system. Any time spent with the maintainer can impact the schedule and budget. How this issue is resolved is a major concern for the maintainer.

Communications with the User The users are often in a dilemma. During the transition, do they talk with the developer or the maintainer? This is the case if the system is operational (fielded) or not. To whom do they report problems or recommended enhancements? The period of transition is critical for the maintainer. For them, the issue is how do they demonstrate to the user that they possess knowledge of the system and are prepared to provide maintenance support? The credibility of the maintainer is at great risk during the transition.

Formal Turnover Process Transition demands a formal turnover process. When does it start? How does it impact the development? The developer? The maintainer? The user? When are the necessary transition documents written? Who writes them? Who must live with what they say?

Training What amount and kind of training is provided to the maintainer? For users and hardware maintenance people, the training is nor-mally very formal and sometimes institutionalized. For the software maintenance people, typically a short lecture-type training session is provided by the developer for the maintainer. The structure of the system and operation are covered. When should training be provided? Is the training sufficient? Most importantly, how will the maintainer train additional people to maintain the system? Perhaps some computer-based, online software maintenance training is needed. If not, the maintainer must deal with this lack-of-training problem over the life of the system. This is not normally an issue for the users' training needs, but very frequently it is an issue for the software maintenance people.

The Speed of Transition The time to complete the transition might be extensive and costly (Pigoski and Sexton 1990). The development schedule might slip. People may have to stay on transition longer than desired. The time for the maintainer to become "comfortable" in supporting the system could be lengthy. Who pays? How long will it take?

Who Performs the Transition Who actually performs the transition? Organizationally, how is it accomplished? Do you assign people who already have day-to-day maintenance responsibilities on other projects, or do you assign a separate group? If the development effort does not meet its scheduled delivery date, can you justify the resources dedicated to transition? Finally, how do you staff for transition? Is transition performed by programmers? Do they get assigned two years before the responsibility is transitioned?

The Cost of Transition What are the costs of transition? How do you account for the time of people involved in transition? Is travel involved? Do these efforts take away from current maintenance activities?

THE LESSONS LEARNED FROM TRANSITION EXPERIENCES

The above provided numerous questions. What are the answers? What are the solutions? For the past 10 years, many transition lessons have been learned. The details are contained in case studies (Chapters 10 and 11). The following sections provide some solutions for the transition issues presented above.

Transfer of Knowledge

Transfer of knowledge is one of the most difficult issues. Trying to get the developer to pass on that knowledge is an uphill battle. Training provided by the developer *should* be the primary means of transferring knowledge. However, usually little or no training is provided. The maintainer must set out to acquire this knowledge, and must be aggressive to obtain it. To transfer knowledge, the maintainer should first perform software configuration management functions (tracking problems, putting the system under automated SCM, establishing software library procedures, and testing), and later evolve to fixing low-priority problems. Much of this relates to training, which is covered in detail in Chapter 18. Maintenance escorts should be used. Try to get *some* of the developers to come with the system. One or two people really make a difference! This is normally very difficult to make happen. If this is not possible, then the maintenance organization must go to the developer. In a perfect world, the maintenance organization should also participate in acceptance testing and integration as well as quality assurance. If the maintenance organization performed these functions prior to transfer of maintenance responsibility, the system surely would transition smoothly.

One of the big issues is how long it takes to become "comfortable" or proficient in supporting the system. Experience and case study data (See Chapter 10) provide 11 "comfort" variables that impact that determination. The variables are:

Number of personnel who participated in the development.

Complexity of the system being supported.

Computer programming language being used.

Size of the supported system.

Operational background of the personnel who will support the system.

Software experience of those personnel.

Formal software training provided.

Commercial vendor software training provided.

System-specific software training provided.

Documentation of the supported system.

Familiarity with the operating system.

A number of variables can be determined well in advance. Maintainers should use these variables to determine when people enter the "comfort zone" and are comfortable (or proficient) in supporting the software.

Documentation

It is important for the maintenance organization to get involved early and to obtain some information about the system. Although not ideal, out-of-date specifications are acceptable for this activity. The key is to get current source code and be able to analyze it, even against out-of-date specifications.

Communications with Developer

The maintenance organization needs to communicate early and often with the developer.

Communications with User

Communications with the user should also be early and often. It is important to learn the operational aspects of the system, and to build credibility with the user. A good approach to building credibility is to do something for the user. Some suggestions are to provide training for system administrators and managers, help them to identify problems, and then document the problems for the user. However, it is good practice to have the user submit enhancement requests through their management to the maintainer for action by the SCM process.

Be on-site when installations are occurring. The user is getting a new system and does not know what the system is supposed to do. The maintainers can ease stress and concern by being there for the user.

Formal Turnover Process

A formal turnover process is mandatory. The maintenance organization should draft the transition plans and force the issue early, and then use this process to get what it really needs to provide maintenance.

Training

The traditional, stand-up lectures at the end of the transition are hardly worth the effort. The maintenance organization needs to be involved much earlier, and should get trained by spending time with the developer and performing functions such as tracking problems, performing SCM, performing testing and integration, and fixing code *before* the responsibility begins.

The Speed of Transition

Slowness is relative. The normal position of a program manager or a developer is that the maintenance organization does not need to be involved two to three years early—and can effect a transition over a three-day weekend. Full-scale Waterfall developments often take three to five years to build a system. Even Incremental and Evolutionary developments might be in process over extended periods of time; yet the assumption is that maintainers should be able to learn the new system in a relatively short period of time. This is not realistic. Case study data do not provide enough data points to provide a scientific basis for lengthy transitions and early involvement; however, case study data clearly indicate the schedule and budget overruns of the systems delivered without significant early and continuing involvement by the maintenance organization.

If slow is over a period of years, then transition should be slow.

Who Performs the Transition

A separate transition organizational element should be formed. It could be part of a planning organization. Experience indicates that a separate transition group works best. If people have current day-to-day software maintenance responsibilities, they cannot effectively plan for the transition and eventual maintenance of a new system. It simply does not work. Most people cannot perform "today" and "tomorrow" functions well simultaneously. "Today" always does, and should, take precedence. A different mentality and focus is necessary for future planning. The separate transition organization should be staffed by senior people first and then as the system takes shape, more junior people who will perform the actual maintenance work on the system should be brought on board to work in the transition organization. The senior people can plan for transition and, due to seniority and experience, might be able to impact software development. Experience indicates that junior-level software engineers or programmers cannot impact software development, and their involvement is primarily to obtain knowledge about the software. Organizations need to pay the price of a transition organization in terms of people and funding *before* they have the maintenance responsibility.

The maintenance organization should be involved early in the development of a system.

The Cost of Transition

In the early stages of transition, the costs are minimal. There is very little involvement. Some travel and training might be required. The planning for transition is performed by a separate group that has responsibility for transition, and the group can and should support multiple systems. Therefore, the cost per system should not be significant. The costs are gradual, peaking during the testing phase. Estimating costs and staffing for transition is a real art. It is certainly not a science.

Perhaps the best way to estimate is by the eventual size of the maintenance organization. If, for example, a system required ten full-time support personnel (FSP) per year, and there was a two-year transition, how many people should be allocated in year one and year two?

Year one is primarily used for planning, and then some technical work. A senior person would use about two months, and a junior person would require about six months. Thus, for the first year, you would want to allocate two person-months plus six person-months for a total of eight person-months for the first year of transition.

In year two you might add another senior person, making the total of senior people equal to two. They work for three months, giving the total of six person-months for the senior people in year two of the transition. Add another junior person for a full year, and the total for the junior people is 24 person-months in year two of transition. Towards the end of year two, three other people for two months are added, or six person-months. Total all the person-months, 6 plus 24 plus 6, and you have 36 person-months for year two for transition.

In summary, for a system that requires 10 FSP to support it, in year one the total percentage of people working on transition in relation to the total amount of people allocated for the annual maintenance effort (10 FSP or 120 person-months) is 6.7%. So, in the first year of transition, you should allocate 6-10% of your total personnel allocated for annual maintenance. In year two, using the above example, the 36 person-months represents about 30% of the annual staffing for maintenance. So, in the second year of transition you should allocate 30-35% of your total personnel allocated for annual maintenance. The above is an example of what has been used for planning purposes. You can expand or collapse time frames and adjust the staffing estimates accordingly.

The most important lesson learned is that the maintenance organization must be involved early in the development effort. This is certainly not the case when maintenance is outsourced, or when a prototype suddenly becomes a production system and requires maintenance; but even for incremental and evolutionary developments, it is important for the maintenance organization to be involved early.

TRANSITION MODEL AND PROCESS

The lessons learned from transition helped put together a transition model and process. The following discusses the key to transition—Software Configuration Management (SCM)—and then the model and the associated processes.

Software Configuration Management (SCM): The Key to Transition

Based on experience, it is necessary to get the maintenance organization involved early and start the transition. The maintenance organization needs to demonstrate that it is capable of supporting the system and the users. One of the best means for getting the maintenance organization involved early is to perform SCM functions (Pigoski 1991b).

Typically the developer has a status accounting database, and at the end of transition it is (hopefully) transferred to the maintenance organization. However, these data are often only viewed by the program manager and the developer. The information does not reach the users—many would say that they do not need it. Most importantly, the information does not reach the maintainers. The maintenance organization can learn much about the system by analyzing the modification requests.

The maintenance organization needs a tracking database after transition, and should take over that mundane function early to establish some credibility. A good way to do it is to tell the PM that you, the maintenance organization, will perform that function and relieve the developer of that burden. The maintainers then know what is going on, and what the backlog is. The transition of the backlog is done early. The maintenance organization gets a chance to exercise its SCM procedures, and provides something for the users. To effect this change, the PM must tell users of this change in responsibility, and this too adds to the credibility of the maintenance organization. The maintenance organization can then participate at the CCBs and eventually provide data from the maintenance organization's status accounting database for the meeting.

The next area to get involved in is version control. Once the maintainer has control of code in libraries, and a target system, the maintainer should try to perform integration and testing. If done properly, the maintainer can get new software to its facility for integration and testing prior to the new version going to the user. This changes the user's view in that new versions, even with the developer in charge, start coming from the maintainer.

The maintenance organization later performs other functions, but none are so dramatic as those of SCM. The maintainers can take control through SCM, one of the crucial areas of transition.

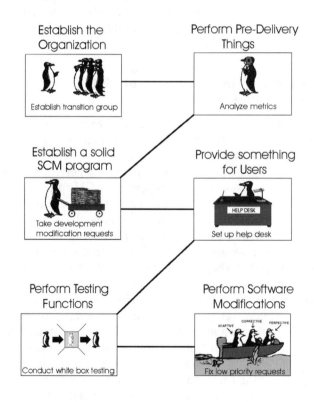

FIGURE 9.3   The transition model.

Transition Model

There are many elements of the transition process. The key elements are captured in Figure 9.3.

The transition model is further refined, as depicted below.

A Sample Transition Model

The model consists of the following phases:

- Establishing an organization for transition.
- Performing predelivery functions until the time of turnover.
- Establishing a solid software configuration management program.
- Providing something for users (customers).
- Testing the new system.
- Performing software modification functions.

Within the model's phases, the following activities are performed:

Establish the organization for transition

- Get identified as the maintenance organization.
- Establish transition group or element.
- Influence development contract.
- Hire SCM personnel first, testers second, and programmers last.

Perform predelivery functions

- Attend reviews.
- Do IV&V (if possible).
- Analyze metrics.

Establish a solid SCM program

- Take development Modification Requests.
- Place requests in a status accounting database.
- Provide requests to users and all others concerned.
- Take code from developer and put under automated SCM.
- Perform version control.
- Exercise build procedures.

Provide something for users

- Set up an early help or trouble desk.
- Provide system training to users.

Perform testing function

- Conduct white-box testing (because the developer does not do it).
- Perform a maintainability assessment of the software.

Perform software modifications

- Fix low priority development Modification Requests.

Transition Model Summary

The transition model presented above is still in use and, like any process, it is continually improving. It can be used for large developments. Outsource maintainers can use it, but they must severely compress the time frames and, in many cases, will not have the luxury of performing many of the activities.

SUMMARY

Experienced practitioners state that early involvement by the maintainer in the transition process is necessary for success. Unfortunately, there is little or no empirical data to substantiate that claim. Intuitively, it appears that it must help. However, management must be convinced of the cost benefits. This chapter provided details regarding transition of software from a developer to a maintainer and a suggested transition model. The next two chapters provide case-study data that amplifies the transition data contained in this chapter.

1. Describe how you would plan a software transition and a maintainer transition.

2. Draft a transition plan.

3. Describe your approach to resolving each of the transition issues presented in this chapter.

4. Apply the transition model to a system coming to your organization.

Transition Experiences, Part I

Not much is published on actual transition case studies. As can be seen from the previous chapter, there are a number of issues that arise during the transition, and decisions must be made as to how to close those issues. While I was at a Navy software maintenance activity, a number of newly developed systems transitioned for maintenance. Regrettably, the first few systems did not have maintainer predelivery involvement, and thus the maintainer did not have the opportunity to affect the plans for the transition. For systems that transitioned later there was early involvement, and that helped transition.

This chapter provides practical experiences in software transition in the form of case studies. The first study provides the results of an empirical study that was conducted to determine how long it took Navy maintainers to become "comfortable" with supporting systems. The second addresses how the training issue was attacked. Chapter 11 discusses the third case study, which compares the transition of systems and provides the lessons learned.

WHEN MAINTAINERS BECOME "COMFORTABLE" WITH THE SYSTEM: A CASE STUDY

The transitioning of large systems from a developer to a maintainer, particularly an outsourced maintainer, should put fear in the hearts of people. When faced with receiving a large system, of say 300, 400, or 500K LOC, or over 5,000 function points, how long would it take to

have the people become proficient in the code and operation of the system such that they could provide effective support? How long do you think it would take to be proficient with a very large system? Would the time frame be different if the maintainer had performed some predelivery functions?

In the early days at the U.S. Navy software maintenance organization, that was of prime concern (Pigoski and Sexton 1990). How long would it take to become comfortable with the new system? No one knew. Intensive searches and calls to peers in the software maintenance business provided no answers either. Therefore, a decision was made to learn from the first two systems that were supported. A data-collection plan was developed, current capabilities were benchmarked, and data were collected. The intent was to learn from those experiences. These lessons would help in the planning for transition and eventual maintenance of other systems.

How the Software Transition Process Worked

How the transition process should work was discussed in Chapter 9. Unfortunately for the Navy maintenance organization, their transition process was a little different. Although established as a separate

organization for maintenance, the maintenance organization was designated as the maintainer essentially *after* the first systems were developed, and thus did not participate in the various development checkpoints that Martin and McClure (1983) suggest. Further, the Navy maintenance organization was in the process of growing an organization from the ground up as well as establishing facilities and the work environment. These, naturally, had an impact on the transition process and the length of time that it took to become proficient at maintaining the newly transitioned systems.

Data Collection There was a unique opportunity to collect data regarding how much time and effort it took software maintenance personnel to prepare to assume maintenance responsibility for two Navy software systems. Data regarding these experiences and profiles of the personnel performing maintenance for these two systems were collected. Finally, empirical data about the involvement (or lack of it) of the maintainer during the development cycle was gathered. The following provides specifics regarding these experiences.

The State of the Maintainers It must be noted that the Navy maintenance organization was being established during this time frame, and items such as an operational computer programming environment, standard operating procedures (SOPs), and a detailed training plan were being developed concurrently with the preparation to assume software life-cycle maintenance responsibilities. These factors had to be considered when analyzing the data. For an organization that is fully operational, receiving a system of similar size, with a familiar programming language, using similar hardware to their current equipment, the transition would obviously be easier and would take less time.

The Systems to Support The two systems to support were minicomputer-based using LANs and a WAN to connect worldwide locations.

- *The first system.* This system was developed using Digital Equipment Corporation (DEC) VAX hardware and the DEC VAX/VMS operating system. The application code was written in FORTRAN 77 and the DEC VAX assembler language MACRO. The Oracle relational database management system (DBMS) was used for the database applications. WAND/TEMPLATE were used for the graphics work. The system size was 230K LOC.
- *The second system.* This system was developed using Digital Equipment Corporation (DEC) VAX hardware and the DEC VAX/VMS operating system. The application code was written in Pascal and the DEC VAX assembler language MACRO. The Oracle relational database management system (DBMS) was used for the database applications. WAND/TEMPLATE were used for the graphics work. The system size was 370K LOC.

The State of the Systems When Delivered The systems were received essentially devoid of any documentation. An image copy of six disk packs was provided for both systems. No software library management packages were employed, and thus they were not provided. No maintenance journal was maintained, and thus a history of software changes was not available. Further, no means or procedures to provide initial installation software or routine updates were provided. No documentation was provided to the on-site system management personnel. No test procedures or automated test drivers for unit and module testing were provided. Lastly, and most importantly, no call trees were provided.

Personnel Qualifications of Maintainers The philosophy used when establishing the initial staffing for the Navy maintenance organization was that the organization was to be primarily military in nature. There would be some government service civilian personnel and, as funding

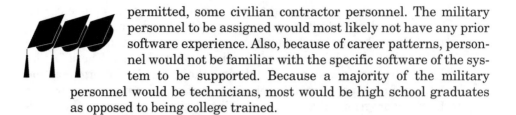

permitted, some civilian contractor personnel. The military personnel to be assigned would most likely not have any prior software experience. Also, because of career patterns, personnel would not be familiar with the specific software of the system to be supported. Because a majority of the military personnel would be technicians, most would be high school graduates as opposed to being college trained.

Background of Personnel   Personnel came primarily from Navy operational (or user) backgrounds. Thus, a number of the personnel were familiar with the operations that the new systems were to automate. Some had prior software experience. Some had four-year college degrees, and a few even had advanced degrees. However, only five had ever worked in software maintenance. Only one of the 30 personnel had ever seen the supported systems in operation. None had participated in the development effort. The following sections provide empirical data regarding the backgrounds of the personnel involved in the transition of software maintenance responsibility.

Distribution by Category   Table 10.1 provides data regarding the various categories of the 30 personnel. The preponderance (70%) of personnel were U.S. Navy, career-enlisted personnel.

Education   As can be seen from Figure 10.1, the majority of personnel were high school graduates. This contrasts dramatically with Swanson and Beath's (1989) study of 12 information systems organizations. In their study, the mean years of college for the maintenance personnel was 3.49 years, with a range of 2.30–4.31 years of college. The Navy's maintainers had domain expertise, but were lacking important formal education. This would be a factor in determining how long it took to become "comfortable."

TABLE 10.1   Personnel Categories

Category	Number
Officers	4
Enlisted	21
Government Service	4
Civilian Contractor	1
Totals	**30**

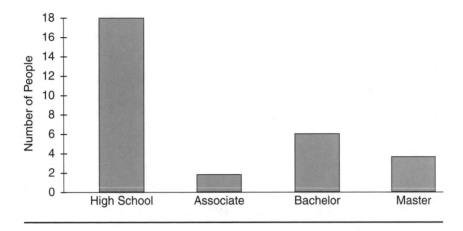

FIGURE 10.1 Education levels of personnel.

Target System Operational Experience As both of the systems to be supported were new systems, essentially none of the personnel had any experience with these systems. One person had spent three years working with the prototype system at an operational location. Additionally, this individual had learned about the system management aspects of both systems, but had not actually performed any software maintenance functions. Towards the end of the transition, a second individual who had worked with the developer of one of the systems arrived. The timing was clearly too late to aid in the transition of responsibility, but data regarding this individual is included in the study.

Although essentially none of the personnel had any operational experience with the systems to be supported, a majority of the personnel had worked on the manual systems that the new automated systems replaced. Thus, personnel were somewhat familiar with the functions being performed.

Software Training Thirteen of the 30 personnel involved had received 13 weeks of FORTRAN programming instruction at a formal Navy school. A total of 12 of the 30 individuals attended another 13-week Navy school that taught Pascal, ORACLE, and VMS. This formal Navy training was augmented by specialized DEC and ORACLE schools, which ranged from two to four days in length.

As can be seen from Figure 10.2, during the two-and-one-half-year period involved, a significant number of specialized courses was provided.

As an example, seven people attended four courses, and three people attended 11 courses.

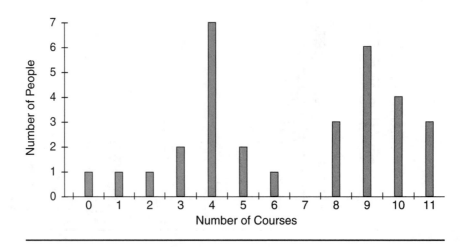

FIGURE 10.2 Specialized vendor training.

Target System Software Experience Only one individual had target system software experience, and that was only as a systems manager and not a developer or maintenance programmer.

Software Experience Figure 10.3 depicts the years of software experience for each of the 30 surveyed individuals. Clearly the preponderance of personnel were not very experienced.

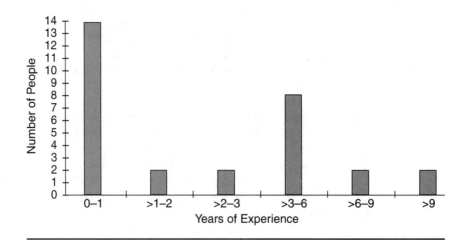

FIGURE 10.3 Software experience.

Analysis of Data You now have a picture of the kind of personnel involved, their experience, and their training level. When did they get into the "comfort zone"? Data to determine when each individual got into the "comfort zone" was collected via a questionnaire and then corroborated by management personnel. In some cases it was very obvious. The "light" literally went on for some people, and you could see it in their eyes and their daily routine.

"Comfort Zone" Figure 10.4 represents how much time it took to enter the "comfort zone." As can be seen, most personnel required between 6 and 12 months to be comfortable in their support role. Naturally, personnel were supporting the system throughout this period.

Years of Experience Versus "Comfort Zone" The results of analyzing years of experience and number of months to enter the "comfort zone" were not very conclusive.

The only patterns that emerged were as follows: Personnel with three to six years of software experience required from three to twelve months to become "comfortable"; personnel with less than one year of experience required six to twelve months to become "comfortable." Whereas it took lengthy periods of time to become "comfortable," keep in mind that support was provided throughout the entire period.

While the above data might be alarming (in terms of the number of months it took to become comfortable), remember the state of the systems being delivered, the fact that personnel had not participated in the development at all, and the people had limited experience. The

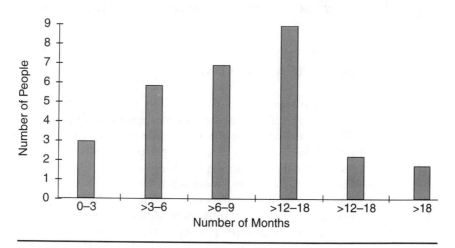

FIGURE 10.4 "Comfort zone."

important variables were previously introduced in Chapter 9. A number of the variables can be determined well in advance. Intuitively, if you control some of these variables, you can get a reasonable estimate of the time required to enter the "comfort zone."

Of what use is the case study? Hopefully it provides empirical data not otherwise available, in conjunction with the variables presented in Chapter 9; customers and maintainers can use it to plan transition better. Lastly, keep in mind that the later the maintainer gets involved, the longer it takes to become proficient. The amount of training is certainly a factor. Education and previous maintenance experience are also important variables.

Based on the fact that the Navy maintenance organization had not been involved in the software development, and that personnel did not have significant maintenance backgrounds, it was estimated that it would take 12 months to provide solid maintenance support (or be "comfortable"). It took about nine months. As software managers, you should be prepared for this extended period and should not expect miracles. Based on the empirical data collected and analysis of the variables, it took a *long time* to become comfortable. Better educated, more experienced maintainers should become "comfortable" much sooner.

For an average maintenance organization to become "comfortable" with an average (although large) system, it is not unreasonable to build in three months to your schedule for the staff to become "comfortable" in providing support. Outsource organizations need to factor these startup items with plans to perform outsourced maintenance effectively.

It will take at least three months to ramp up to provide quality maintenance support for a large system.

TRANSITION TRAINING: A CASE STUDY

When large software systems transition from a developer to maintainer, system-specific software maintenance training is a transition issue. Who trains the maintainers? Unfortunately, in most cases—the maintainer. Training as a general topic is addressed in Chapter 18. The topic of transition training is addressed here to keep the focus on transition. The case study presented previously gives an idea of how long it takes to get staff proficient to the point where they can provide quality support. Of note is that *three of the eleven "comfort" variables mentioned are for training.* If proper training is provided, the time frame for becoming comfortable in supporting a software product can be accelerated.

With the emphasis on quality, many organizations are outsourcing the maintenance of systems so that they can concentrate on core business activities. Outsourcing is a growth industry, and potential outsource maintenance organizations must be prepared to train their people to maintain new systems.

The problem that faces the maintenance organization is how to prepare its people to perform the task of maintenance on say, a software system greater than 300K LOC or greater than 5000 function points. For a typical large system, the developer may have spent from two to five years developing the system. How long will maintainers have to get ready to support the system? How early will they get involved? Of extreme importance is the question, how will they be trained to support the new system? The real questions are: Who is concerned about this issue, and who is responsible for ensuring that the issue gets resolved?

The Navy maintenance organization previously mentioned had to provide the software maintenance training for new systems (Pigoski and Looney 1993). This case study addresses the training issues of transition, discusses how to attack the problem, and provides the lessons that were learned.

Background of the Case Study

During a typical software development effort, great care is normally taken to ensure that operations and hardware maintenance personnel are fully trained to perform their functions on a new, large software system. However, formal training is rarely if ever provided to the software maintenance organization. Why is this normally the case? Who is responsible for providing the training?

For most large development efforts, a program manager is responsible for all aspects of the development, including training. For whatever reason, training and documentation are seemingly the first items to be cut from the development effort when the project runs into budget difficulties. Even worse, PMs have not recognized the need for software maintenance training. The end result is that the maintenance organizations must deal with the problem. Thus, the maintainer needs to have a process for training its people for system-specific software.

As a separate maintenance organization, large software systems were transitioned to the Navy software maintenance organization from defense contractors (Pigoski 1991c). As the Navy software maintenance organization was not involved at all in the development process, it was not able to influence program managers regarding needed training. As is often the case, the software was handed to the maintenance organization without them having any prior involvement.

The maintenance organization was tasked to perform software maintenance for the two systems discussed in the previous case study (see the section "Systems to Support"). The organization was provided with old specifications, no maintenance manual, and the source code, albeit not under automated control. No system-specific software maintenance training was received.

Collect Data

As the software maintenance organization prepared to perform maintenance, it was concerned with how to train maintenance people. The organization was also concerned with developing a training process, because numerous systems would transition for maintenance support, and (as with most maintenance organizations) personnel turnover would be inevitable. Of extreme concern was how long it would take for maintenance people to become proficient at maintaining each system.

During the normal transition process, one of the key issues is the transfer of knowledge from the developer to the maintainer. Training is critical to transferring knowledge. However, the Navy maintenance organization, like many other maintenance organizations, had to train its own people. A training process (discussed in the following sections) was used to "institutionalize" the transition training.

Transfer of knowledge is a key transition issue, and is difficult to accomplish.

Ensure a Smooth Transition

In resolving the transition training issue, it was important to ensure that all of the maintenance people involved in the maintenance effort received training. Thus, the process included personnel from software configuration management, testing, quality assurance, and programming.

The process used the following steps, some of which came from Fay and Holmes (1985):

- Understand the problem domain.
- Learn the structure and organization of the system.
- Determine what the software is doing.
- Practice fixing low-priority items.

Understand the Details of the Problem

It was important for the maintainers to understand the problem domain—the type of application. For example, if the software related to accounting, the maintainers should have a knowledge of accounting principles. Domain knowledge is very important to the success of the maintainers. The Navy maintainers all possessed a certain amount of domain knowledge in that most of them had worked with predecessor systems. They did understand the operational usage of the system but did not, however, understand how the software worked. To understand the domain better, the following were performed:

- Read existing documentation.
- Discussed the system with the developers.
- Operated the system.

Successful maintainers possess domain knowledge of their application.

Although the existing documentation (system specification, software specifications, and user's manual) was out of date, it did give the software maintenance people an idea of what the system was supposed to do. Reading the documentation was followed up with discussions with the developers and various project management people. Once a copy of the software was received, it was loaded on the system and training of maintenance people as users commenced.

Learn the Structure and Organization of the System

The next step was to learn the structure and organization of the system. To accomplish that, the following actions were taken:

- Inventory the software.
- Place the system under automated configuration control.
- Rebuild the system from the automated software libraries.
- Produce call trees.
- Analyze structure.

All the source files, header files, libraries, and build procedures were inventoried. The maintainers also needed to be sure that they could rebuild the systems. As the systems had not been placed under automated configuration control by the developers, that was accomplished before attempting to analyze the code.

The maintainers placed the systems under automated configuration control. Because structure of the system was unknown, this was a difficult task. A source code analyzer was used to produce call trees. This provided library dependencies and some clues into the structure of the system. Determining the structure was very important from a personnel management perspective (people needed to be assigned to various portions of the code). Until the call trees were obtained, the structure was not known. The call trees helped to assign people to different functional areas such as processing subsystems.

After reviewing the source code analyzer output, the SCM organization put each of the files under automated control and developed procedures for rebuilding the software system. They rebuilt the systems and provided them to the test organization.

The test organization needed to develop test plans and procedures for use in functional or black box testing. The effort to train the testers consisted of reviewing the old specifications and then developing the test plans and procedures. Through this effort the test organization became familiar with the software, and were later able to test it in-house and at field locations.

The next step was to draw structure charts. Using the source code analyzer, a rudimentary relationship between low-level routines was determined, but what was really needed was an overarching representation of the entire system. This was accomplished by analyzing the code and the call trees. This effort was to determine:

- Which functions call other functions.
- How various functions are called.
- How data is set.
- Where data is used.

Data flow diagrams were then developed (now CASE tools will perform this function) so it could be determined how functions were related. Finally, common components and special libraries were identified.

Determine What the Software Is Currently Doing

The most difficult area in software maintenance is program comprehension. Empirical data indicates that somewhere between 40% and 60% of the programmer's time is spent trying to comprehend the code.

Program comprehension begins by reading lines of code in simple algorithms, but in order to interpret the true intent of a program, comprehension must iteratively expand into larger and larger sections of the system code. Relationships must be described between other system domains and the program in question (Brooks 1983). It was also recognized that subsystems or logical divisions of the code had to be determined. Use of the source code analyzer helped in that regard.

Another area that was looked at in relation to program comprehension was the complexity of the code. This effort did not directly aid in code comprehension, but it did provide an indication as to where the most difficult code was and thus helped in the assignment of people.

The specific process that was used to determine what the software was doing consisted of:

- Review specifications.
- Review overall structures.
- Analyze call trees.
- Read the code.
- Make oral presentations.
- Add comments to code.

Reading old specifications is very valuable. Do not wait until the most current documentation is provided, because valuable time needed for the training of maintenance people will be lost. On the surface, reading old specifications seems like a waste of time, but it is not. For the Navy maintenance organization, the maintenance people quickly learned what the system was originally designed to do, and it set the stage for their eventual code reading. Valuable background information is not contained in the code. Some specification information is needed to augment the code.

Old specifications are acceptable for starting a maintenance effort. Current code is what counts!

The overall structure of the software system was then analyzed. People related the specifications to various subsystems. This was accomplished by using the source code analyzer as a static analyzer to locate strings, symbols, and data structures bearing some relationship to the specifications.

A detailed analysis of the call trees followed. This analysis helped to solidify the structure of the system. Next came code reading. The reaction of the maintenance people was as expected. *What do you mean, 'read the code?'* The software engineers and programmers had been assigned areas of responsibility for the code. They were tasked to read their section and then provide a presentation to the other members of the programming team, appropriate SCM people, and the testers for their system. Initially, the head of the programming team provided an overview of the system. This effort provided a necessary systematic training method for program comprehension (Deimel and Naveda 1990), which allowed the programmers to become very familiar with their areas of responsibility.

The code reading created some difficulty. Once the programmers had learned about the code, they wanted to add their own comments to the code. This request brought up some interesting issues of its own. As the system was under version control, did adding comments change the version? Was it a good idea? Yes it was, as these people would perform the maintenance tasks for up to three years. What impact would adding comments have on the metrics effort? If you count Annual Change Traffic (ACT) as a measure of productivity, how do you account for the code reading and subsequent generation of comments?

The approach used was to let the programmers check out the code and make comments in development libraries. They were free to update the comments. When they checked the libraries back into SCM, they accounted for comments by completing a Software Configuration Management form listing all additions, deletions, and modifications to the source code.

Fix Low-Priority Problem Reports

The next area was actually changing code. This was interesting, as the responsibility for software maintenance had not yet transferred to the Navy maintenance organization. As there was a significant backlog of outstanding modification requests (both problem reports and enhancement requests), the Navy maintenance organization coordinated with the developer and took some of the low-priority problem reports to fix. The risks were minimal. If they were fixed, that was fine. The users and the program manager would be pleased. The Navy maintenance organization fixed low-priority problem reports and provided them to the developer for review. The developer, busy with large enhancements, reviewed the corrections and approved the maintenance organization's work. Naturally, all the SCM procedures were followed. The backlog was reduced and the new maintainers (the Navy maintenance people) became familiar with the code and accomplished the goal of trying to change the code.

Understand the Importance of Peer Reviews

The in-place maintenance process (which included peer reviews) was used. These (like the oral presentations) did not sit well with the programmers, but the results justified the effort. From a management perspective, the peer reviews provided a forum to exchange ideas and accelerated the overall understanding of the software. After two or three peer reviews, the programmers became accustomed to the reviews and viewed them as a positive experience. With everyone concerned about getting ready to support the system, the peer reviews were a welcome part of the maintenance process.

Peer reviews accelerate the understanding of the software.

The most significant benefit of the peer reviews was that they aided team formation. As a result of the peer reviews, the programmers evolved from individuals into software teams openly sharing ideas and information. Not only did this produce less error-prone code at an earlier stage, but it identified particular training needs that might not have been discovered by other means. Specifically, during the peer reviews, it became apparent that certain people did not understand how to perform unit testing, nor did they comprehend relational database concepts.

THE LESSONS LEARNED FROM THESE CASE STUDIES

By pursuing a very aggressive internal software maintenance transition training process, by volunteering to take on the software maintenance items no one else wanted (low-priority items), and by having the programmers "digging in the dirt" for a period of time, the Navy maintenance organization was successful in getting ready to support the software. Some of the more important lessons that were learned the hard way are as follows:

Transition Training Lessons Learned

1. *The software maintenance organization should be involved as early as possible in the development life cycle.* Ideally, involvement should begin immediately following the point at which the need for a new system is defined. When the software maintenance organization is not involved early in the development effort, there is usually no planning for system-specific software maintenance training.

2. *The software maintenance organization should be the one most concerned about system-specific software maintenance training.* Plan for the worst. The maintenance organization will probably not get any system-specific training. Program managers often are so consumed with delivering their projects on time and within budget that they spend very little time worrying about transition issues. When they do, they are anxious to get the system transitioned quickly. Experience indicates that system-specific software maintenance training is rarely, if ever, provided.

3. *The software maintenance organization needs a software maintenance training process in place.* Turnover is one of the main problems in maintenance (Dekleva 1992) and having a system-specific software maintenance training process in place is vital for continuity of support. This process should be used during transition phases, and should start well before the maintenance organization assumes responsibility for the software.

4. *A software engineering environment should be in place early.* New tools are always accompanied by a steep learning curve. The sooner that you get started the better. Once the environment is set up, place the system under SCM control. The SCM people need training, too.

5. *Transfer of knowledge from the developer is difficult at best.* Program managers usually do not account for knowledge transfer. Do not plan on any help. Get some specifications, even old ones, and start the process. Initially, the Navy maintenance organization did not believe that the old specifications would be beneficial, but they did provide a basic understanding of the original systems. Do not dismiss the old specifications as being useless because they do not accurately reflect the current code. There is no guarantee that a more recent specification is a good reflection of the code, either.

6. *Oral presentations are tremendously valuable.* These force maintainers to learn the system. Verbalizing the code is difficult, at first, but it accelerates the learning process. The peer reviews helped people to become a team.

7. *Adding comments helps understand the code better and aids the ACT effort.* Initially, most of the work effort was in fixing problems. The typical fix required changing one line of code. The comments were used in the ACT count because of the effort involved, even though they were categorized as comments and not source code changes.

8. *Change must occur.* Only recently have organizations begun to realize that the most costly phase of the software life cycle is that of maintenance (Moad 1990). Hopefully, they will soon recognize that system-specific software maintenance training must be provided, and that it must be institutionalized due to personnel turnover.

SUMMARY

This chapter provided detailed case studies regarding how long it takes the maintainer to become "comfortable" with the system and how to train for transition. Hopefully, these case studies will aid other maintainers in transition efforts. The next chapter gives another transition case study.

1. Determine how much time it will take for your organization to become comfortable with an incoming system.

2. Determine the process you should go through to learn how an incoming system works.

3. What are some things you can do to ensure a smooth transition?

Transition Experiences, Part II

This chapter continues the discussion of transition case studies. In addition, it also includes lessons learned. The third and final case study (Pigoski and Cowden 1992) on software transition deals with the challenges a Navy maintenance organization faced and the experiences gained in having three large systems transitioned for maintenance. The transition for each system was quite unique, and was based on how much involvement the Navy maintenance organization had in the predelivery activities.

HOW TO TRANSITION SYSTEMS: A CASE STUDY

The transition of the first two systems was painful. Based on experience, the transition model (see Chapter 9) was developed and used for later systems. The results are finally seen during the transition of the third system. Experiences with two categories of transition, one that did not have predelivery involvement and one that had full predelivery involvement, are discussed in the following sections.

No Predelivery Involvement

The details of the first two systems to transition, which had no predelivery involvement, are discussed below.

The Systems to Support The two supported systems are the same as discussed in Chapter 10.

Predelivery Interaction The first two systems were developed before the maintenance organization was designated. Thus there was no involvement at design reviews and no participation in acceptance testing or the delivery of the first system to an operational location. Due to significant difficulties with the systems, it was a number of years before the initial version was updated and delivered to other locations.

When delivered, the systems had major problems. The developers were still in charge, and no thought was given to transition. The users reacted very negatively to the systems because the systems had so many problems—many of the problems were never documented. No real SCM existed. When plans were made to finally field another version of the system, the transition process began. It was during this period that the maintenance organization finally got involved.

When the maintainers got involved the status was:

- The systems were already delivered.
- The maintainer had not participated in any predelivery activities.
- The developer was providing support.
- The systems would be delivered to additional locations.
- In the middle of these additional deliveries, the software transition was taking place.

The fact that the maintenance organization had not been involved at all in the transition of these two different systems created huge transition issues. These issues (see Chapter 9) follow along with the solutions the maintenance organization used.

Transfer of Knowledge Knowledge was transferred for these two systems by traveling to the developers' location and remaining with them for weeks at a time. During this period, people became familiar with the code and attempted to assist the developers by fixing low-priority problems. The developers still retained responsibility for the system, as it had not been transitioned.

Perhaps the most important action taken by the maintenance organization was to offer to put the system under automated software configuration management. The maintenance organization first began tracking all the problem reports and enhancement requests. This facilitated the transfer of knowledge, and also let the users know what was occurring with the system. Secondly, the maintainers took all the code (source and object) and placed it under a CASE tool for automated control. This provided valuable information regarding the structure of the system and how to build new releases. Later this was very important, as all new code from the developers was added to the automated libraries that the maintenance organization controlled. Having control of the libraries put the maintainers in a position to perform test and integration functions. The early execution of these functions was invaluable in preparing the maintenance organization to support the systems.

Level of Documentation   All the hard-copy documentation was out of date. Five-year-old design specifications were all that were available. However, the code was available and documented reasonably well with comments. The maintainers determined that the out-of-date specifications together with the current source code were sufficient information to aid in the transfer of knowledge during transition.

Communications with Developer   Maintenance people spent time with the developers, who welcomed the help. As with most developers, they did not want to do maintenance. Thus, fixing low-priority problems did not interest them. The maintenance people fixed them, and everyone won.

Communications with User   The tracking of problem reports and enhancement requests provided for an opportunity for excellent communications with the user.

Formal Turnover Process   Although a number of documents were drafted, including a transition plan, the formal turnover process never occurred. Agreements were never reached; turnover just evolved. However, a majority of the items in the draft plan were resolved.

Training   The developers did not provide any actual software maintenance training. All training was acquired by actually doing the work (on-the-job training). The best approach to training at the time was to get involved early by putting a system under SCM and learning by fixing low-priority problems.

The Speed of Transition   There are those who state that transition is complete when the developers get tired of the system. That was the case here. Because of the lack of predelivery involvement, it took from six to nine months to start performing quality maintenance on the systems (Pigoski and Sexton 1990).

Transition is complete when the developer gets tired of supporting the system.

Who Performs the Transition   The maintenance organization had no real maintenance duties until these systems transitioned. Plus, it was too difficult to perform day-to-day responsibilities for an operational system and, at the same time, plan for transition. Therefore, a specific transition organization was established and made responsible for the transition. Additionally, there are different skills necessary for transition that a maintenance organization might not necessarily have (such as budgeting funds for maintenance). People with these skills were placed in the transition organization.

Cost of Transition   Considerable funding was used to send people to the developer to fix low-priority problems. This process prepared four or five people per system for maintenance.

Predelivery Involvement

The details of the second transition, which had *full* predelivery involvement, are as follows.

The System to Support   For the next system, there was total involvement from the very beginning. This system was developed by a U.S. DoD organization using AT&T hardware and the UNIX operating system. The application code was written in C; the system size was 109K LOC.

Predelivery Interaction   For the 109K LOC system, the maintainers were involved early. They participated in design reviews, reviewed all technical documentation, received general and specific training, participated in formal testing, and even coded some modules. The maintainers participated in the design of the software maintenance environment that was put in place during the predelivery stage.

The system attained operational status and the maintenance organization assumed support on time in accordance with the schedule put forth in the Transition Plan, and within budget. When the customers received the system, they were aware of the maintenance organization and had been working with the maintainers during the predelivery stage. For this transition, everything worked like clockwork. Why? A look at the transition issues and how they were addressed for this transition gives the answers.

Transfer of Knowledge   From the very beginning, maintenance and supportability were made major concerns. Planning called for placement of several personnel who would later "transition" with the system from the developer to the maintainer. These are the "maintenance escorts," and they actively participated in the development effort. Two of them transferred with the software to the maintenance organization. In addition, several other members of the maintenance organization participated in all the reviews and coded several modules. Code was available and accessible. This was possible because prior planning arranged for it to happen.

Level of Documentation   All the documentation during the transition was current and held by the maintenance organization.

Communications with Developer   As some of the developers were the eventual maintainers, communications were excellent. Additionally, constant communications with the developer occurred. In view of the fact that this was the first system in C/UNIX that the maintenance organization would support, this communication was very necessary.

Communications with User   This system had thousands of users and many locations. Direct communication was almost impossible, and not a real issue for this system. However, there was constant communication with the one or two largest user locations in order to get user input.

Formal Turnover Process   A formal turnover was executed. A transition plan was developed (by the maintainer) and followed rigidly by all parties.

Training   A considerable amount of informal training was given to the maintainers so that they could code several modules. A formal system-specific lecture course was not provided by the developer. However, the maintainers went to numerous courses to receive training in new areas such as the C language, CASE tools, and the UNIX operating system. The needed training was identified very early in the transition plan.

The Speed of Transition The transition process evolved over a period of two years, and was effective. The maintenance organization effectively supported the system when it was supposed to assume maintenance responsibility. The transfer of responsibility was almost transparent to the users.

Who Performs the Transition Transition was effected by the separate transition organization previously established. Senior people did the planning and junior people performed the coding and testing. As this technique had worked before, and the rest of the Navy maintenance organization now had real day-to-day maintenance responsibilities for the other systems that had transferred, it was deemed appropriate to stay with what worked previously.

Cost of Transition The maintenance organization used about one and one-third of a person-year per year for two years preparing for maintenance support for the system. A significant amount of funding was spent on training and travel to the developer's location. Based on the fact that the system was on time, and the maintenance organization was ready to support the system, it was money well spent.

THE LESSONS LEARNED ABOUT TRANSITION

The most important lesson learned is that the maintenance organization *must be involved early in the development effort*. This certainly cannot be the case when maintenance is outsourced, or when a prototype suddenly becomes a production system and requires maintenance; but even for incremental and evolutionary developments, it is important for the maintenance organization to be involved early.

The maintenance organization should be involved early in the development of a system.

There are costs associated with that level of involvement, but experience shows that it is cost-effective.

SUMMARY

This chapter provided a case study and the effect of predelivery maintainer involvement. Early participation is essential. The issues and how they were involved should help maintainers resolve similar transition issues. Next, you'll learn how to set up a maintenance organization.

1. List some things maintainers can do to smooth transition if they get involved late in the process.

2. Discuss how SCM can aid transition.

3. Think about a previous transition you might have been involved in, and how it might have been different if the maintenance organization would have been involved earlier.

Setting Up
the Software
Maintenance
Organization

12

Up to this point in the book, you've been introduced to many aspects of maintenance. You've learned software maintenance's history, a new definition, how to apply that new definition, the maintenance process, when maintenance should begin, how to go about planning for maintenance, and how to have a successful transition. However, there has been no discussion about the actual functions that a maintainer will perform, nor how to organize the maintenance people to produce a quality maintenance effort. This chapter discusses these maintenance functions in an organizational context.

WHAT ARE THE ROLES AND RESPONSIBILITIES OF MAINTAINERS?

The roles and responsibilities (as well as the functions) of the software maintainer must be clearly defined. For individual systems, software, or software products, these are contained in the maintenance plan. However, there must be some higher-level document or directive that refines the overall roles, responsibilities, and functions of the maintenance organization. Sometimes the directive is a stand-alone directive and is called a *charter* or the *software maintenance policy* (see the section "A Sample Software Maintenance Charter"). Sometimes it is included in corporate or organizational manuals. In any event, there must be some documentation to clearly identify the roles, responsibilities, and functions of the maintainer. The directive delineates:

- All responsibilities, authorities, and functions of the maintenance organization.
- Operations of the software maintenance organization.
- The need and justification for changes.
- Responsibilities for making the changes.
- Change control and procedures.
- The process and procedures for controlling changes to software.

What the document is called is not important. What is important is that the roles, responsibilities, and functions of the organization are documented and understood by the maintainers as well as also the users and the supplier.

Ensure that roles, responsibilities, and functions are documented.

WHAT ARE THE FUNCTIONS OF A MAINTAINER?

Once the roles, responsibilities, and functions of the maintainer are documented, how the maintenance functions are placed organizationally must be determined.

First the functions must be aggregated, and then parceled out to various organizational elements. The following list designates the particular functions the maintainer must perform:

- Management.
- Software modification.
- Software configuration management.
- Training.
- Documentation support.
- Integration support.
- User liaison and help desk.
- Testing.
- Quality assurance.
- Technical assistance.

Now that you know which functions need to be performed, read on to understand details about those functions and who performs them.

Management Function

The maintainer has definite software maintenance management functions. These are the purely management-oriented functions necessary for the success of the organization and related maintenance efforts. Management functions include:

- Development of the organizational documentation (e.g., a charter).
- Development of planning documents (e.g., the maintenance plan, transition plan, migration plan, and retirement plan).
- Development of budgetary items for the organization.
- Transition of systems.
- Software process improvement and metrics.

Responsibility for performing the management functions falls to a number of people. A software maintenance manager (SMM) would normally have overall responsibility, and would perform the functions of developing organizational documents and conducting general oversight of maintenance activities. Planning could be performed by a head planner in a separate organizational element. If not, the SMM could provide planning. The same is true for transition planning and execution. A separate planning element is a nice fit for transition planning. A good way to handle the planning and related issues is to have a *plans, programs, and resources* organizational element. This element can perform all planning, budgetary, resource, and transition issues. It can also plan migration and retirement of the software.

A separate planning organization works well.

Software Modification Function

Software modification is the analysis of problems, the isolation of faults, the analysis of enhancement requests, and the designing, coding, unit testing, and documenting of changes to a software product. Software modification includes correcting software errors, modifying software to enable it to work with interfacing systems, and adding enhancements to the software. Software modification includes database modification (e.g., a schema, or data dictionary). These modifications are grouped into three categories: corrective maintenance, adaptive maintenance, and perfective maintenance (see Chapter 2). In addition, the scope of the modification, including size, cost and time, are determined. Finally, the criticality and the modification's impact on performance, safety, or security are analyzed.

Senior software engineers are normally responsible for the technical success of the software for a system. They coordinate with systems engineers, who have overall responsibility for the systems. The senior software engineer will have a group of software engineers performing the software modification function. These software engineers, who specialize in specific applications software, have the responsibility to analyze, design, code, test, diagnose, and modify the application portion of the system, including its database. Modifications are identified and then classified and prioritized.

Software Configuration Management Function

Software configuration management (SCM) is the set of activities that is developed to manage change throughout the software life cycle. The SCM function ensures that all software in a system is identified, documented, produced, and delivered in accordance with the design requirements and specifications. Specific functions under SCM include:

■ Coding and tracking problem reports and enhancement requests.
■ Determining the feasibility and costs of enhancements.
■ Maintaining knowledge of the intricacies of reconstructing and testing a working component of code after a modification has been designed and coded.
■ Baselining the system to deliver it to the customer.
■ Managing version control.
■ Auditing to determine compliance with requirements, plans, and contracts.

SCM is vital to the success of software maintenance. Systems are now very interoperable, and interfacing of systems is a major concern.

SCM requires numerous people to perform the functions; it is almost always understaffed, because it is undervalued. People are often recruited for analysis, design, coding, testing, and SCM positions in the same manner; therefore, many organizations do not have separate job descriptions or qualifications for SCM functions. This is a poor practice; separate job descriptions with different qualifications are required. SCM positions include:

■ SCM manager.
■ Software librarian.

- Software builder.
- Auditor.
- Secretariat.
- Change control tracker.
- Configuration specialist.

In some organizations the SCM organization has a distribution function. The SCM organization, which produces the new version, also makes copies and sends them out to users. Larger organizations tend to have a separate distribution organization and often separate the distribution function from SCM. SCM fulfills the maintenance requirement of maintaining a database to track proposed and implemented changes. It usually is in the form of a tracking database.

Training Function

Training is a key support function upon which the success of a maintainer depends. It is the provision of whatever the user needs to ensure that the user understands the operation of the software process works (such as problem reporting). Most importantly, the maintainer must train user personnel and provide technical demonstrations of the software. User training might take the form of traditional schoolhouse training, on-site training, training manuals, help guides, computer-based training (CBT), or electronic performance support systems (EPSS). Part of the software maintenance training function is to maintain training material. Some maintainers have a separate training organizational element. That is normally the case with very large organizations. However, for most instances, user training is provided by the individuals who perform software modifications.

Maintainers often overlook the training function. They shouldn't.

Documentation Support Function   Considerable documentation must be maintained throughout the software life cycle. The documentation function includes all activities of preparing, updating, and distributing software documentation. The following documentation must be maintained:

- User or operator manuals.
- Program maintenance manuals.
- Software installation guides.
- Requirements.

- Training materials.
- Specific software documentation (software development folders, software requirement specifications, and independent requirement specifications).
- Process manuals.
- Maintenance manuals.
- SCM process.
- Test process.
- QA process.

With the advent of CASE tools, much of the documentation is now in computer form. The media might be different, but the maintainer still must maintain the documentation as the software changes. Organizationally it is still a challenge; the documentation function is one of the most difficult. Large organizations have separate people to handle documentation. Smaller organizations tend to have the technical people (those analyzing, coding, testing) update software documentation without a separate organizational element.

It is well recognized that software engineers and programmers do not document very well. It is not their strength. Most of them only do it because it is required. A better approach is to have a separate person (such as a technical writer) working with a particular software project to perform the documentation.

A major documentation issue for a maintenance organization is "How much documentation is enough?" As discussed under transition, do the maintainers want all the current documentation? Are they willing to wait until it is provided?

What documentation is really necessary in order to perform *maintenance?* Based on the cost to obtain maintenance documentation, this  area needs considerable attention. Recent efforts focus on the automation of documentation. This is a step in the right direction, but some real effort needs to be expended, and empirical data collected and analyzed, to determine the cost-effectiveness of producing the massive amounts of documentation that are currently required for maintenance. Old specifications and current source code are somewhat sufficient documentation to support a system. Adding a programmer's maintenance manual ensures success!

Maintainers can be successful with old specifications, current code, and a programmer's maintenance manual.

Integration Support Function

An additional function of software maintenance has emerged, and must be considered when tailoring a postdelivery software maintenance scope for software products. Due to the use of Open Systems Architecture and the extensive integration of a variety of products, "integration support" is now a significant maintenance responsibility. Many systems are fielded with all commercial products, and the traditional maintainer *has no code to maintain!* Is maintenance still required? Absolutely! What about upgrades to the commercial products? The maintainer must integrate and test them before sending out a new version. The maintainer must perform all software maintenance functions except the software modification functions.

Systems based solely on commercial-off-the-shelf (COTS) products still require extensive maintenance support.

What does a maintainer do for a COTS-based system? The maintainer serves as an interface between COTS software vendors and the system software users for reporting COTS anomalies and receiving new versions of COTS software. If system users identify a problem with COTS software, they generate a modification request or problem report and forward it to the maintainer. The maintainer contacts the vendor to work out the problem. All revised COTS software is sent back to the maintainer, where it is integrated with the rest of the system software. Regression testing is then performed before the revised software is delivered to user configurations. The software maintenance concept must incorporate continuous liaison with commercial vendors and other agencies to adequately support today's systems.

Unfortunately, there is not much available to help maintainers maintain COTS-intensive systems. There is very little literature available and almost no research. Mitre Corporation (Agresti 1994) is addressing this important topic. Organizationally, often the commercial products and system/network portions of the system are put together. Included in maintainers' responsibilities are all commercial products (e.g., word processors, operating systems, and network operating systems) and if necessary, the maintainers might write low-level code to effect interfaces. They typically have no application code responsibility.

User Liaison and Help Desk Function

One functional area that is often overlooked is that of user liaison, customer liaison, or customer service. Software maintenance organizations need to realize that they are in the customer service business (Pigoski 1991d). Establishing a user liaison function reinforces that concept.

This function is often implemented in the form of a "help desk." Whatever it is called, performance of this function is critical to the success of a maintenance organization. The individual or organization assigned is responsible for the communications liaison between the users and the maintenance team.

An ideal help desk serves as a focal point and screens calls. Only those calls that cannot be solved by the help desk are referred to the software maintenance organization. This is a win-win situation. The customers get answers, and the arrangement is cost-effective. Every maintenance organization needs a dedicated user liaison individual or office.

If it is impossible to set up a help desk, designate someone on the team to be the user liaison representative. It will save money and buy goodwill with the users.

Many organizations are now using "system help desks." Users call these for any and all problems or questions. The system help desk tries to resolve the problems, and if it cannot, it passes it on to the system (hardware) or software maintenance organization. For very large systems, this concept works very well. If this concept is used, the maintainer should still designate one individual as the primary person to perform user liaison.

Testing Function

Testing is a critical function in the software development process, and is also extremely important for maintenance. There are many issues relating to maintenance testing. Is it the same as development testing? Is it different?

What is a good definition of testing? Some possibilities include the process of demonstrating that errors are not present, showing that a program performs its intended functions correctly, or the process of establishing confidence that a program does what it is supposed to do. According to Myers (1979), it is none of the above. Testing should add value, raise quality, or increase reliability by finding and removing errors. Myers defines testing as the process of executing a program with the intent of finding errors.

Is testing for software maintenance the same as for development? Myers' definition is a development definition. There are those like

Beizer (1992), who state that maintenance testing is very different. Beizer states that the focus of maintenance testing should merely be to ensure that the system still works.

As with development, there are various types of maintenance testing. Pressman (1992) lists the following types of tests:

- Unit testing.
- Individual subprograms, subroutines, or procedures in a program testing.
- Integration testing.
- Errors associated with interfacing testing.
- Validation (acceptance) testing.
- Functional and performance testing.
- Outside software engineering.
- Hardware, software, and information testing.

Maintenance testing includes performing the different types of testing, and developing test plans, specifications, procedures, reports, results, and databases.

Unit and component testing should be performed by the software engineer who did the analysis, design, and coding. Integration and acceptance testing should be performed by an *independent* test organization. Regardless of the size of the maintenance organization, a separate organization for testing is vital.

Maintainers, like developers, need an independent testing organization.

Quality Assurance Function

Another area that is often not used by maintenance organizations is quality assurance (QA). QA is defined as a planned and systematic pattern of all actions necessary to provide adequate confidence that the item or product conforms to established technical requirements (ANSI/IEEE 730 1981). QA functions include:

- Definition of standards, practices, and procedures.
- Assurance that a high quality product is delivered.
- Performance of independent review of the program.
- Establishment of tracing requirements.
- Evaluation of documents.
- Evaluation of test plans and procedures.
- Monitoring of problem reporting and SCM activities.

- Performance of procedural and documentation audits.
- Writing of QA plan.
- Conducting audits.
- Moderating software inspections.
- Attending walk-throughs or peer reviews.

These functions need to be performed by the maintenance organization, and should be documented in the charter or software maintenance policy.

Technical Assistance Functions

The technical assistance function is the catch-all function. It is the "miscellaneous" category. If some function is not included elsewhere, it is included here.

The technical assistance function includes actions such as:

- Performing installations at user sites (if appropriate).
- Sending out additional documentation, including copies of installed software (This might be performed by SCM under distribution).
- Answering/resolving questions from the help desk.
- Responding to requests for technical assistance from the users.
- Performing ad hoc studies or analysis.

Due to the nature of the technical assistance function, the various organizational elements often each exercise some of the actions for this function. Experience indicates that maintainers spend 10% to 20% of their time performing technical assistance.

Resources expended for technical assistance must be documented.

Other Functions

Are these all the functions of a software maintenance organization? What about running the local area network (LAN)? What about the functions of adding new users to the LAN? What about adding *content* to the corporate databases? Who does the backups of the files or databases?

The software maintenance functions delineated above are for a typical software maintenance organization providing software maintenance support for a software system. For example, the system might be an inventory system to support some retail organization such as Wal-Mart. The responsibilities of the software maintenance organization would be to support the system, which in this case is used by many retail locations. The day-to-day operation of the system is a function of the user or operational organization. Therefore, they are responsible for the backups, security, data entry, and other nonmaintenance functions. When problems occur or new requirements arise, they get passed to the software maintenance organization for resolution. If, for example, the backup of a database is particularly slow, the maintenance organization might develop a new utility program to improve or expedite the backup operation. However, the running of the backup is the responsibility of the operational organization. In addition, if a security problem were uncovered by the users, the maintainer might write software to correct the problem.

There are, however, integration functions (previously discussed) that the maintenance organization must perform. These functions include diagnosing and isolating network problems. They do not include performing backups.

There is another reason to not include these areas in software maintenance functions: cost. Maintenance costs are high and increasing. It is not in the best interest of the maintainer to perform routine operations functions.

Practical Experience

The people performing the analysis, design, and coding (also known as programmers or software engineers) need to be part of a team. It is common knowledge that the least effective debugging method is a programmer working alone. All work needs to be reviewed either by a software inspection, a structured walkthrough, or a peer review. Small teams focused on a particular system, software, or software product are very effective.

In the early days of setting up the U. S. Navy software maintenance organization, it became apparent that building the team concept was important. In lieu of separate offices, modular, adaptable furniture was used and team members were located in contiguous areas. Further, openings to their "cubicles" were back-to-back so that they could slide chairs back and forth easily to discuss matters. That idea worked for us, and promoted the team concept.

HOW SHOULD A MAINTENANCE ORGANIZATION BE ORGANIZED?

Now that you know the functions of a software maintenance organization, how should it be organized? What would a typical organization chart look like? Everyone wants a textbook answer to their unique situation. That is almost impossible to do, but the following information should help maintainers determine how to establish their organization.

Development of an organization for a software maintenance organization is dependent on many factors, some of which are more political in nature than technical. Size is one factor. Questions to ask include: Are development and maintenance performed by the same organizational group? Is the full range of maintenance functions performed? But the most important factor is—what are the goals of the organization? What corporate goals is the software maintenance organization supporting? If the goal of the organization is zero defects, the QA and testing elements would be significantly larger than those elements in an organization whose goal is to get products on the market quickly.

Most software maintenance organizations would typically be part of a corporate information systems (IS) organization. The IS organization, like corporate operations, would report to the CEO. An average IS organization might look like Figure 12.1.

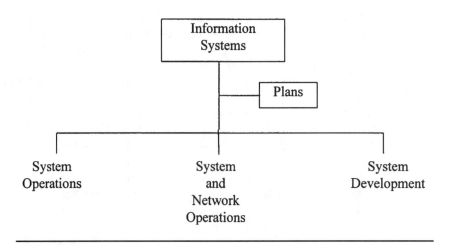

FIGURE 12.1 Typical information systems organization.

Responsibilities for this example include:

- *Plans*. Development of IS strategies, plans, and budgets.
- *System Operations*. Operation of the data-processing installation.
- *System and Network Operations*. Operation of distributed mini- or micro-computers.
- *System Development*. Development and maintenance of the applications portfolio.

Below is a discussion of each organizational element.

Plans. While some organizations have separate planning organizations, others perform the listed responsibilities within the system development organization.

System Operations. This organization primarily operates mainframes. Of note is that there are still large numbers of mainframes in operations, and these will continue to exist for some time to come. System operations is also sometimes called just computer operations.

System Network Operations. Many organizations have opted for separate organizations to introduce and operate new distributed technologies (e.g., Client/Server).

System Development. This organization is the area that is of most concern for maintainers. Many organizations combine development and maintenance into one organizational element. Other titles include product development and application development. Regardless of the title, this organization is responsible for development and sometimes maintenance.

Because the focus here is maintenance, the system development organization is discussed. A typical system development organization might look like Figure 12.2.

This example illustrates how the software organization fits in with other system-related activities. Responsibilities include:

- *Plans*. Development and maintenance of systems plans.
- *System Engineering*. Development of system.
  Maintenance of system.
  Development of hardware.
  Development and maintenance of system specifications.
  System analysis and diagnosis.

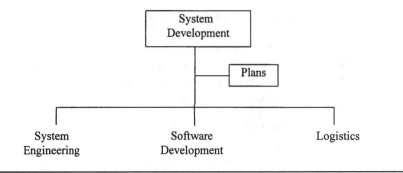

FIGURE 12.2   System development organization.

■ *Software Development*. Development of software.
Maintenance of software.
■ *Logistics*. Maintenance of hardware/firmware.
Provisions of material.

Below is a discussion of each organizational element.

Plans. Some organizations have a separate planning organization. Sometimes the planning functions are combined with logistics functions.

System Engineering. This organization oversees the development and maintenance of the systems, concentrating on system and hardware aspects.

Software Development. This organization can be organized many ways, but this example assumes that both development and maintenance are combined into one organization called software development. It is sometimes referred to as software engineering to align itself with system engineering, software applications (as its focus is code), or software production (as it develops and maintains software products). The software development organization is further broken down by application or product. Small teams are formed and have overall responsibility for a particular application or product.

Logistics. This organization has overall responsibility for support and hardware maintenance. The logistics organization coordinates with system engineering for systems-related support items and software development for software-related support items.

The issue of whether the maintainer is the developer is not addressed—yet.

Previously, there was considerable discussion (Chapters 9–11) regarding transition of software responsibility from a developer to a maintainer. What if the developer retains the maintenance responsibility? Figure 12.3 depicts an IS organization in which the developer and maintainer are the same.

The following shows various responsibilities:

- *Quality Assurance.* Quality of the system.
- *Plans.* Planning for the system.
- *Training.* Train users and the maintainers.
- *Help Desk.* Accepts, resolves, and refers problems and questions from the user to appropriate organization.
- *Product Services.* Development and maintenance of software products.
- *Test.* Testing of software.
- *SCM.* Software configuration management of the software.

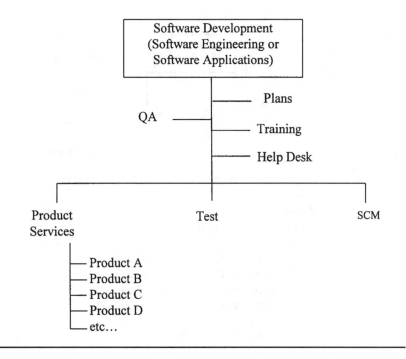

FIGURE 12.3 Software development organization.

Below is a discussion of organization elements that have not been discussed thus far.

Product Services. This organization is often referred to as application or application services. This organization is divided into teams for each product (e.g., one software team develops and maintains product A, another for B, etc.). Integration and maintenance-related network services would be performed within this organization element.

What if maintenance is performed within the software development organization, but a different group? This normally is not the case, but that type of an organization would look like Figure 12.4.

The organization depicted in Figure 12.4 has separate maintenance responsibilities. It could perform maintenance on products developed by the in-house software development organization or from anywhere else, such as an outsource development organization. Both software development and software maintenance use the services of the other organizations, as depicted in Figure 12.4.

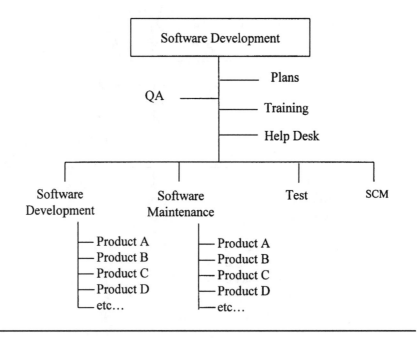

FIGURE 12.4 Maintenance organization within software development.

What about a separate maintenance organization, perhaps one that only does maintenance? For example, you might have an out-sourced maintenance organization that does nothing but maintenance. A separate maintenance organization might look like Figure 12.5.

Let's say that the software maintenance organization has respon-sibility for a software system and is given ten full-time personnel to support the system. (See Chapter 8 for a discussion about estimating staffing resources.) An organization chart might look like Figure 12.6.

The organization depicted in Figure 12.6 separates the support functions of QA, test, and SCM. Could they all be rolled into one orga-nization? Could people perform multiple functions? For example, could the programmers analyze, design, code, and unit test in the morning and perform testing in the afternoon? Yes—and it is done in very small organizations. The key is that they should test other products. If, for example, Programmer A maintains Product A, Programmer A could test Product B. Programmer A should not test (as in integration or acceptance testing) Product A.

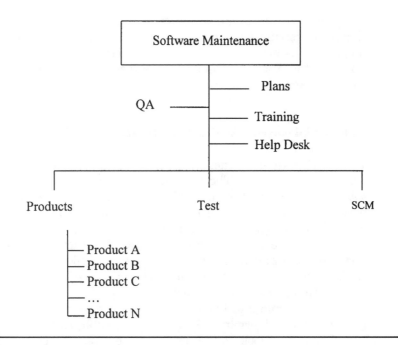

FIGURE 12.5 Separate maintenance organization.

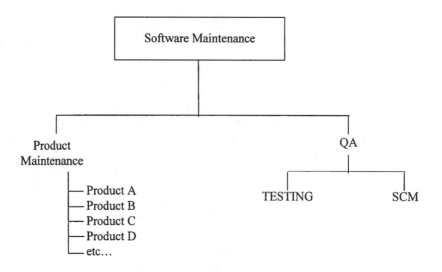

FIGURE 12.6 Small maintenance organization.

Even with an organization of ten people, the functions can and should be distributed among the staff. Management can perform planning, and product maintenance personnel can perform help-desk functions. As the number of maintainers increases, the organization can change to approach the one depicted in Figure 12.5.

HOW SHOULD PERSONNEL RESOURCES BE DISTRIBUTED?

The organizational structure is dependent upon many factors, size being a primary one. The next questions are: How do personnel resources get allocated to the various organizations? How many people perform management functions? How many perform analysis and design? How many perform testing?

As for determining the organizational structure, it depends on corporate and software maintenance goals. Take the example of a small software maintenance organization of ten people. How many people should be performing testing functions?

Take a moment or two and write down some numbers, or parts of numbers, for each organizational entity in Table 12.1.

Now take a look at the breakdown between those producing the

TABLE 12.1 Personnel Distribution

Function	People Needed
Management	
Product Maintenance:	
Analysis	
Design	
Coding	
Unit Testing	
SCM	
QA	
Testing	

code and those supporting it. Simply, those people performing product maintenance (analysis, design, coding, and testing) are the people producing the code. Everyone else supports them. What percent of the entire organization is analyzing, designing, and coding versus what percent is supporting? Is that ratio 9 to 1? 8 to 2? 1 to 9? Fill in Table 12.2.

And the answer is—it is impossible to do without knowing the goals of the organization. If one of the goals of the software maintenance organization is to put more functionality in the operational systems, perhaps quality would not be that important. Think of Microsoft, Inc. trying to get Windows 95 to the marketplace. What do you think their ratio was? The goal must have been to get it to the marketplace quickly! If the goal of the organization was zero defects, the ratio would be entirely different. During informal discussions with people at the NASA Houston Space Center, where software development and maintenance support is provided for the Space Shuttle,

TABLE 12.2 Number of Personnel Producing/Supporting Code

Function	People Needed
Produce Code	
Support Code	

> **Practical Experience**
>
> In the early days of establishing the U. S. Navy software maintenance organization, we used a 6 to 1 ratio. That did not work. Over a period of time we evolved to about 6 to 3.5 or 6 to 4. With that type of ratio we were able to perform credibly. For an average system, with average people, and with average goals, you should use 6:5 or 1:1. Most organizations will have trouble getting management to agree that five people are needed to check on five others who are producing code; but in order to have a well-functioning maintenance organization, this is a good ratio. Three years ago, I used to get answers from tutorial participants in the range of 9:1 and 8:1. Now, most recent participants are saying that the ratio should be 1:1. The good news is that those who are attending software maintenance tutorials and seminars have a good idea of what the ratio should be. However, most state that it is no where near 1:1 at their organizations. Most see more like 4:1.

a ratio of 1 to 5 is used. That means for every one person producing code, there are five people testing the code, performing SCM, and otherwise supporting the code. For systems where safety is involved, zero defects is far more important that putting more functionality in the operational system.

That concludes the discussion about setting up an organization. Hopefully, the charts and ratios give you something to ponder. The next section provides a sample charter (discussed earlier in this chapter) for a maintenance organization.

A SAMPLE SOFTWARE MAINTENANCE CHARTER

Software maintainers need a charter, as mentioned earlier in the chapter. The following is a sample that can be tailored depending upon organizational responsibilities. The generic software maintenance organization (SMO) is used as an example. Maintenance organizations might use the terms *department, division, product services, software engineering,* and so on.

Software Maintenance Charter

1. Designation of the software maintenance organization

The software maintenance organization (SMO) of the information systems department (ISD) of our company, WE DO WIGGETS, Inc.(WDW) is assigned as the software maintenance organization (SMO) for all software systems supporting the company.

Responsibilities include those systems developed in-house and those developed externally and transitioned to WDW for software maintenance.

2. Designation of the software maintenance manager

The software maintenance manager (SMM) is the head of the SMO. The SMM will designate the specific system software maintenance managers.

3. Software Maintenance Organization (SMO) Tasking

The SMO is responsible in accordance with company directives, regulations, and program direction for:

1. Providing predelivery and postdelivery software maintenance support within the scope of this charter, and the approved maintenance concept for the designated systems as provided for in the individual maintenance plans for the systems. The SMO will assist program managers in the development of these plans. If the PM does not develop a maintenance plan, the SMO will develop it.

2. Supporting program managers in areas relating to software support for the developed systems.

4. Software Maintenance Organization Responsibilities and Authority

The SMO will plan, coordinate, and control software maintenance activities in support of the designated systems. These responsibilities include:

1. The SMO will plan, coordinate, and control software maintenance activities in support of designated systems.

During the predelivery phase, the SMO will assist the planning for: software maintenance, identification of requirements, software quality, software supportability, and transition. Specific activities to be performed during the predelivery phase include:

- Develop transition and support plans.
- Attend design and technical reviews.
- Review documentation.
- Conduct independent verification and validation (IV&V).
- Participate in testing support.
- Evaluate quality.
- Do software configuration management.
- Manage problem reporting and tracking.

During the post-delivery phase, the SMO will implement approved software changes and maintain quality software. The primary activities of the SMO during this phase are to support user requirements through evaluation of proposed changes, and developing and incorporating those changes that are approved into the system software. Other activities performed during this phase include:

- Provide information about the functions, nature, and uses of the software.
- Explain and possibly correct anomalies when they are identified during operations.
- Train support and user personnel.
- Design, code, verify, test, and document software modifications.
- Maintain knowledge of the intricacies of reconstructing and testing software after a modification has been designed and coded.
- Determine feasibility and cost of enhancements.
- Record and track modification requests.
- Provide technical demonstrations of the software.
- Maintain documentation.
- Conduct delivery process and procedures.
- Provide commercial-off-the-shelf integration and support.
- Maintain a customer help desk.

2. The SMO will develop a tailored software maintenance plan, when appropriate, for each designated system. (See Chapter 7.)
3. During the predelivery software maintenance stage, the SMO will ensure that the accepted software is supportable, that software requirements are satisfied, and that plans are made for transition and postdelivery software maintenance.

4. During transition, the SMO will implement the transition plan and demonstrate that the software can be supported.

5. During the postdelivery stage, the SMO will maintain software quality, and coordinate related postdelivery software maintenance activities.

6. During the postdelivery life cycle, the SMO is responsible for the software configuration identification, status accounting, and configuration audits of controlled baselines associated with the designated systems.

The SMO will have the following authority:

1. The SMO, an organizational element of ISD, is the representative of the head of ISD and has the following authorities:

   ■ Management and direction of contractors (if appropriate).
   ■ Intra- and interdepartment liaison to resolve support requirements.
   ■ Direct communication between the user community and the SMO is authorized to help identify and isolate software problems and to foster attitudes of support and cooperation.

2. Configuration control authority is held by the SMO. The configuration control authority and responsibilities of the SMO are defined in the appropriate designated system Software Configuration Management plan.

5. Resource Control

1. The SMO will ensure that financial and personnel requirements to accomplish the above responsibilities are submitted in accordance with established procedures.

2. Funding to accomplish the above responsibilities will be provided to the SMO. The SMO will, in turn, allocate the necessary funding and provide direction, as applicable, to participating organizations for services in accordance with current regulations, policies, and procedures.

3. As early as practical and continuing throughout the predelivery software development phase, the SMO will solicit approval and advocacy from the program manager or the integrated logistic support (ILS) manager regarding acquisition and support of the engineering environment and the testing environment in accordance with the approved postdelivery concept.

4. Postdelivery resource requirements will be identified in the maintenance plan (MP). When an MP does not exist, then the SMO will coordinate postdelivery resource requirements with the SMM.

6. **Resource and Facility Support**

1. Resource support: The ISD will coordinate and provide support to the SMO in accordance with the MP or appropriate directive.

2. Facility support: Facility support (office space, utilities, phones) for the SMO and for other agencies assigned postdelivery activities will be provided in accordance with the MP.

7. **Communication Channels**

Direct communication must occur between people involved in implementation of the post operational software maintenance concept and people involved in the support of the designated systems to ensure timely and effective coordination and exchange of information.

SUMMARY

This chapter summarized the functions of a maintenance organization. It discussed how different maintenance organization are arranged and provided sample organization charts. In addition, this chapter contained a sample charter.

1. What are some other tasks that the help desk might perform?

2. Establish a goal for a software maintenance organization and develop an organizational structure.

3. Allocate personnel resources to the organizational entities and defend your numbers.

Tools and Environments

Previous chapters discussed the software maintenance process and the organization that will provide maintenance, but in what kind of environment will the maintainer work? What tools are available for the maintainer to perform maintenance activities? This chapter addresses CASE tools, CASE environments, and CASE's impact on maintenance. Additionally, the chapter provides a case study of developing an integrated CASE environment.

What is an environment? What are tools? Is an environment a set of computer aided software engineering (CASE) tools? The IEEE and ISO/IEC are addressing these issues, and Dr. Tom Vollman (ANSI/IEEE 1209 1995) has spearheaded related standards efforts. This section discusses some definitions that have their genesis in the IEEE/ISO/IEC standardization efforts for the adoption of CASE tools.

WHAT IS CASE?

 CASE is an acronym that stands for Computer-Aided Software Engineering. A CASE software tool aids in software engineering activities. These activities include requirements analysis and tracing, software design, code production, testing, document generation, and project management. CASE tools can provide support in one functional area or in many areas.

Programmers and analysts were using CASE-type tools long before CASE became a buzz word. Experienced programmers and analysts used language processors—called *back-end* or *lower CASE* tools—that worked with code (both source and object) to aid in interpreting and modifying code. These tools were used in the program implementation and maintenance tasks. The recent emphasis on tools focuses on the front-end (or design) stages and encompass activities like business modeling and analysis, systems planning, requirements specification, and logical design. These are referred to as *front-end* or *upper CASE* tools—terms that should be somewhat familiar—but there are other, newer terms.

IEEE 1348 *A Recommended Practice for the Adoption of CASE Tools*, (ANSI/IEEE 1348 1995) states that the vision for CASE is an interrelated set of tools supporting all aspects of the software development and maintenance process. Some of these tools are called *vertical* tools; they provide support for specific phases of the life cycle. Examples of vertical tools include analysis and design tools, code generators, and testing tools. There are other CASE tools, referred to as *horizontal* tools; they provide functionality across the life cycle and include tools for project management, software configuration management, and documentation. A third category of tools called *integration frameworks* has emerged, and these provide a set of mechanisms to facilitate the interaction of other CASE tools. The effort to get an interrelated set of tools resulted in *integrated CASE*, or ICASE.

WHAT IS ICASE?

 CASE tools have evolved and recent efforts focused on integrating the tools in order to improve productivity. Integrated CASE tools, or ICASE, are defined as the combination of two or more CASE tools to form an integrated whole. There are two requirements for integration: an understanding of the relationship between the services or functions provided by the components, and a physical means by which to combine the components. The physical means permits them to operate as a unified whole and improve productivity.

WHAT IS AN ENVIRONMENT?

Sommerville (1989) tells us that an *environment* encompasses all of the automated facilities that a software engineer has available to perform the task of software development. Although not explicitly stated, Sommerville would probably apply that definition to maintenance.

What Is a Software Engineering Environment (SEE)?

What is a software engineering environment? A software engineering environment (SEE) is an integrated collection of CASE tools which are brought together to support the methods, policies, guidelines, and standards that support activities within some software engineering process such as software development or maintenance. ICASE environments must be networked through a database.

There are several other terms used to identify CASE environments. These terms include software development environments, programming support environments, and integrated program support environments. You will see all these terms used, and most people simply refer to them as CASE environments.

What is the typical environment at a maintenance organization? There are computers and software in which the operation software runs. This is often referred to as the target system. A maintainer needs one of these to test new software. Some maintainers refer to these as the software test environment (STE).

Can, or should, the maintenance activities be performed on the target machine? For very small systems that is acceptable, but for medium and large systems it is not recommended. Computers, editors, linkers, code analyzers, and other CASE tools are needed to support a system, software, or software product.

Most often it is not practical to run on the target system because the tools require significant more memory and storage than the typical target machine would have. Thus a separate computer, the host machine, is used for the maintenance activities. All the CASE tools are used with the host machine, and are commonly referred to as the software engineering environment. The target machine with its software, including simulators, is often called the software test environment.

Maintainers need a Software Engineering Environment for CASE tools.

Now that you know the terminology, let's discuss the SEE in more detail. SEEs are designed to support all phases of the software process including the specialized activities of software development and maintenance. Included in the SEE is a software toolset to aid the software engineers. Sommerville (1989) provides some examples of tools which might be in an environment:

- *Host / target communications software*. Links the development computer (host) to the computer on which the software is to execute (the target machine).
- *Target machine simulators*. These are used when target machine software is being developed so that it can be executed and tested on the host machine.
- *Cross-compilers*. These are language processing systems that execute on the host machine and generate code for the target machine.
- Testing and debugging tools.
- Graphical design editors.
- Test processors.
- Project management tools.

Any maintenance organization must have an automated environment in which to work. In addition to Sommerville's list, the following tools are essential:

- Automated software configuration management tools to provide for source code control and software library functions.
- An automated trouble report/enhancement tracking database. If the process is to be improved, there must be a database to track the efforts of the maintenance organization.
- Automated test tools to assist in regression testing.
- Auditing tools.
- Performance monitors.
- Code analyzers.

What Is a Good CASE Environment?

Whatever you call your collection of tools, the resulting environment must provide the software engineers with user-friendly facilities to perform all software development and maintenance activities. Figure 13.1, from Elliott Chikofsky and Ron Norman (1994), provides the general architecture of a CASE environment. Chikofsky and Norman also detail the properties required for a comprehensive CASE environment. These are listed in Figure 13.2.

These are the properties that you would like in your environment, whether it be for development or maintenance.

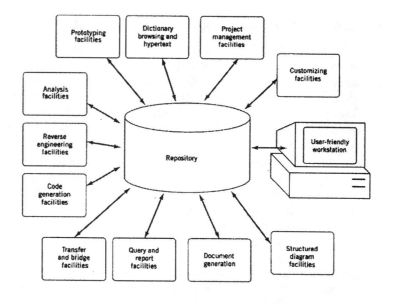

FIGURE 13.1 Architecture of a CASE environment.

Properties of a CASE Environment

- Repository.
- Maintaining intergrity.
- Integration of tools.
- Capability to retrieve information.
- Facilities to update information.
- User-friendly interfaces
- Support for different representation forms.
- Ability to transform data.
- Capability for analysis.
- Customization and extendability.
- Project control and management.
- Methodology support.
- Bridge capability.

FIGURE 13.2 Properties of a CASE environment.

What Is a Good Maintenance-Specific Environment?

Unfortunately, very little has been accomplished in the area of maintenance environments. Throughout the 1980s, most CASE vendors ignored the operation and maintenance phase of the life cycle. Beginning in the early 1990s, reengineering came into vogue and CASE finally discovered maintenance. CASE vendors decreed that the "software maintenance crisis" would be resolved by reengineering or redeveloping with CASE tools.

The maintenance industry can greatly benefit from CASE tools. Unfortunately, a method has not yet been defined to apply CASE tools to a maintenance environment. Most experts agree that tools are not effective without a supporting method to guide their use, CASE for software maintenance is hampered by a lack of a defined process, and available tools only address a portion of the maintenance activity (Forte 1992). Plus, CASE still has a bias towards software development and little or no emphasis on software maintenance (Sharon 1996). It is encouraging to see some efforts by Sharon to address the challenges of a maintenance environment and how CASE can help to solve them.

CASE has focused on development and has done very little in the maintenance area.

The future of maintenance environments will be to have ICASE environments with a formal, automated process. Automated, integrated environments facilitate the sharing of common information and can help to enforce process standards.

The previous sections discussed all the latest buzzwords. But how can these ideas be used in your environment? Many organizations are using CASE tools and eventually will evolve to integrated CASE environments. For now, many maintainers, particularly smaller organizations, cannot afford to go to full ICASE or ICASE-type environments. Some very small maintenance organizations do not use any tools at all. Thus, discussions of full ICASE environments is mere fantasy for some organizations.

What could a typical maintenance organization have in the way of tools? One way to address this is to look at the maintenance process and decide where the tools can be used and which ones can be obtained. The *IEEE Standard on Software Maintenance* (IEEE 1219 1993) relates generic tools to the activities of the IEEE maintenance process. For example, under IEEE's design activity, diagramming tools are used for flow-charting and data-flow diagramming. Additionally, *visualizers* are used for visualizing the code and *documenters* are used to document changes in the design activity. Another approach is to look at requirements for a particular environment and then decide what is needed. IEEE 1209 *Recommended Practice for Evaluation and Selection of CASE Tools* (ANSI/IEEE 1209 1992) addresses the evaluation and selection of tools supporting engineering processes, including project management processes, development processes, and integral processes.

The following discusses sample functional requirements for a maintenance environment and related tools for the environment. These requirements are considered the minimum functional requirements for a maintenance environment.

- Analysis and design.
- Software configuration management.
- Testing.
- Reverse engineering.
- Documentation management.

Tools should be used to satisfy these requirements. There are other requirements to be satisfied but some can be performed manually (as they have been for years), and others are not needed unless the maintainer goes to CASE or ICASE environment. Some of these are software requirements, such as tracking, process automation, a framework for the environment, electronic mail, and environment management. These are the minimum requirements:

Analysis and Design. There are many of these so-called "front-end" CASE tools available today. These provide code beautifying, diagramming, mapping, code visualization, code generation, and code analysis. These are not very prevalent in maintenance organizations. One of the difficulties is that if the development efforts did not provide full analysis and design in automated form, then the maintainer must go back and build it! That is time-consuming and normally not done. These tools are normally fairly expensive and complex to use. Training is mandatory if a maintainer is going to use one of these tools.

Software Configuration Management. These tools are the most mature. These tools are used throughout the maintenance process and provide for problem report and enhancement request tracking, version control for code and documentation, and auditing. Every maintenance organization, even if it consists of 2 people, needs to have SCM tools. There are now SCM software packages that are inexpensive and can be used by small maintenance organizations. They normally provide code and documentation control and tracking of modification requests.

Testing. These tools provide for test analyzing and test data generation. They should be used by all maintenance organizations, but alas that is not the case. Although these tools are available, in most cases they are expensive and complex. The maintainer must have an automated means of running regression testing, and the best way is to automate that function. As a minimum, maintainers need to put test cases in a text file and run them.

Reverse Engineering. These tools are used during analysis and design. Diagrammers are needed for flow-charting and data-flow diagramming.

Documentation Management. Tools are used throughout the maintenance process to develop, store, and update required documents.

All maintainers should have tools that satisfy the above functional requirements.

Adoption of CASE tools How does a maintainer go about adopting CASE tools? The IEEE standard on CASE tool adoption (ANSI/IEEE 1209 1993) recommends the following activities:

- Define CASE needs.
- Review CASE practice.
- Assess the organization.
- Define organization needs.
- Evaluate and select tools (ANSI/IEEE 1061 1992).
- Conduct pilot effort.
- Transition tools to routine activities.

How successful have adoption efforts been to date? What has been learned from practical experience? CASE is oversold by the vendors, sufficient training is not provided, and most CASE adoption efforts fail. Why?

Vollman and Garbajoza-Sopena (1996) says that some obstacles are:

- Lack of understanding of organizational needs.
- Misunderstanding what tools do.
- Inability to adequately evaluate tools.
- Incomplete integration of new technology.

Of interest is that only the third item is technical in nature. Vollman and Garbajoza-Sopena state that the "... Overall adoption effort is the key which guarantees that the tool will actually be used and not simply purchased."

These obstacles are now being addressed through CASE and other tool-related standards. Tool specific standards include ISO/IEC 14102, *Information Technology—Guideline for evaluation and selection of CASE tools*, and IEEE 1348 (1995). Vollman and Garbajoza-Sopena report that an ISO/IEC version of IEEE 1348 is expected to be published in 1997 as a technical report.

The standards are relatively new, and hopefully they will make an impact. Perhaps, the most significant action to take when adopting

---

Practical Experiences

My experiences with CASE tools have been less than satisfying. The CASE tool vendors keep talking about the life-cycle cost savings, but there is no empirical data to support those claims. Vendors say that integrated environments will save money; still, there is no empirical data to support their statement.

Upper management goes off to executive seminars and comes back and tells the software people to use CASE tools because they will save money. Tools are bought and *no training is provided*. What happens? At the ICSM-95 session in Nice, France, one panelist stated that after one year, 85% of the people who were trained in CASE tool usage continued to use the tools. However, 85% of the those not trained did not use them after one year. About 90% of the CASE tool adoption efforts fail. Why? A lack of training is the primary cause. The IEEE/ISO/IEC are to be applauded for their standardization efforts, which will markedly improve adoption efforts.

Productivity goes down in the first year of a CASE tool effort—it does not go up. People need to be trained in new methodologies and use of the tools; that takes time. If you are a maintainer and you are adopting CASE tools, you need to convince everyone that productivity will go down. Maintenance production does not go up until the third year. The discussion at ICSM-95 substantiates Jones' data. Capers Jones (1991) studied this, and reports that productivity goes down and quality goes up. Management needs to be prepared for this.

The following statements are important:

- CASE tools can help.
- An integrated environment is the way to go.
- Automating the process is in the best interest of the maintainer.
- It takes time (and money) to do all these things.

CASE tools is to have all the vendors assist in adoption. Most organizations do not buy time from the vendor (it is costly), and they struggle to get the product working.

Most CASE tool efforts fail due to a lack of training and management commitment.

If your organization is going to use CASE tools, everyone needs to be educated as to what the adoption will likely bring.

WHAT ARE DISTRIBUTED COMPUTING ENVIRONMENTS?

Thus far, this chapter has discussed environments that have included CASE tools. One area that is not often mentioned in maintenance discussions is the hardware for the computing environment. What impact does the computing environment have on maintenance? If a user organization moves from a mainframe to a client/server environment, what is the impact?

Research Results

Surprisingly, this topic did not receive much attention until 1994. At that time, Scott Schneberger (1995) was working on his doctoral dissertation and started researching the problem. He noted that most of the documented information on maintenance is concerned with mainframe-based centralized architectures. Is maintenance harder or easier with distributed systems? Schneberger notes that Bozman (1993) opines that computer systems with smaller, cheaper computers will have lower software maintenance costs; but is that really the case?

Schenberger's research focuses on the issue of the difficulty of maintaining distributed computing software and the characteristics of two key diametrics of information system architectures: *component simplicity* and *system complexity*. The details are contained in the dissertation (Schneberger 1995), some working papers (Schneberger 1996), and a paper presented at the International Conference on Software Maintenance-1995 (Schneberger 1995).

Schneberger's research concludes that:

1. Software for distributed systems seems harder to maintain than for centralized systems.

2. The complexity of a computing environment appears to affect software maintenance difficulty.
3. All computing environment complexity factors appear to affect software maintenance difficulty.
4. Some system complexity factors apparently have greater effects than others.
5. Effects from component variety seem to outweigh the effects of component numbers.
6. Some individual distributed computing environment factors seem to make software maintenance easier.

The key conclusion to the research is that distributed architectures appear to be more complex and difficult for software maintenance than centralized architectures even though distributed architectures involve components that might be individually easier to work. Smaller, cheaper computers might not lower maintenance costs.

Maintainers need to follow this type of research as this area has been overlooked. Further, when planning for maintenance (see Chapters 7 and 8), a system's number and variety of computing components and their rate of change need to be taken into account.

Client/Server

Newer environments like client/server will also pose challenges to maintainers. What costs are affected by client/server? Client/server system management costs *ten to twenty times* more than present mainframe system management budgets. Often overlooked is the fact that system management labor costs are seventy percent of the client/server costs.

Virtually all of the system management disciplines common to mainframe data centers need to be practiced in client/server computing. Some have substantially different meanings in the new environment. Thus, maintainers must still address disciplines such as change management, software configuration management, fault management, problem management, and help desk services. In the distributed and client/server environments, there are other disciplines with which maintainers must be concerned, such as software distribution, virus control, and license management (Semich 1994). In sum, client/server imposes additional disciplines that must be practiced and that cost much more than mainframe computing.

It is important for maintainers to understand the impact of client/server architecture and to plan for addressing these challenges.

WHERE CAN YOU GET MORE INFORMATION?

Zvegintzov's *Software Management Technology—Reference Guide* (1994) provides a comprehensive listing of software tools and services. Additionally, the U. S. Air Force's Software Technology Support Center at Hill Air Base in Utah, USA, maintains a database of tools and periodically publishes a survey of tools. The latest series provides detailed surveys for requirements analysis and design, documentation, test technologies, and process technologies. The preceding sections provided definitions and some discussion about tools, environments, CASE, and ICASE. How would an organization develop an integrated CASE environment? The Navy maintenance organization referred to so often in this book was faced with that challenge. The following case study discusses how the challenges were attacked, what lessons were learned, and the results.

HOW TO CREATE AN INTEGRATED CASE ENVIRONMENT: A CASE STUDY

When the U. S. Navy software maintenance organization commenced operations, software engineering and maintenance were conducted on a single-vendor programmer's workbench (PWB). The PWB was a

set of tools that worked on only one type of system and was not portable to other systems. Each homogeneous system had its own PWB; thus, each programmer had to learn the unique PWB for each supported system. In addition, the maintainers also had to adjust to the planned delivery of dissimilar systems. Each delivery presented enormous obstacles for continuing software maintenance on the existing PWB. Furthermore, the escalating cost of hardware maintenance for the current PWB dictated that an alternative solution be identified.

As a result, a new project (which is still ongoing) was initiated in an effort to upgrade the PWB into a fully *integrated software engineering environment (SEE)*. The integrated software maintenance environment under development was called the *common software engineering environment (COSEE)*.

Background of the Case Study

The PWB at the maintenance organization was originally designed to provide software engineering support for Digital Equipment Corporation (DEC) VAX/VMS systems. At that time, planning indicated virtually all future systems were to be DEC-based. Full hardware and software life-cycle support, including training, was put into place. The first systems supported by the maintainer were sized at 848K lines of code (LOC). Like the PWB itself, these systems were built entirely on DEC hardware platforms, and the applications software was created and deployed in the DEC VAX/VMS software environment. The PWB provided support for programming activities, but only limited support for software analysis and design. Software configuration management support was achieved through the use of DEC-layered software applications in conjunction with locally developed programs. The PWB consisted of DEC's code management system, module management system, source code analyzer, performance coverage analyzer, and test manager (Pigoski 1991e).

As a result of a number of changes in long-range plans, there was less emphasis placed on DEC hardware than had been anticipated. The majority of systems being developed by defense contractors for eventual transition to the organization for support consisted of many different hardware platforms and operating systems, including UNIX. All of the systems were non-DEC and non-VMS operating systems, with applications developed in several different programming languages. Effective software support for these systems required a robust, integrated software engineering environment (which did not exist at the maintenance organization).

Why Develop a New SEE?

Due to a lack of commonality between the systems initially supported by the maintainer and systems that arrived, multiple PWBs were in use, one for each system. This practice was not cost-effective and presented an obstacle to ensuring consistency in the process and quality of software support from one system to the next. Thus, an initiative to develop a new SEE—COSEE—at the maintenance organization began.

One of the primary purposes of the new SEE was to reduce hardware and software maintenance costs. Cost reduction would come in the form of less hardware, fewer CASE tools, and less training.

What Are the Maintenance Issues?

Each of the 15 systems supported by the maintenance organization was contractor-developed and had a lengthy development cycle. The majority of the systems were over 200K LOC. The software and documentation were voluminous and difficult to use. Further, most systems did not provide a supporting tool set. For those that had a supporting tool set, the set was usually limited and inadequately documented. Furthermore, sponsors did not typically provide adequate funding for tools or tool support. Consequently, a substantial part of a maintainer's time was spent trying to determine exactly how the supported software system functioned.

The maintenance organization was also concerned with personnel turnover, because the staff was primarily made up of military personnel that transferred to new assignments every three years. Without a rigid, well enforced process, productivity could have been a problem. The lack of CASE tools for the software maintainer, combined with the fact that the maintainer used manual processes, caused the process to be relatively slow.

The cost of software maintenance is well documented, and the Navy Maintenance organization needed a means to reduce life-cycle costs. (As stated previously, cost savings would accrue due to the common environment).

What Is COSEE?

The COSEE concept is to provide a common, integrated software engineering environment that will reduce software maintenance costs over the life cycle of the supported system. The COSEE design provided a flexible and open software engineering environment that was able to evolve. In an effort to reduce its own life-cycle costs, the COSEE design was based on existing commercial software and hardware technologies.

The Navy maintenance organization established a Working Group consisting of application users, maintainers, and government and con-

tractor software engineers to develop COSEE. TECHSOFT functioned as the contractor for the COSEE effort. The team designed, developed, and implemented the new SEE. The working group was established, and shortly after, a concept of operations (CONOP) for the COSEE development effort (which defined roles and responsibilities of the working group) was finalized (Looney 1993).

How Do You Build the SEE? The direction was to build an SEE incrementally, based on commercially available software tools. The various tools had to communicate with each other, and a data repository had to be established within an integrated software framework.

What Kind of Models Do You Use? The COSEE concept called for developing two models: one for software engineering, and one for process management. The software engineering model consisted of all tools and processes that were concerned with the technical aspects of software maintenance, such as CASE tools. The process management model consisted of automation of the day-to-day communication within and among offices to assist in managing daily activities. It was described by building a data-flow model to show the tasks and organizational structure required by the maintenance life cycle.

How Do You Develop COSEE?   The COSEE development used a series of phases: initial analysis, requirements analysis, preliminary design, detailed design, and implementation over a four- to five-year period. This concept afforded the opportunity to evaluate the design, become familiar with some of the tools, and permit fine-tuning of the final design. This incremental development approach facilitated the transition from the DEC-based PWB to a UNIX-based, integrated software engineering environment.

What Kind of Process Do You Use?   Current CASE products and SEEs are tool-oriented—they focus on the tools provided to support the maintenance personnel, and do not address the maintenance process. Maintenance personnel need to know what tasks need to be accomplished, what data to manipulate, what tool to use to manipulate that data, and often where on the network to find each piece. Current tool-oriented environments do not provide a process-oriented solution for a software maintenance organization.

Accordingly, for the COSEE effort, the concept was to use a process-oriented approach. With this approach, the tools used in the environment adapted to the people. The tasks required to perform the

maintenance activity, from receipt of the initial software modification request through version release, drove the process. This was accomplished through use of process automation software that guided maintenance personnel through the maintenance activity by allowing them to focus on the task at hand. The process-oriented approach called for presenting software maintenance personnel with a to-do list of tasks necessary to complete the next maintenance activity. Upon selecting a task, the process automation tool then presented the individual with all of the tools and data objects (already loaded into each tool) that were needed to complete the task. All of this was accomplished without requiring the individual to be knowledgeable of the environment configuration.

What Is the Important Documentation?   Documentation was required throughout the development to ensure satisfactory progress. For COSEE, the working group determined what the deliverables were and developed them accordingly. Documentation ranged from documents used to aid in the management of the development effort to actual user and maintenance manuals to be used by the application maintainers after the environment transitioned into the work area. Documentation required for the COSEE included (Looney 1993):

- Concept of operations.
- Procurement plan.
- Training plan.
- Implementation plan.
- Validation plan.
- Functional requirements document.
- Process model.
- Integration model.
- Tool evaluations.
- User and maintenance manuals.
- On-site survey.
- Security plan.
- Strawman, preliminary, and details architecture models.

What Are the Requirements of COSEE? The best approach in developing a new system, or, in this case a SEE, is to have approved requirements. Thus, after approval of the COSEE CONOP, the functional requirements were developed by the working group and documented in the "Functional Requirements for the Common Software Engineering Environment (COSEE)" (Looney 1994a). The following summarizes the COSEE requirements.

Functionality. The functional requirements were:

- The architecture of the COSEE must be based on open technology concepts that will encourage vendor independence in the use of commercial products.
- The COSEE must be an integrated environment that promotes distributed processing and the sharing of resources.

Framework. Based upon analysis of prevalent commercial practices and technologies, an integrated framework model was chosen as the basis for COSEE design. The COSEE framework conformed to the National Institute of Standards and Technology (NIST) Reference Model for Frameworks of Software Engineering, commonly referred to as the *toaster model*, as shown in Figure 13.3 (NIST 1991).

The toaster model segments the SEE framework into functional elements called services. The services are grouped according to key characteristics of SEE frameworks: objects that are manipulated, the tasks or processes that are performed, interaction with the user, tool integration, and administration of the entire SEE.

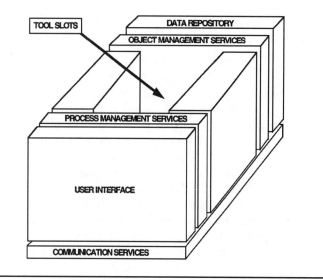

FIGURE 13.3 NIST toaster model.

The framework technology operates much like a network bus technology. Messages pass through the framework to and from tools in the environment. The messages contain instructions for a given tool to perform some action on some piece of data.

Maintenance Support. The COSEE was required to support discrete activities for maintenance. Software tools and applications were identified to support one or more of these activities. The major activities identified for support included:

- Requirements.
- Analysis and design.
- Prototyping.
- Coding.
- Reverse-engineering.
- Testing and quality assurance (QA).
- Software configuration management (SCM).

In addition to these activities, the COSEE was required to present a consistent, intuitive user interface and to provide a mechanism for automating the software maintenance process—the way in which the maintainer conducts business.

Finally, the COSEE was required to provide underlying support for the data artifacts created during these activities. This form of support included:

- Object management.
- Data repository.
- Communications services.

Communications services, in the context of COSEE operations, refers to the ability of the tools to exchange data among themselves and the repository and to the capability of users to access COSEE applications in a networked environment. Tool communication was provided within the SoftBench framework by the HP Broadcast Message Service (BMS). Network communication is managed at the user interface level by X Windows/Motif windowing technology. The network protocol for this phase of the COSEE was IEEE 802.3. In no way did this limit the expandability of the network. Other protocols, such as 802.4, might be integrated at a later date.

Electronic mail services were enabled by the various UNIX and HP SoftBench e-mail utilities. E-mail to PC LANs were accomplished through conversion software.

Detailed requirements for each of the above features were described in the COSEE requirements document (Looney 1994a).

How Do You Evaluate Software Tools? After approval of the COSEE functional requirements, an evaluation of software tools for the COSEE was conducted by the working group, using a four-step process consisting of classification, preliminary evaluation, quantitative assessment, and a tailored summary. The study was conducted and documented in a tools report (Looney 1994b). Products were reviewed for each of the following functions: framework, software engineering, QA/testing, software configuration management, project management, document management, environment management, and electronic mail.

The COSEE Tool Summary Tools and applications were grouped and presented according to the user's role. Process enactment software presented an overall view of the organization's activities, covering requirements, analysis and design, coding, and testing. The user was able to choose a particular stage of the process, and the appropriate tools were presented. For example, in the design phase, users were presented with design tools such as entity-relationship diagrams, data flow diagrams, and pseudocode tools. In the coding phase, programmers were given access to language-sensitive editors, linkers, compilers, and debuggers (Fugetta 1993). Table 13.1 is a recap of the tools and applications recommended for integration into COSEE.

TABLE 13.1   COSEE Tools

Function	Product
Framework:	Hewlett Packard SoftBench
Process Automation:	Hewlett Packard Synervision
S/W Engineering:	Software through Pictures
S/W QA/Testing:	McCabe's ACT/BATTLEMAP
Configuration Management:	CCC
Project Management:	PC-based Project Manager (e.g., WinProject)
Document Management:	Interleaf
Environment Management:	Native O/S utilities and Tool features
Electronic Mail:	Native O/S E-mail with interfaces to LAN-based cc:Mail

Application Mapping To Functional Requirements After the working group completed the tools evaluation, the design effort commenced. The final design was promulgated in the "Detailed Design Document for the Common Software Engineering Environment (COSEE)" (Looney 1994c).

Figure 13.4 depicts the software applications that were used to provide the services that were identified in the "toaster" framework model, including support for software life-cycle activities.

What Is the Design of COSEE?

The following sections describe the overall design and functionality of the COSEE.

What Is the COSEE Topology? The logical view of the COSEE topology was a simple method of presenting design goals. The environment was required to support multiuser network access to applications and data. Figure 13.5 depicts the general design concept for the COSEE.

Personal computers, X-terminals, and workstations were able to access COSEE applications and devices from anywhere on the network (where security allowed). The network infrastructure of the maintainer was represented in generic fashion, as were the COSEE servers and workstations.

What Is the COSEE Access? User access to COSEE tools and applications was accomplished through several methods:

Common User Interface			X Window/Motif		
Analysis Tools	Design Tools	Coding Tools	QA/Testing Tools	Reverse Engineering Tools	Prototyping Tools
CADRE TeamWork Toolsuite IDE Software through Pictures Toolsuite			ACT/BATTLEMAP/STW		UIMX

Requirements Traceability	RTM
Configuration Management Tools	CCC
Process Management Tools	SYNERVISION
Documentation Tools	WordPerfect
Object Management Services	ENCAPSULATOR, HP BMS, ORACLE, UNIX O/S
Data Repository	ORACLE and proprietary databases
Communication Services	HP BMS

FIGURE 13.4   Application mapping.

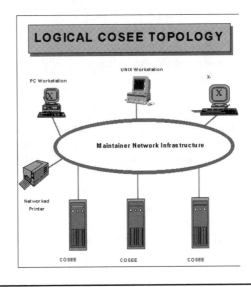

FIGURE 13.5   Logical COSEE topology.

- PC/X-terminals were able to log on to COSEE servers across the network infrastructure.
- UNIX workstations executed COSEE applications, with the workstation performing most of the processing locally.
- Casual users were able to accomplish file transfers from UNIX hosts to local PC platforms.

The network infrastructure for accomplishing these activities was IEEE 802.3 with TCP/IP protocols.

What Are the PC/X-Terminal Operations? Access to COSEE tools and applications from PCs and X-terminals is depicted in Figure 13.6. The COSEE server was configured to be accessible by the appropriate user stations. X-terminals downloaded the necessary X Windows software from the server. X Windows client/server software was installed on the appropriate PCs or PC LAN.

COSEE Software Distribution Software tools and applications used in the COSEE were not installed on a single server. Software was distributed among three main servers, with a fourth used as a backup.

As shown in Figure 13.7, two of the COSEE servers were used for application framework, process enactment, and individual software life-cycle tools and applications, with associated program files and user files. The software configuration management software, along with the data repository, resided on the third COSEE server.

As an example, a user wishing to analyze code executed COSEE life-cycle applications on server A or B, and the code was checked out via the software configuration management tool (CCC) from server C.

An additional benefit of this architecture was the ability to execute programs and applications installed on machines other than the COSEE servers. For example, given appropriate access, a user on one PC LAN segment was able to execute applications physically located on a machine connected to the *high powered workstation (HPW)* LAN segment. This capability allowed maximum use of resources and assisted the maintainer in preserving its existing investment in technology.

What Are the COSEE Goals? Phase 1 of the COSEE project focused on determining functional requirements and developing a design. That phase ended thirteen months later with delivery of the functional requirements.

Phase 2, which lasted eleven months, delivered a working prototype of the COSEE, including the core set of commercial software engi-

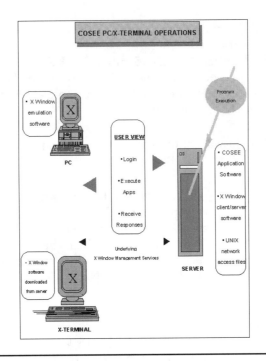

FIGURE 13.6 COSEE PC/X-terminal operations.

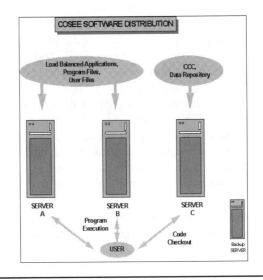

FIGURE 13.7 COSEE software distribution.

neering tools to enact a subset of the software process. (A process is "enacted" by using on-line automated software applications to simulate the workflows and dataflows that occur in real life.)

The goal of Phase 3 was to integrate a supported operational system into COSEE and to continue the automation of the maintenance process. This goal was satisfied in February 1996.

Phase 4, in progress, further refines the automation of the maintenance process.

What Else Is Occurring? Software process improvement and metrics collection/analysis is another ongoing parallel effort that significantly impacts the COSEE prototype. The SEI's *capability maturity model* has been modified to more appropriately fit a software maintenance environment. The software process has also been defined and documented in the *Software Maintenance Process Manual* (Nelson 1994). This document provided the basis for constructing an automated process using HP Synervision on the COSEE. As a result of the COSEE effort, a new software maintenance process was developed. While the multi-year COSEE effort is ongoing, this much improved manual process is now being used by the maintainer for current support efforts.

Summary of the Case Study

The project is ongoing and has a long way to go. What was learned is that implementing the tools is difficult and time-consuming. Training for the tools and the eventual users is mandatory. The maintainer learned that the project is a multi-year effort. Do not define requirements, design a system, acquire the tools, integrate the tools, refine the process, develop a prototype, and automate the process all at once; it takes time. That is why the maintainer used the prototype approach. The prototype completed at the end of Phase 2 is in use now. The software maintenance personnel are using the new tools, although not in a fully integrated, automated environment. Phase 3 automated the process at a high level and touches on all activities of maintenance. All tools are automatically launched and are immediately available for use by maintenance personnel. In parallel, the process is further automating the process under Phase 4.

Developing an integrated CASE environment is a multi-year effort.

WHAT IS THE OUTCOME AND WHAT ARE THE LESSONS LEARNED?

There are many lessons that were learned. The most notable outcome is that the foundation of a new SEE for the maintainer exists. Whereas the maintainer did not have a tool suite to use for the non-DEC VAX/VMS-supported systems, it now has one. The new system is UNIX-based. Support personnel are transitioning to the new UNIX-based SEE, they are being trained in tool usage, and they are using selected tools to support current operations.

Although the COSEE effort will continue for a number of years, the impact of the effort is being felt today. The maintenance process was tailored and is in use. Thus, when the process is enacted incrementally over the next few years, the transition will be relatively simple.

There are specific lessons learned during the first three phases of the COSEE development. Some relate to contracting and project management, while others are related to technical integration.

The Non-Technical Lessons

- *Obtaining resources was difficult and time-consuming.* The maintainer has priority commitments for its hardware and software resources. As a result, the components for the COSEE prototype were assembled from those resources that the maintainer could spare. Hardware, software, and financial resources should be identified and committed prior to attempting projects like the COSEE.
- *Stay with the concept of prototyping first.* Users are anxious to operate new systems. There is always pressure to give them *something* new as soon as possible and to make it available for everyone. The incremental approach worked well. Products should always be prototyped, tested extensively by a small group of users, and then modified to reflect the lessons learned during testing. The prototyping/testing/modification cycle is critical to the success of a project such as COSEE.

The Technical Lessons

- *One of the most important lessons learned is that a rigid and documented process is necessary in order to construct an automated model.* The ongoing process improvement effort produced a process manual. This is the basis for the automated model using HP Synervision.

■ *It is important to determine how to implement the model.* The approach to enacting the software process should consider the breadth and depth of coverage. The options were either to automate a very finite portion of the process down to the smallest detail, or automating several key areas across the spectrum of the maintenance process in much less detail. The process enactment efforts concentrated on automating the introduction of modification requests (MRs) into the COSEE, implementation of a software development folder (SDF) that contains data artifacts concerning each MR, and the ability to check out/check in source code and build specific versions of systems.

■ *Some tools install easily—some do not.* Some tools installed quite smoothly, and the documentation was straightforward. Some provided a set of demonstration modules. Some were very user-friendly, and some were very difficult to install.

The CCC software configuration management tool was a part of the maintainer's application portfolio. However, it did not include the necessary modules for SoftBench encapsulation. The maintainer has ordered the updated version of CCC.

Problems were experienced with interfacing the PC-based X Window emulation software eXceed with the network. Much of this difficulty can be attributed to running multiple protocols on the network. The problem was resolved by using PCTCP protocol stacks, which appear to be more robust for this type of environment.

■ *No database supports all tools, and some tools do not integrate with any database.* Unfortunately, when attempting to choose the best available applications, a trade-off must sometimes be made. Even the most feature-rich tools often generate proprietary formatted files and data artifacts.

Also, there is no single commercial database that *can* support such a myriad of software tools off the shelf. However, most true relational databases can serve as a repository for even proprietary data artifacts, with a small amount of tailoring. In this way, at least software configuration management can be implemented.

■ *Be flexible; evolve.* It should be noted that neither the design nor any particular tool will endure. An SEE that will endure for years is under development. The initial design is now in use. The COSEE architecture will be reviewed for areas of improvement, and future incremental deliveries will provide design changes.

For general CASE information read a summary of CASE in the *Encyclopedia of Software Engineering Volume 1 A-N* (Wiley 1994). For more advanced reading, look at the papers that Elliot Chikofsky (1993) put together for IEEE. He collected a group of CASE-related papers that address CASE technology, the evolution of environmental concepts, technologies applied to provide advanced user functionality, tailoring environments, and key issues in evaluating CASE technology.

Another valuable information source is ISO/IEC 14102 "Information Technology—Guideline for evaluation and selection of CASE tools" published on November 15, 1995 (ISO/IEC 14102 1995). This international standard provides a sequence of processes and a structured set of CASE tool characteristics for use in the technical evaluation and the ultimate selection of CASE tools. This can be used to define a software engineering environment for maintenance.

SUMMARY

You now should understand that CASE tools have the promise to improve productivity, but they have not fulfilled that promise. The use of CASE tools in a maintenance environment is a fertile one for both researchers and tools developers. Hopefully the case study gave you an approach to automating your integrated environment. In addition, there are standardization efforts underway, and these will help significantly. It is imperative to understand how to adopt these tools correctly and how lengthy the learning curve is.

1. Describe the maintenance tools environment at your organization. (If you are a student, describe the environment at the university.)

2. Describe how the environment fits within the architecture of the CASE environment.

3. Describe how the environment satisfies the properties of a comprehensive CASE environment.

4. Develop functional requirements for a maintenance environment.

5. Design a SEE for a maintainer.

Software Maintenance Metrics

14

Earlier I discussed the software maintenance process (Chapter 5) and the need for a software maintenance environment (Chapter 13). But how do you know if your process is working? How can you improve it? How can you contain costs? How can you defend your resource requirements? Where are the bottlenecks in the process? Those, and many more questions, are constantly on the minds of software maintenance practitioners.

Software life-cycle costs are growing and every maintainer needs a strategy for maintenance. Software metrics need to be a part of that strategy. Just like with CASE tools, everyone now feels the need to get involved with metrics. The corporate emphasis on quality has had much to do with the recent emphasis on metrics, but hard-core software maintenance practitioners have used metrics in one form or another for decades. This chapter discusses implementation strategies for metrics and gives some practical advice regarding metrics and metrics programs.

WHAT IS A SOFTWARE METRIC?

Before continuing, some terms need to be defined, and some background information is needed. What is a software metric?

- Grady and Caswell (1987): A software metric is a standard way of measuring some attribute of the software process. Examples of these attributes are size, cost defects, communications, difficulty, and environment. Applying metrics leads to a better understanding and increased predictability of the process. However, you must have a documented process. If you do not know what your process is, then you cannot use metrics to improve it. If you can understand why defects are or are not present, you can modify the process and eliminate these types of defects.

- Card and Glass (1990): When evaluating the software process, most organizations focus on the quality of the product. However, they do so through inspections and reviews, which are manual in nature and merely enforce standards. These practices, according to Card and Glass, do not ensure software quality. A better approach is to use numerical methods to judge quality.

- The IEEE: A "metric" is synonymous with a "software quality metric" and defines a software quality metric as a function with input and output. Software quality metrics have software data as inputs and a single numeric value as output. The output is interpreted as the degree to which software possesses a given attribute that affects its quality (ANSI/IEEE 1061 1992).

- The international community (ISO/IEC 9126 1991): A software quality metric is a quantitative scale and method that can be used to determine the value a feature takes for a specific software product.

Simply put, metrics are a means of measuring some aspect of software and in most organizations it directly relates to quality.

Practical Experience

I was called in by a U. S. government agency and asked to establish a metrics program for a large software maintenance organization. No—I was really asked by a very intelligent person to give him one or two metrics that would enable him to know all he needed to know about his organization. My response was that if I could do it that simply and quickly that I would charge him significantly more for my time! I told him that it was not that simple. There was more to it; metrics must be tailored to corporate goals. If the corporate goals were zero defects, (such as with the space shuttle software), one set of metrics would be required. If the corporate goals were to get a product to market quickly (such as Windows 95), a different set of metrics would be required. The point here is that some thought must be given to metrics before launching a metrics program.

WHO DOES METRICS WELL?

If you were asked to start a software metrics program at your company or organization, how would you start the program? Where would you begin? A suggestion is to look at the efforts of Hewlett-Packard first.

The most widely publicized corporate program is at Hewlett-Packard. They developed a task force, set up a Metrics Council, and developed long- and short-term goals (Grady and Caswell 1987). They decreed that software metrics are vital for software process improvement, but the process must be measurable. Most importantly, they state that software metrics can only be a *part* of a successful plan for software process improvement. If done by itself, software metrics will not result in software process improvement.

Grady and Caswell's book contains many charts or graphs that your organization could use. Herein lies the problem: Which ones do you use? How can you sift through all of that material and establish a program for your organization?

WHY DO YOU WANT A METRICS PROGRAM?

Let's get back to the question at hand—how do you start a metrics program? First, you need management support. Without it, don't waste your time; the program will fail. However, with proper management support and a long-term management commitment, a software metrics program can be successful. Also, it takes about three years of collection and analysis before sufficient data trends are available.

When you try to implement a program, you will collect numbers on the things people in your organization do. The people whom you collect data about might resist being measured. Only education can help to alleviate the situation. You must make sure that all of the people concerned, from upper-level management to entry-level employees, understand the use of the measures—to satisfy the goals of the company and create a better product and environment. If people understand why the metrics are being collected, they can embrace the project. Otherwise, individuals might become suspicious and question their job security. Employees must understand that the way they do their job right now is fine. Collecting metrics will enable them to do their job better.

Measurement is a long-term activity, and evolves to satisfy organizational needs and goals. Maintenance metrics is almost always discussed in terms of software complexity metrics. Most people believe that the first (and perhaps only) metrics needed are those that relate to software complexity. While McCabe (1976) and Halstead (1977) state that metrics need to be a part of most software development efforts, it is premature to agree that a maintainer needs either of these metrics until the goals of the effort are determined.

Collection of metrics should not commence until organizational goals are defined.

Grady (1992) provides some excellent information regarding the collection of software maintenance metrics at Hewlett-Packard, and provides three primary goals:

1. Maximize customer satisfaction.
2. Minimize engineering effort and schedule.
3. Minimize defects.

Once the goals are determined, *then* an organization can decide which measurements to collect. The key here is for the organization to have goals. You cannot and should not establish a metrics program without goals. As the example above indicates, the metrics that you would collect with a goal of zero defects are very different from those that you would collect if you wanted to put more functionality in the hands of the users.

There is a significant cost associated with implementing a metrics program. Estimates range from five to fifteen percent of software costs (Card and Glass 1990). However, with some basic measures suggested by Card and Glass, this figure can be kept at about five percent.

HOW DO YOU IMPLEMENT A METRICS PROGRAM?

Successful implementation strategies were used at Hewlett-Packard (Grady and Caswell 1987; Grady 1992) and at the NASA/Software Engineering Laboratory (Card and Glass 1990; Basili 1985). The Hewlett-Packard approach is to:

- Define objective for the program.
- Assign responsibility.
- Do research.
- Define initial metrics to collect.

Practical Experience

Basili's approach was used to establish a metrics program (Pigoski 1991c) for a U. S. Navy maintenance organization. Initially it was thought that some sophisticated McCabe cyclomatic complexity analysis would be the core of the metrics program— but it was determined that none of the people who were providing money and other resources would really care if a module had a cyclomatic complexity of 5, 10, or 500.

The goals of the Navy maintenance organization metrics program were twofold: to provide quality, timely products, and to let customers know what they were getting for their money. The goals were referred to as metrics for quality and metrics for survival (Pigoski 1995).

Metrics for Quality. The first goal was satisfied by tracking modification requests from initiation to successful installation at the user site. From the modification requests the following data were collected:

- Date of submission.
- Originator.
- Type of problem.
- System affected.
- A one-up annual number.
- Priority that the user placed on it.

The modification requests were tracked through the maintenance process, and data such as the following were collected:

- Name of the individual performing the maintenance.
- Lines of code touched (changed, modified, deleted).
- Type of modification request (was it perfective, adaptive, or corrective?).
- Type of programming error found.
- Rejection or acceptance by the test group.
- Time required to go through the various activities until the code was released.
- Effort expended by various individuals (such as managers, programmers, and people from SCM and testing).

These metrics helped look at backlogs, schedule work, determine how resources were being used, and determine how long it took to fix and release code. These metrics supported the goal of providing quality, timely products.

The supported systems were developed by other organizations and might have had high or low complexity. The users knew four things: The system worked, a large backlog existed, they did not want a less complex system (in terms of cyclomatic complexity), and they wanted quality, timely products. Thus, the metrics chosen to collect were based on the goal of providing quality, timely products.

These rather mundane metrics worked. The maintenance process in use included evaluating the code and evaluating unit testing and independent testing. At one point it was determined that a large number of code fixes were rejected by the independent test organization. Further analysis revealed that most of them were from one particular programmer. Analysis indicated that the individual involved did not have a good appreciation for unit testing, and thus the training process was improved to include more information on unit testing. The metrics helped to isolate a problem, ensure quality, and improve the process.

In another testing-related incident, the programmers were producing code at a rapid rate, but they got backlogged because of testing. This was identified through analysis of the metrics. More people were then added to the independent test group. These are just two examples of how the metrics relating to the goals were helped by metrics. As a matter of fact, some of these metrics were very helpful in determining the ratio of programmers to support people that was discussed in Chapter 12.

Metrics for Survival. The second goal was to let the customers know what they were getting for their money. Most outsourced maintainers are acutely aware of the problem of having to defend costs and resources.

When I discussed estimating maintenance resources earlier in the book, I mentioned that it was relatively easy to get resources for our initial systems. However, I recognized that it would be more difficult later, and thus developed our practical estimating methodology. To be able to defend those "estimates" later, it was important to clearly show what the maintenance organization was providing. The maintenance organization needed to use metrics to document staffing resources and what was produced.

> In order to defend staffing resources, it was decided that the submitted modification requests would be categorized as corrective, adaptive, or perfective. Great pains were taken to track the lines of code touched, and the effort to complete the fixes. The maintenance organization was able to go to the configuration control board and convincingly state that over 80% of the effort was for enhancements. The metrics provided the data, and these were published in order to let everyone know that maintenance is more than fixing bugs. These data were very useful in defending resources in later years.

- Sell (convince people of merit of collecting) the initial collection of these metrics.
- Get tools for automatic data collection and analysis.
- Establish a training class in software metrics.
- Publicize success stories and encourage exchange of ideas.
- Create a metrics database.
- Establish a mechanism for changing the standard in an orderly manner.

The Card and Glass approach is to:

- Define the object of measurement (such as software).
- Identify the characteristics or attributes to be measured (such as quality).
- Specify the purpose or intended use of the measurement results.
- Collect data as indicated in the preceding steps.
- Verify and modify the model based on analysis and application experience with the collected data.

Basili's (1985) approach states that a metric program should consist of:

- Identifying organizational goals.
- Defining the questions relevant to the goals.
- Selecting measures that answer the questions.

Using Basili's approach, data collection commences, a measurement suite customized to organizational needs and capabilities results, and the measurement data takes on a special local meaning.

Basili's work is referred to as GQM, for *goal, question*, and *metric*. It is a simplistic approach that works. Henderson-Sellers (1996) provides some GQM examples and an adaptation and extension to the GQM paradigm.

HOW DOES THE TYPICAL PRACTITIONER APPROACH METRICS?

How do most metrics programs start? Normally, some management person attends a seminar and gets motivated about metrics. A quick meeting is held and someone—maybe you—is appointed to establish the metrics program. Some attendees at my tutorial on software maintenance at ICSM-95 in Nice, France called and told me that they too had just been "appointed" to spearhead the corporate metrics efforts. All of a sudden there was this great support and interest in metrics for maintenance at their organization, but with no apparent plans or goals.

The typical metrics program starts the same way. A practitioner is directed to begin collecting data right away, without any specification of goals or objectives. The mandate comes down because someone, usually management, believes all maintenance problems will go away and costs will decrease with a metrics program. Also, it becomes imperative or fashionable to say "We have a metrics program."

Bob Grady states that *over 90% of all metrics efforts fail within one year*. Why? In many cases, management support wanes. There is a massive data collection effort, very little analysis, and no reporting. In order for a metrics program to work, the collected data must be analyzed, goals must be stated, and management must support the effort. Without any of these requirements, the metrics effort will fail.

Successful metrics programs must evolve. Start slowly and do not collect too much.

In most situations, far too much data is collected, and far too little analysis is conducted to support a viable metrics effort. These efforts must be evolutionary; start slowly and keep it simple in the beginning. Resist the urge to create a metrics program that collects too much data. The more data collected, the bigger the chance that the effort will fail. Stay focused on the goals of the organization, and collect only the data necessary to complete these goals.

Practical Experience

At the IEEE Computer Society's Software Measurement and Reliability for Software Maintenance Workshop-1993, held in conjunction with ICSM-93, a group of software maintenance practitioners came together to discuss maintenance metrics. What unfolded there might help you embark on the difficult task of setting up a metrics program for your organization.

At the workshop I served as the head of a discussion group to discuss maintenance metrics and gave a speech titled "Software Maintenance Measurement: A Practitioner's Perspective of Processes and Metrics." I had the pleasure to follow speaker Ted Keller as he discussed his 17 or so years of collecting maintenance metrics on the space shuttle project, a project where the metrics are extensive and impressive. I mentioned that there was a good chance that no one in the audience would ever need a metrics effort as complex as Keller's space shuttle project or NASA's Software Engineering Laboratory (Valett 1994).

I then got to the heart of my speech. I asked how many people had a metrics measurement process. Of those people, how many followed the process? Only 50% did. Then I asked the participants how they thought that they could collect effective metrics. Their response was that they wanted the organizers of the workshop to give them a list of 25 or so metrics; with those in hand, they would have effective measures! That did not happen at the workshop in 1993, and it has not happened in succeeding workshops. Many people want a small list of metrics to satisfy all their needs. That is the wrong approach. You must develop goals and then determine the metrics. In addition, if improved quality is your goal, quality must be analyzed for quality's sake—not for the sake of saving money.

WHAT DOES THE SOFTWARE ENGINEERING INSTITUTE (SEI) SUGGEST?

There are, however, some metrics that just about every organization needs. The SEI looked at this problem and came up with its core metrics. In 1992, the Department of Defense (DoD) commissioned the SEI's Software Process Measurement Project to develop materials and guidelines for a core set of measures to be used in DoD software acquisition, development, and support programs. The objective was to produce measures that would serve as a basis for collecting well understood and consistent data throughout the DoD. The focus was the collection of management measures for size, effort, schedule, and quality that would serve as a foundation for achieving higher levels of development process maturity, as defined in the Capability Maturity Model (Carleton, 1992) (See Figure 4.2). These are:

- *Size.* Source statement counting.
- *Effort.* Staff-hours.
- *Schedule.* Milestones, deliverables, and completion criteria.
- *Quality.* Problems and defects.

The central theme is the use of checklists to create and record structured measurement descriptions and reporting specifications. These checklists provide a mechanism for obtaining consistent measures from project to project and for communicating unambiguous measurement results (Carleton 1992). Even though the above categories were designated for software development, with some minor tailoring all of these measurement areas have application to software maintenance activities. Each of these basic areas is discussed in more detail below. If a maintenance organization is looking for a textbook answer for a metrics program, the SEI core metrics is a place to start.

Size

The SEI research and recommendations on software size measurement are contained in a report titled "Software Size Measurement: A Framework for Counting Source Statements" (Park 1992). In an abstract of the content, the author writes:

> This report provides guidelines for defining, recording, and reporting two frequently used measures of software size— physical source lines and logical source statements. The report proposes a general framework for constructing size definitions, and uses the framework to derive operational methods for reducing misunderstandings in measurement results. It further shows how the methods can be applied to address the information needs of different users while maintaining a common definition of software size. The report does not address measures of difficulty, complexity, or other product

and environmental characteristics that are often used when interpreting measures of software size.

While the report described above provides a methodology for counting both physical lines of code and logical source statements, the authors conclude the study by advocating the use of physical lines of code rather than logical source statements as a starting point for most organizations. Physical lines of code are both simpler to count and less subject to unstated assumptions than logical source statements. They add that logical source statements can be added later after clear and exhaustive rules for identifying statement deliminators and statement types have been specified (Park 1992).

 All maintenance organizations *must know* the size of their application portfolio and the size of each product (or application)— whether size is determined by lines of code or function points. The maintenance organization must then track the change in size for each product and use size to determine annual change traffic (ACT). As discussed in Chapter 8, ACT is needed for personnel resource estimates.

Maintenance organizations should also track comment lines of code. Many systems are transitioned for maintenance without the benefit of good documentation. Very often the code is not well documented with comments. The maintainer must become familiar with the system, and should count the number of comments added. Naturally this can be abused, but the maintainer might well spend the next 2–3 years maintaining the product, and those comments (initially generated when the maintainer is learning the code) are very valuable. Similarly, comments developed for problem reports and modification request should be counted.

The SEI metrics provide some useful hints that are useful in maintenance.

Use the SEI core metrics as a starting point for a metrics program.

Effort

The SEI research and recommendations on measuring effort are contained in a report titled, "Software Effort and Schedule Measurement: A Framework for Counting Staff-Hours and Reporting Schedule Information" (Goethert 1992). Using the same general approach of developing a framework and then using a series of checklists for implementation, this report provides guidelines for defining, recording, and reporting staff hours. The checklist uses seven attributes to describe the kinds of measurement included in a measurement of staff hours. These attributes are type of labor, hour information, employment class, type of pay, labor class, activity, and product-level function (CSCI-level functions, build-level functions, and system-level functions). The report recognizes that various circumstances will require different definitions; thus users can determine which attributes they will include and which they will exclude when measuring and recording staff hours. With its capacity for tailoring, the checklist supports the objective of a structured approach for dealing with details that must be resolved to reduce misunderstanding, communicate the exactness and details of the measurement, and specify attribute values for the individual reports that are desired. There is extensive rationale in the report for using staff hours. The effort described in terms of staff hours can be collected, analyzed, and communicated among projects and organizations in more precise and unambiguous terms than other measures such as staff weeks, person-days, or person-months. Managers need well defined and universally understood measurements for software project estimating, planning, and tracking. Staff hours, collected and categorized in a predescribed and structured manner, provide the best unit of measure to satisfy those measurement needs.

Maintainers must track effort in terms of staff hours for maintenance activities. It is important to know the number of hours spent on analysis, design, coding, unit testing, and other activities. It is important to determine the number of staff hours spent on problem reports and enhancement requests. This data will help planning and estimating efforts. It will help maintainers defend resource requirements. It will also help estimating efforts.

Collecting staff hours for small maintenance organizations is difficult. If it is not possible to track staff hours, then track hours by the number and type of people used in maintenance on a monthly basis. For small organizations, it is acceptable to say that .5 person-months were expended by management, 2.5 for programming, .5 for QA, and .5 for SCM. The total is 4 person-months. Correlate that staffing factor to the size, and the maintainer learns a lot about staffing for various products. This macro approach does not help much with determining the effort expended on problem reports versus enhancement requests, but it does provide something for the small maintenance organization to use for defending resources.

Schedule

The discussion of schedule is combined with effort in the Goethert report (1992). The framework for schedule definition addresses two different but related aspects of schedule measurement. The first aspect concerns the dates of project milestones and deliverables. As with effort, the dates aspect of schedule definition is captured in two tailorable checklists: One lists milestones, reviews, and audits; a second lists deliverable products. In the first list, the user specifies the frequency of measurement, whether the dates recorded are planned or actual, which specific elements are included or excluded, whether the measure is to be tracked on each build, and the relevant dates to be reported. Examples of major project milestones can include holding internal reviews, holding formal reviews with the customer, closing all action items, and obtaining customer sign-off. For deliverable products the user again can specify which products are included, which are excluded, whether the measure is to be tracked on each build, and the relevant dates to be reported.

Schedule data is important for maintenance. Each modification request (MR) must have a schedule to ultimately end up in a new version of software for release to the user. At a higher level (project level), all the MRs must come together for acceptance testing, installation, and release. Actual, historic metric data is useful for refining the estimating process for future MRs.

The second aspect of schedule concerns measures of *progress*, or the rate at which work is accomplished in order to meet any given milestone or completion of a deliverable. Tracking milestone dates and deliverables provides a macro-level view of the project schedule. However, much greater visibility is gained by tracking the progress of activities that culminate in reviews and deliverables. The principle is that by tracking the rate at which the underlying units of work are completed, management has an objective basis for knowing where the project is at any given point in time and a basis for projecting where it will be in the future. The checklist addressed in the Goethert (1992) report provides a means of describing, specifying or communicating the units to be tracked during software engineering activities such as analysis, design, coding, and testing. The activities contained in the report can be tailored for maintenance.

In both the dates and progress aspects of schedule measurement, the key is a comparison of the planned versus actual schedule. This requires realistic estimates that can only be made by continually feeding back data on the accuracy of those estimates based on what is actually experienced.

Quality

The fourth element of the SEI core metrics program is quality. The SEI discussion on software quality metrics is contained in a report titled "Software Quality Measurement: A Framework for Counting Problems and Defects" (Florac 1992). This report provides a framework for the discovery, reporting, and measurement of software problems and defects found by what the author terms the primary problem (as opposed to secondary) and defect-finding activities. These activities include product synthesis (all of the effort from requirements to finished code that result in an actual software artifact), inspections, formal reviews, testing, and customer service. The report goes on to discuss that although defects and problems are reported in different data formats by the different defect finding activities, they have in common certain attributes and attribute values. These attributes apply the "who, what, when, where, why, and how" questions that are essential to a software measurement framework. The report then presents a series of checklists and supporting forms to reduce the misunderstanding of measurement results. The objective is to provide methods that will help obtain clear and consistent measurements of quality based on a variety of software problem reports and data derived by analysis and corrective actions.

SEI Metrics Summary

All organizations need some core metrics and every maintainer should have metrics such as the ones presented by the SEI.

A SET OF MAINTENANCE METRICS

Managers at NASA's Mission Operations Directorate at the Johnson Space Center wanted more insight into cost, schedule, and quality of software-intensive systems for the space shuttle. Thus, a software metrics set that contains 13 metrics related to corrective and adaptive maintenance actions was defined and implemented.

The metrics were published in an article (Stark 1994) intended to assist software maintenance managers in developing a software maintenance metrics program. Of interest is that the GCM paradigm (introduced earlier in this chapter) was used to identify the set of metrics. The GQM are contained in Table 14.1.

TABLE 14.1   Software Sustaining Goals/Questions/Metrics

Goals	Questions	Metrics
Maximize customer satisfaction	How many problems are affecting the customer?	Discrepancy report (DR) and Service request (SR) open duration Software reliability Break/fix ratio
	How long does it take to fix a problem?	DR/SR closure DR/SR open duration
	Where are the bottlenecks?	Staff utilization Computer resource utilization
Maximize effort and schedule	Where are the resources going?	Staff utilization SR scheduling Ada instantiations Fault type distribution
	How maintainable is the system?	Computer resource utilization Software size Fault density Software volatility Software complexity
Minimize defects	Is software sustaining engineering effective?	Fault density Break/fix ration Ada instantiations Software reliability

The software maintenance metric set includes:

- Software size.
- Software staffing.
- Maintenance request processing.
- Software enhancement scheduling.
- Computer resource utilization.
- Fault density.
- Software volatility.
- Discrepancy report open duration.
- Break/fix ratio.
- Software reliability.
- Design complexity.
- Fault type distribution.
- Ada instantiations.

The *Software Sustaining Engineering Metrics Handbook* (Kern and Stark 1992) documents the standardized set of metrics. The Stark (1994) article discusses each metric in detail. If you need a set and can't figure out what your goals are, you might want to look at the NASA metrics set.

WHAT ARE THE LESSONS LEARNED FROM PRACTITIONERS?

There are two primary lessons from metrics practitioners. First is to focus on a few key characteristics. The second is to not measure everything. Rely on simple measures extractable from common design products. Most organizations collect too much. It is better to use a few measures that are well understood rather than many measures that are not understood. Grady and Caswell (1987) state that measurement identifies problems, it does not solve them.

Starting a metrics program for a maintenance organization is difficult. Donnelly (1992) discussed the first year of his effort and stated that the resistance from middle management is one area that surprised him. Please keep in mind that any measurement program must support organizational goals. Before establishing a program, the goals must be clearly identified and all personnel must understand their use. Unfortunately, the measure of people is not a very satisfying one.

As Grady (Grady and Caswell 1987) so eloquently states, software metrics is not so established as a science that a specific set of measures

---

Practical Experience

When a Navy maintenance organization started a metrics program, people were concerned that their annual evaluation would be based on the number of modification requests they implemented or the number of lines of code that they fixed. In spite of education, the maintainers still resented collecting metrics! Finally, the maintainers were told that the metrics were collected so that resources could be defended and thus retained. Simply put, the metrics were needed to save their jobs. Do you remember Chapter 8 on estimating personnel resources? In later years it was very important to have metric data to justify resources, and the maintenance organization had the data.

are the right set. There is not one set of metrics that can be used by all organizations to satisfy organizational goals. Even the IEEE Standard for a Software Quality Metrics Methodology (ANSI/IEEE 1061 1992) merely "suggests" use of some metrics. It does not mandate use of specific metrics. You need to establish goals and then determine which metrics support those goals.

WHAT ARE SOME METRICS RESOURCES?

The good news is that these metrics efforts have made progress. There are attempts at metrics standards. The *IEEE Standard for a Software Quality Metrics Methodology* (ANSI/IEEE 1061 1992) does not describe specific metrics, but the annexes include examples of metrics with examples of the use of the standard. The metrics contained therein are also for maintenance.

The IEEE Computer Society's International Conference on Software Maintenance (ICSM) has addressed the issue of software maintenance metrics. Workshops were held in conjunction with ICSM-93 and ICSM-94. The International Workshop on Empirical Studies of Software Maintenance was held in conjunction with ICSM-96 in Monterey, California. This workshop focused on maintenance metrics and lessons learned. The proceedings from the workshop and follow-on workshops should be great interest to maintainers interested in metrics.

Practitioners need to follow the efforts of the International Workshop on Empirical Studies of Software Maintenance.

Before closing out the discussion on metrics, one other area, acquisition metrics, must be discussed. First, there is discussion about some acquisition metrics and then there is discussion about why maintainers need to be concerned about acquisition metrics.

U.S. Army

The U.S. Army (USA) is using metrics to provide a quantitative and qualitative assessment of the processes and products in the software development life cycle. The Army Software Test and Evaluation Panel (STEP) Subgroup of Measures applied the principle of total quality management (TQM) to the development and maintenance of Army software. The Measures Subgroup conducted case studies, searched through metric literature and visited government, academic, and industry organizations to develop a minimum set of metrics (Figure 14.1).

Cost/schedule. Measures the total funding estimates for the software development or maintenance effort compared with the actual expenditure schedule.

Schedule. Measures the degree of completeness of the software development effort and the readiness to process to the next stage of software development. It portrays adherence to and changes in planned major milestone schedules by computing and analyzing the percent of *computer software units (CSU)* that are 100% complete in the three categories of design, coding and unit testing, and integration at the computer software component (CSC), computer software configuration item (CSCI), or system level.

Computer resource utilization. Measures the degree to which target computer resources used are changing or approaching the limits of resources available, and the specified constraints. It ensures that target utilization is not exceeded. It guarantees that sufficient excess capacity remains for future growth and for periods of high-stress loading.

Software engineering environment. Measures the capacity of a contractor to use modern software engineering techniques in his development process, and therefore his capability to instill such principles and characteristics in the product. It shows a relative comparison of the ability of contractors. It also encourages contractors to improve their software development process to increase their ratio.

Requirements traceability. Measures the adherence of software products capabilities (including design and code) to their requirements at various levels. It traces all required operational capabilities (ROC), software-related requirements to the software specifications. Identifies omissions using a software requirements traceability matrix. This matrix will be heavily tied to meet requirements definition document (RDD) requirements proposed for all software development. It establishes criteria for levels of requirements traceability at designated stages of development.

Requirements stability. Measures the degree to which changes in software requirements or contractor's understanding of the requirements affect the development effort. A high level of volatility at the critical design review (CDR) stage indicates serious problems that must be addressed before proceeding to coding.

Design stability. Measures the level of change in the design of the software. Furthermore, it monitors the potential impact of design changes on the software configuration.

Fault profiles. Plots the cumulative number of open and closed software anomalies as a function of time for each priority level of define fault in performance. This gives insights into quality of the development and testing process. The government should not accept software for any formal system level testing until (at a minimum) all priority one and two faults have been closed.

Breadth of testing. Measures the degree to which required functionality has been successfully demonstrated. It will also display the amount of testing that has been performed. The functionality that should be in place at each phase of development must be identified.

Depth of testing. Measures the extent and success of testing for coverage of possible paths/conditions within the software. The plotting of depth of testing metrics over time provides indications of the progress of successful testing and also of the sufficiency of the testing.

Reliability. Measures the number of faults in the software, as well as the number of faults expected when the software is used in accordance with its OMS/MP.

Complexity. This metric uses established industry standards for complexity of function. It should be generated for each module in the system to provide indications of potential problem areas where the government test efforts should be focused.

FIGURE 14.1 A minimum set of metrics.

The results of the study are documented in a U.S. Army Armament Research, Development & Engineering Center (ARDEC) report of June 1992 [ARDEC 1992]. These were later formalized in U.S. Army acquisition documents. The subgroup recommended a set of twelve metrics, grouped into three categories as shown in Figure 14.2.

The Army approach is to use these metrics to determine the system characteristics that have a measurable impact upon software maturity. They recommend a baseline set of metrics, and an optional set to be collected for all Army software development efforts. Today, if you are going to develop software for the U. S. Army, you are required to use these metrics throughout the development. The baseline set of metrics contribute to the decision to proceed to formal testing. Additional metrics may be used to augment the recommended set. The STEP measures can be used to define maintainability measures.

Other Metric Resources

Schneidewind's (1994) work with software maintenance metrics for the space shuttle give great insight into the goal of reliability for main-

CATEGORIES	METRICS	PROVIDE
Technical	Computer Resource Utilization Requirements Traceability Breadth of Testing Complexity Depth of Testing	Quality of Software Development Process and Production
Maturity	Development Progress Breadth of Testing Depth of Testing Fault Density Prediction Fault Profiles Reliability Stability	Maturity of the Software requirements, design, coding, testing and CM
Management	Software Engineering Environment Manpower Cost	Items of interest to PM

FIGURE 14.2 STEP metrics.

tenance. Munson and Khoshgoftaar's (1992) relative complexity work and Munson's later work on the space shuttle are state-of-the-art.

Why do maintainers care about these *acquisition* metrics? Because maintainers should work hard during the predelivery stage to ensure that the developer *provides* these metrics. The maintainer should influence program managers and ensure that the development contract includes provisions for these acquisition metrics. MIL-STD-498 suggests the use of some acquisition metrics, but much more detail is required in the development contract if the needed metric data is to be obtained. It will help the maintainer—particularly if the maintenance is outsourced—to understand the technical status of the software and its maturity. There are other acquisition-related metrics efforts including *Practical Software Measurement; A Guide to Objective Program Insight* (JLC 1995). This guide describes how to define and implement an effective software measurement program. Again, the focus is acquisition; but maintainers must be involved during acquisition.

There are numerous metrics conferences today—far too many to mention. The only ones specifically addressing maintenance needs are the workshops associated with ICSM. There are also numerous books and periodicals on the topic of metrics but none dedicated to maintenance.

SUMMARY

The definition of organizational goals is the initial step in establishing a software metrics program. This should be the first priority. A program can be established, but it will not be successful if it is not tied to organizational goals. A successful program establishes well defined uses for measures.

The next chapter provides a case study to reinforce metrics concepts introduced in this chapter. Chapter 16 then discusses a topic very closely aligned with metrics: maintainability.

1. Describe goals for a typical maintainer.

2. Use Basili's GQM methodology and drive out metrics for those goals.

3. Describe how you would provide training to all software maintenance people to educate them regarding the metrics program at your organization.

Software Maintenance Metrics Experiences

15

The previous chapter introduced the concepts of metrics, and detailed some of the difficulties in establishing programs and determining which metrics to use. This chapter provides some case studies to give specific, practical information regarding metrics. The first case study discusses the evolution of a metrics program and its current state. Practitioners will see how a program was started, evolved, and then almost died (like most programs do). The second case study discusses maintenance metrics collected and analyzed over a six-year period but, more importantly, over the entire operation and maintenance phase of the two systems. Both case studies relate the experiences of a U.S. Navy software maintenance organization.

EVOLUTION OF A METRICS PROGRAM: A CASE STUDY

The first case study gives more details on establishing a metrics program than were presented in the introductory chapter on metrics and addresses the establishment of the initial metrics program and goals for a Navy maintenance organization. The Navy maintenance organization established a metrics program based on its goals and then evolved the program as the goals changed. This case study also addresses how the program evolved since the late 1980s, and it is presented in three parts: the initial program, how it evolved, and its current status. The lessons learned in establishing and evolving a software maintenance metrics program are provided.

Background of the Case Study

The Navy software maintenance organization discussed herein was new, and thus its establishment afforded a very unique opportunity. As the organization did not exist, there was no excess baggage of "that's the way we've always done it." There was an opportunity to install a rigorous software engineering approach to software maintenance and to learn as the organization and related processes evolved. Metrics would help, and the Navy maintenance organization was not encumbered by tradition or in-place metrics or procedures.

State of the Organization

Being a new organization, the maintenance organization did not have a maintenance process (see Chapter 4), and did not have any metrics (see Chapter 14). The organization was presented with numerous obstacles, some technical, but most were political. The following summarizes the state of the organization when it was initially established.

State of the People

As the maintenance organization did not have a career path for computer professionals, the majority of the personnel were inexperienced software people. Details of these levels were presented in Chapter 9. As is the case with many systems, the transition plans for the newly developed systems did not provide for any software maintenance training (Pigoski 1994), and thus the maintenance organization implemented its own software maintenance training program (Pigoski and Looney 1993).

State of the Supported Systems

In the late 1980s, two systems were transitioned to the maintenance organization for maintenance support. One system was sized at 230K lines of code (LOC), while the other was 370K LOC.

Software maintenance for the two systems was to transition when the maintainers were ready to assume support in accordance with the transition plans that they had crafted. Part of the transition effort was to take control using software configuration management (Pigoski 1991b). As part of the transition effort, the maintainers collected all backlog information on outstanding modification requests in the form of problem reports (PRs) and enhancement requests (ERs). Problem reports reflected problems in the system, and enhancement requests documented proposed enhancements to software. These data were gleaned from the developers. The approach the maintainers took was to document the backlog and hopefully control expectations. They let everyone know that the newly established maintenance organization was starting with a significant backlog.

For the initial two systems, the problem report backlog was 11 and the Enhancement Request backlog was 31. Over two hundred person-months of effort were required to remove the backlog! Staffing  for each system amounted to one person for each system. Full staffing was about 13 people per system. It was very important to tell everyone what the maintainers were faced with—and they did. Within the next 12 months, all staffing was on board, and then the maintainers attacked the backlog. Just picture a metrics chart with the backlog and one person on board!

The data gleaned prior to transition, and the fact that all personnel were not on board, were very important data that needed to be preserved. That data became a key element of the software maintenance metrics program.

The Problems the Maintenance Organization Faced

There were many technical challenges. The maintenance organization had to establish a smooth-running organization with a software maintenance process that could be repeated and that could provide timely, quality support. Many questions arose. For example, how do you ensure a repeatable process? How do you improve it? How do you measure the improvement? (Please keep in mind that these issues surfaced *before* publication of Watts Humphrey's (1989) work on the software process, and well before introduction of the Capability Maturity Model.) Lastly, the maintainers were concerned about how they would convince the users that they were providing timely, quality support? The perception of the users was that maintenance was "merely fixing bugs," and that maintainers were slow and costly. These questions led to the establishment of the metrics program.

How the Maintenance Organization Attacked the Problems

The approach taken was to attack the perceptions. The maintainers had to prove that they were performing better than any other maintenance organization. The good news were that there was no data available to measure their performance. The only thing that was real was the perceptions.

For one of the most important issues (staffing for software maintenance) there were no data available. No one could confirm, deny, refute, or support future staffing estimates. Historical metric data regarding staffing would have been very valuable. A number of new systems would transition over the next few years, and the lack of historical data resulted in considerable disagreement over software maintenance staffing for each new system. (See Chapter 8.) As each new system was transitioned, there would always be a major battle over the staffing estimates. However, with no historical empirical staffing or annual change traffic (ACT) data, it would be a difficult task to defend staffing estimates. There was no means to measure the productivity of the maintenance organization and thus no basis for comparison. The maintenance organization needed to collect staffing data, and did so as part of its metrics program.

ESTABLISHING THE INITIAL METRICS PROGRAM

Prior to establishing the metrics program, the Navy maintenance organization established its software maintenance process. The process was documented and used numerous check-off sheets to document the various stages in the process. For each problem report/enhancement request, the sheets became part of a software development folder. Signatures were required at the various stages.

After documenting the process, the effort shifted to determining what the metrics program should be and what should be collected. In the beginning, the maintainers did not have the benefit of Hewlett-Packard's metrics efforts (Grady 1987). It was very apparent that everything could not be collected, and thus the metrics program would start small and then evolve. The maintenance organization used the GQM (goal, question, metric) approach advocated by Vic Basili (1985) to determine what to collect; the approach was to state goals, ask questions that satisfied the goals, and then determine which data answered the questions. That data would then be collected.

The Stated Goals

Recognizing that it was not feasible to collect all data concerning the system, the maintenance organization decided to at first collect only data that would support its primary goals. These primary goals were:

1. Provide quality, timely products.
2. Let customers and users know what they were getting for their money (Pigoski 1991c).

The Collection of Data

To satisfy the first goal, the maintenance organization collected data on the types of software errors found. A list of 20 errors derived from a list provided by Martin and McClure (1983) was established; this was a starting point. Analysis over the years indicated that only about five types of errors were recurring, and thus the list was eventually reduced to five. Of note is that all of the initially backlogged problem reports were latent defects from the development effort. Knowing where most of the latent defects were in the software helped isolate problems. However, the maintainers found that programmers gravitated to only a few types of errors, and the maintainers never did get the benefit they expected from this type of error analysis. The problem reports that were of most interest were those which could be traced to the maintainers' efforts. Accordingly, a code was established to see how many of the problem reports were attributable to the maintenance organizations' efforts.

Modules that are error-prone initially will always be error-prone.

Another metric was used to track the phases in which the problem reports were rejected during the maintenance process. This allowed the maintainers to see where errors were found, and how the process to remove the errors could be improved. These numbers helped to define their training needs. For example, the maintenance organization found that several of the programmers really did not know how to conduct unit testing. After some additional training, the quality of unit testing went up and the rejections by the independent testing organization went down.

The maintenance organization collected timeliness and backlog data for each phase (e.g. analysis, design, and coding). Metrics helped to determine where the bottlenecks were and eliminated them. It was important to determine the differences between problem reports and enhancement requests. If the customers and users perceived that the maintenance organization was slow, it would be interesting to find out where the time sinks were and to let everyone know what they were. These type of data were very useful in the early years as the maintenance organization learned that problem reports/enhancement requests were becoming backlogged in the test area. The maintainers evaluated the situation and determined that they had understaffed the test organization.

The second goal was to let the customers and users know what they were getting for their money. This directly relates to productivity.

What is a measure of productivity for a maintenance organization? Clearly, the number of problem reports/enhancement requests completed was one measure of productivity. The number of releases was also important. A very common perception is that the maintenance organization is merely fixing problems. Certainly the customers and users do not want, nor do they claim, any ownership of problem reports. Their perception (and perhaps rightly so) is that the developers failed to find the errors during development. Thus Swanson's (1976) three classical categories of maintenance: (corrective, perfective, and adaptive) (see Chapter 2) were used to try to determine what was actually being performed during the software support phase. These categories had not been used by the other Navy maintenance organizations; this naturally led the users to conclude that "maintenance is merely fixing bugs." The categories of maintenance would help provide the necessary data to show what the customers and users were receiving for their money.

The maintenance organization collected metric data regarding the number of software releases and dates. Also, the systems were baselined and lines of code (LOC) data were captured. Data regarding LOC that were added, deleted, or changed during each software modification were kept. Actual staffing was recorded each month.

The determination of goals, and subsequent determination of needed data, was fed back into the process in order to ensure that the proper data were collected and that the process supported the goals. The maintenance organization eventually modified the initial process to include peer reviews and an independent test organization.

Metrics Repository

The maintenance organization determined that the amount of metric data would grow, and that some automated repository was needed. As the maintenance organization was new, it had no databases, and thus an enterprise model was developed. This was later mapped into a database design that held all organization data.

Types of Reports

Weekly reports were provided from the database. These reports provided backlog information and the status for each problem report/enhancement request. The maintenance organization learned how well problem reports/enhancement requests were moving through the process. These data also were useful to parcel out the maintenance workload.

On a monthly basis, the status of each problem report/enhancement request was tracked. This was useful for seeing how many had come in, how many were resolved, and what the trend was. The reports helped determine bottlenecks and how to take action to resolve them.

Productivity data based on the metrics were provided on a quarterly basis. Trend analysis charts were provided to the customers and users so that they would know what was being produced. The charts also served to see what the trends were.

For configuration control boards (CCBs), detailed information was extracted from the database and provided for the CCB members. This information made it easy for the chairman of the CCB, the customer, to determine what was important for the next release and to direct the maintenance organization to work on those activities. Everyone needed to understand that the maintainers worked for the customer and users. Thus, there was no work performed on enhancements (enhancement requests) without CCB approval.

The initial metrics program provided valuable information for ad hoc technical reports. One of the most important reports was one that analyzed the relative proportions of the modification request that fell into the maintenance categories of corrective, perfective, and adaptive. Analysis for each system indicated that enhancements (perfective or adaptive) accounted for 78% to 83% of the effort at the maintainers. This information was provided to the customers and users in an attempt to show that maintenance was more than fixing problems.

Another ad hoc report that proved to be very helpful was one concerning the time spent on each phase of software maintenance. Policy dictated that problem reports could be acted upon and resolved by the maintenance organization upon receipt. However, for enhancement requests, the CCB had to approve any work. Analysis and subsequent reporting was very helpful because it indicated that all enhancement requests took significantly longer to resolve, primarily due to the time period between meetings of the CCB. The maintenance organization was able to tell the customers and users that it would typically take 18 months for an enhancement request to be fielded, and that this delay was due in good measure to the time it took for the CCB to convene and approve a scheduled release. Ad hoc reports that detailed the inherent time delays were provided to anyone who would read them. The reports were useful in telling everyone that enhancement requests took a long time to get fielded, but a large portion of the time delay was due to the CCB process and not the slowness of the maintenance organization. This was an important element in controlling the expectations of everyone concerned. The maintenance organization collected the data through the metrics program and was not bashful about sharing it.

THE LESSONS LEARNED FROM THE INITIAL METRICS PROGRAM

The following describes the lessons learned:

- *Collection.* Initially each individual was responsible for inputting data to the database. Policy and procedures existed, but the maintenance organization found that the data integrity was poor. Programmers did not want to count lines of code added, deleted, or moved, and the maintenance organization did not have a good automated means of collecting the data. The quality assurance (QA) organization found many of the data errors, and had to re-input the data. Ultimately, metrics (and in particular the inputting of metrics) was placed with the QA organization.
- *Analysis.* Analysis was performed by an independent, small ad hoc group and a number of internal and external reports were provided. This approach worked well. Based on the metrics data, the maintenance organization was able to plan the workload and was able to tell its headquarters what it was getting. Through the education program, the maintenance organization attempted to combat the natural resistance that each person had to any measurement program. Every three months, the maintenance organization would gather all its people together and present the results of the metrics program to them. They were told what the organization was learning from the metrics program, and what the organization was sharing with its customers and users. There were no surprises. Everyone knew what the data were saying and how the organization was trying to use it. Analysis helped to refine the software maintenance process. The maintenance organization had to increase staffing in the test group because the analysis indicated that testing was the bottleneck.

Share the results of the metrics program with maintainers on a regular basis.

- *Weaknesses.* In the early years, the major weakness of the metrics program was the lack of data to support the specific goals. It was difficult to make major decisions and to come to firm conclusions based on limited data. Recognized metrics experts like Bob Grady (1987) state that you must collect data for at least three years for it to be meaningful. However, there are a number of things that can be learned early on, particularly if you are evolving your process. The metrics program was helpful in that respect. The maintenance organization did not claim that the metric data were overly scientific or perfect, but that the data were useful for identifying trends and alerting management to potential problems.

- *Code Metrics/Error-prone modules*. After initiation of the metrics program, the maintenance organization wanted to get involved in code metrics, and even wrote some original software to determine complexity. These data were useful in assigning the best programmers to the worst code, and helped to focus the testing effort. It was also thought that it would be useful to map the problem reports to modules. The maintenance organization could then identify the error-prone modules and then perhaps rewrite them.

  However, with so few data points it was not meaningful to map problem reports to modules. It is good practice to identify error-prone modules, but you need a large number of problem reports to map. Even items like software defects/KLOC were not practical for the maintenance organization; in reality they had very little meaning. The majority of problems came from the developer. The maintenance organization did not insert them. Of what value then was going back and determining that the system that was delivered had X number of defects/KLOC? For the maintainers, there was no value, and thus they did not include it in their metrics program. Certainly, that was old news and of no great significance to users. It was important to determine what errors were made while fixing problems, and then to improve the process to eliminate future errors.

- *Impact on people*. The reaction of the maintainers to the metrics program was very predictable. They did not like the program. As Problem Reports, Enhancement Requests, and ACT data were collected, the people looked upon them with disdain. Providing metric results quarterly did not allay their fears. They were concerned that their job performance would be tied to the metrics. The approach was to state that the maintenance organization needed the metrics to retain the resources that it had. Unfortunately, all the presentations and training regarding the metrics program did not help.

- *Scheduling work*. The maintenance organization found that the metrics program was especially helpful in preparing for CCB meetings. The maintenance organization functioned as the secretariat and needed to track the status of all problem reports/ enhancement requests. The metrics repository was very helpful. Analysis of how many problem reports/enhancement requests the maintenance organization had completed in the past was valuable information at the CCB. The maintainers had to state how many problem reports/enhancement requests they could complete prior to the next CCB. The historic data let the maintenance organization know what a reasonable number would be.

THE SECOND STAGE OF THE METRICS PROGRAM

At the end of the initial period, there was a formal software maintenance process in place. The number of people involved in the maintenance effort had increased to about 40, and they were trained. However, their tours of duty were ending, so the second stage would be more concerned with training. A solid programming environment was in place, and extensive use was made of CASE tools for code management and source code analysis. More systems were identified for transition to the Navy maintenance organization for support, and the next stage was to be one of dramatic growth. The metrics program was needed to help manage this growth.

State of the Organization

During this period the maintenance organization was fully functional. Additional systems were transferred for maintenance as another Navy maintenance organization was closed. The perceptions regarding cost were still alive and well. A concerted effort was made to convince the customer and users that the cost was cheaper than if support were provided by civilian contractors at an alternate location. A very detailed cost accounting system was implemented whereby each hour of each person's day was tracked. The focus was to determine where and how the labor hours were being expended. The input was extensive, and the analysis cumbersome. Both were performed manually. Additionally, the data were initially collected for the programmers, and after a year passed the software configuration management and test people were also included. The data did permit the publication of some reports that clearly indicated that the maintenance organization was less expensive than other maintenance alternatives. Unfortunately, results of this metric analysis were retained internal to the Navy software maintenance organization; the customer and users did not see the data.

State of the People

During the second phase, the maintenance organization grew at a dramatic rate. The staffing increased from 40 to 150 full-time personnel. The majority of the staff were still U.S. Navy enlisted personnel, with a higher percentage of government service personnel than during the first phase. These maintainers possessed considerable domain knowledge, but they were inexperienced in software support.

GROWTH

State of the Supported Systems

This second phase was one marked with significant growth in the inventory of supported systems. Three large-scale communications systems were transitioned for maintenance along with two smaller intelligence-related systems. One system of 1.5M LOC was added for maintenance and another, with 2M LOC, was identified for transition. Total LOC now exceeded 3.5M LOC. Some smaller systems were also identified. A few prototypes were also transitioned. The maintenance organization did not have the benefit of predelivery involvement, and no acquisition metric data were available. The challenge with the new systems was to put them into the process and to use the metric data to improve the process.

EVOLUTION OF THE METRICS PROGRAM

The second phase was one marked by evolution of the metrics program, but it was also a period that should have seen the program come to maturity. It did not. The following discusses the evolution of the program.

- *Documentation.* During the initial period, unfortunately, not much was documented. The two goals mentioned above (and in Chapter 8) were never formally documented. As a carry-over, no goals were documented for the follow-on period, and there were still no documented goals, policies, or procedures for the metrics program. This period was really a time of isolationism. Considerable metric data were available and used for internal reporting, planning, and scheduling. However, essentially no external reporting took place. Regular quarterly reports were not provided to customers and users and no ad hoc metric reports were published. The metrics program had been set up to support certain goals. The goals might have changed, but they were not documented, nor was the metric collection significantly changed to reflect any new goals.
- *New metric data added.* The database did evolve in an attempt to capture cost data. A number of new tables were added to provide timecard data. Unfortunately, for the first year only programmers entered data. Later, SCM, test, and QA people put in data, but the data integrity was not there. There was significant data collection, but basic information (such as how many people supported a particular system over the life cycle) was not available. There was a huge effort to capture cost data; it was not successful. The pro-

gram was implemented to collect everything, and this attempt to collect everything resulted in collection of cost data that was not useful. The basic tracking data for problems and enhancements was still available, and was useful in scheduling work and preparing for CCBs. Additional data added to the database during this second phase of the metrics program included data regarding the travel of the maintenance people. Historically, there was significant travel, but it was not tracked. In support of the second goal, travel data would let people know that a significant number of technical assist visits were performed.

Make sure that time spent on technical assistance and training for users is documented in the metrics program and reported.

- *Data input.* Input to the database took a turn for the worse. Because of the previous data integrity problems, input was centralized in the QA organization. With a significant increase in the amount of data, a decision was made to input summary data only. Thus, for the software maintenance process, only the major phases in the process were entered into the database. Other data was available in software development folders, but those data had to be extracted manually. As a result, it was impossible to find out things, like how many peer reviews were actually conducted, without a significant manual effort.
- *Metrics training.* In the early years, the effort was small and training was informal. During the next period, the maintenance organization grew in size and stature. The amount of data collected also grew but the metrics training program was never for-

---

Practical Experience

When the original metrics program was established, productivity was measured in terms of problem reports resolved and enhancement requests implemented. One area that was underestimated was the training and technical assistance to the users. Those areas consume significant resources, and any software maintenance metrics program must include more than problem report/ enhancement request data.

malized. By the end of the second phase, the effort was essentially still run by one individual who had set it up. As a result of this lack of increase in staffing, only summary data were inputted and the rest of the maintenance organization really had no grasp of the program. Training, like the resources for the metrics program, dried up.

■ *Metric data*. The systems that were transitioned when the other cryptologic maintenance organizations were closed brought limited historical data with them from the other maintenance organization. Old problem report/enhancement request data were not transitioned, and thus not much was learned about the new systems to be supported. Even worse, the start date for new systems was the date that was inputted into the database. Because there was a backlog of problem reports and enhancement requests, the "time to complete" for many of the existing problem reports/enhancement requests that came with the newly transitioned systems would never be accurate.

■ *Data collection*. As the second phase of the metrics program came to an end, there was extreme concern over the amount of metric data being collected and its utility. There was also concern regarding the amount of time spent in each phase of the support process.

THE LESSONS LEARNED

 By the end of the second phase of the metrics program, it was at a crossroads. This program had survived for a number of years, but had not evolved to keep pace with the activities around it. Organizationally it had not changed. Massive amounts of data were being collected manually, but not inputted to the database. The manual nature of the data collection was a real problem. There were many lessons learned about the metrics program over these first two phases, and these lessons were used to get the program back on its intended track: supporting the goals of the maintenance organization. The following summarizes the lessons learned during the second phase of the metrics program.

Document the Goals

The metrics program was in danger of dying due in great measure to the lack of documented goals. Data were being collected, and no one knew why. No one knew what the metrics supported. The lesson learned here was that the metrics program will die if the goals are not stated and known by everyone concerned. The maintenance organization recognized the need for goals and now has documented the goals for the program. Fortunately, all the data were available for analysis.

Document the Metrics Program

One of the biggest problems was no documentation; people knew nothing about the program. There was not a training program. There was no external reporting. The lesson learned is that there must be a documented program; this has been corrected.

Set Up a Metrics Council

The maintenance organization did not have an oversight organization to support the metrics program, the goals, the metric collection, and the analysis. This organization can ensure that the program evolves.

Set Up a Separate Analysis Group

Initially, data analysis was performed by a separate group. Later, the analysis was performed by the QA organization. A separate analysis group was able to cross organizational lines and respond to the maintenance organization's goals. The QA organization, where responsibility for metrics should reside, or the software engineering process organization, are both good candidates for the analysis. It is important to have a central group responsible for the analysis and reporting.

You need a separate group to perform the analysis and reporting of metric data.

Automate the Process

As the amount of data increased, staffing did not. As a result, only summary data were inputted to the database. Valuable information was not captured and stored in the metrics portion of the database, severely limiting the analysis effort. The lesson learned was that some automated means to capture metric data was necessary. For the Navy maintenance organization, the COSEE project (see Chapter 13) will provide that automation.

Organization Matured—Metrics Did Not

The Navy maintenance organization evolved over a period of 6 years. It took on more systems for maintenance, new people came in, and other people left the organization. The metrics effort also evolved—but did not mature. The separate analysis group was disbanded. As with many other metrics programs, it needed to be revived or it would die. Fortunately, those resuscitation efforts began (Phase 3 of the metrics program) and are continuing.

Too Much Detail Collected

Finite detail is not necessary to have an effective program. You do not have to go to five decimal places and have 15 years of data to make a metrics program successful. If the data supports the stated goals, it is successful. In the second phase of the metrics program, detailed information was collected—and then never analyzed. Simple data collection, like staffing per month/system, was not collected on a regular basis. Further, these data were not put in the database. Instead of going for all the detail and being overloaded with data, it is better to go with simpler data that will satisfy goals.

Metrics Provided Insight into Maintenance Operations

Although the above indicates that the metrics program did not evolve as it should have, changes were made and the program survived. There were positive results from the metrics program. Data were available and much was learned from the data. The case study that follows in this chapter describes metric data from that program. The following provides the current state of the program.

Current Status

The metrics program is under constant review and evaluation. Goals were defined and documented. As a result of the metrics review, the collection process is being improved. External reporting is occurring on a regular basis. An intensive effort was undertaken to collect data from manual sources and place it in the database before the data were lost. Additional data were being added to the metrics repository, such as summary staffing data and LOC data/system. The most significant effort is in the area of process improvement. As part of an effort to upgrade the software engineering process, the software maintenance process was automated via process-modeling software.

Summary of the First Case Study

The previous study described how a metrics program started, evolved, and almost died. It stressed the program rather than the metrics themselves. The good news is that significant data were collected for the goals that were important for the Navy maintenance organization. In spite of attempts to "overcollect and underanalyze," significant metrics data are resident. As part of the resuscitation effort, a separate effort looked at the metrics gathered over the first six years. That period was the full maintenance cycle for two systems that the maintenance organization supported. The following case study provides some of the details of an analysis of six years of metrics data.

ANALYSIS OF SOFTWARE MAINTENANCE METRICS: A CASE STUDY

When you start a software maintenance metrics program, you often wonder: Where is it going? Will it be worthwhile? Will you really learn something from all that data? Will it be helpful in predicting estimates? The data the Navy maintenance activity collected certainly helped change some of the perceptions that were prevalent in the early years; but what about those two initial systems that came to the Navy maintenance organization for maintenance? What about all the data that were collected for over six years, and more importantly, for what turned out to be the entire maintenance phase of these two large systems? Was anything learned from supporting two systems for their entire maintenance phase? Yes. A summary of that data is provided herein to stress what was learned and what was important in the way of software maintenance metrics.

Analysis of Empirical Data

Data were collected on the two systems initially supported by the new maintenance organization. The systems are referred to as system A and system B. Approximately six years of software maintenance data for the two systems were analyzed for this case study. The data covered the entire maintenance phase of the systems from initial period of software maintenance until the systems were retired.

Many metrics, specifically code metrics such as complexity (which might have been useful to the maintenance organization) were not collected because the customers really did not care about those issues. They were simply not important to the customers, and therefore not to the maintenance organization either. The customers were interested in the types of things that drove the goals of the metrics program (listed in the first case study). Thus, what was collected was tied to the goals and part of an overall software strategy as advocated by Grady (1987).

The metrics were grouped into six areas for ease of discussion and analysis:

- Size.
- Measures of Productivity.
- Staffing.
- Categories of maintenance.
- Timeliness.
- Quality.

While not tied directly to the SEI core metrics mentioned in the previous chapter, there is sufficient correlation. The SEI core metrics describes four basis areas: size, effort, scheduling, and quality. The metrics program embodied the essence of the SEI core metrics.

Size of the Systems

The number of lines of code (LOC) is the primary means of measuring the size of software at the maintenance organization, and is used to justify staffing estimates. One of the major problems with systems transitioning to the maintenance organization is determining software maintenance staffing (see Chapter 8). The maintenance organization hoped to justify estimates better by having empirical data to confirm data provided by parametric models such as COCOMO. Thus, LOC data were collected for each release to study the growth patterns to evaluate it against staffing and backlog data. The size of system A is reflected in Figure 15.1.

The overall size decreased in 1989. This was due to significant restructuring of the software to make the system more maintainable, and in great measure to the deletion of a major system A function. From its initial size in 1988 until 1993, the system grew by 9.99%.

Figure 15.2 provides the size of the second system, system B, over the maintenance phase of the life cycle.

System B also had a major decrease in size after a few years. This decrease was due to the deletion of the communications function and a restructuring of its database. From its initial size in 1988, system B grew by 25.48%.

The maintenance organization used this data to tell the customers and users that systems grow in size, and changes in size affect staffing. Previously, no empirical data were available to aid in staffing estimates, but with six years of data, the maintenance organization could use size to adjust staffing levels.

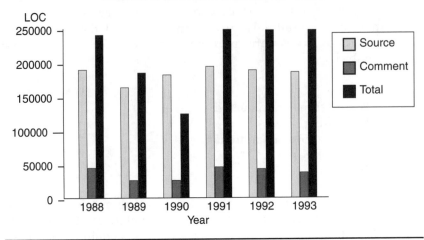

FIGURE 15.1   Historical size of system A.

Whereas the above merely provides the gross sizes and growth patterns of system A and system B, another factor which must be considered is the annual change traffic (ACT). For ACT, the metrics program must track the number of lines of code added, deleted, and

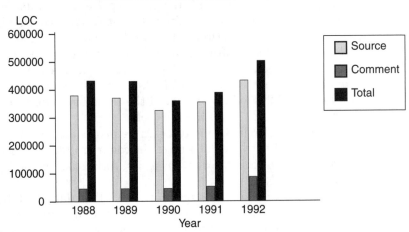

FIGURE 15.2   Historical size of system B.

modified on an annual basis. When evaluating staffing requirements, overall size, the annual growth rate, and ACT must be considered. ACT data for system A and system B are addressed later in this chapter.

Comment Lines

One metric regarding lines of code that the maintenance organization found useful is the percentage of comment lines of code for a particular system (see the next chapter for a discussion on maintainability). The higher the percentage of comment lines of code, the more maintainable the system. The more maintainable the system, the lower the overall software life-cycle support costs. Unfortunately, there is no industry standard to use as a guide to determine if a system has the correct number of commented lines of code.

When a system transitions to a maintenance organization, very often the maintenance organization has not participated in the predelivery stage. There are several references (MIL-HDBK-347; Pigoski 1994; Vollman 1990) that indicate that this lack of involvement is detrimental to the software maintenance effort. In most cases the maintenance organization is not involved in the transition until a few months before the responsibility transfers from the developer to the maintenance organization. The maintenance organization essentially must take the system as it is delivered. The maintenance organization must have some assessment of its maintainability and readability. Thus, it has proven to be useful to collect and report on the percentage of comments in the code. If the opportunity presents itself, the maintenance organization should conduct a full-blown maintainabililty assessment of the system prior to delivery. This too can be tracked in a database and updated over time. However, in the late 1980s those maintainability assessment tools were not readily available, and thus a simplistic approach (like looking at the LOC for comments) was the best that could be done at the time.

Analysis of the number of comments can at least let the program manager and the customers know how the new system measures up in relation to other systems being supported. The maintenance organization, by comparing systems, and by combining this metric with other metrics, can determine if a system is more or less maintainable than another system. Please do not confuse this simplistic approach with full-blown maintainability assessments and a full definition of maintainability (see Chapter 16). Figure 15.3 provides the percentages of comment lines versus source lines of code for system A, system B, and for several systems that have transitioned to the maintenance organization. As can be seen in Figure 15.3, system A and system B fall in the middle. This analysis reveals that system G will be most difficult to maintain.

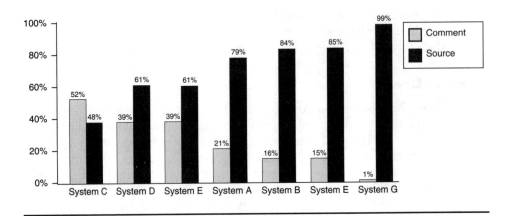

FIGURE 15.3 Lines of code percentages.

This very mundane metric is quite useful to the software maintenance practitioner. Regrettably, the program managers who develop systems are concerned with budget and schedule. No requirements are levied regarding comments in code or for the maintainability of systems (Pigoski 1993). Thus, almost in self defense, the maintenance organization needs to publish source versus comment data to let everyone know the potential impact of a poorly documented system. The Navy maintenance organization has empirical data and can let the customers know, using real data, how potentially difficult new systems (e.g., system G) will be to maintain. The empirical data collected over the past six years gives them a basis of determining the difficulty in maintaining new systems as they are transitioned for support.

Initially, size data were limited to application code, and thus system A and system B size estimates were not very accurate. Lines of code for ORACLE and graphics software were not included. For example, if SQL*MENU was used to build a menu, there was no good method to count LOC. Subsequently, the maintenance organization decided to count the generated LOC, as it was the only true means of determining the LOC count. The fact that the data are somewhat inaccurate is not of much significance. The data are still useful for staffing estimates. The lesson learned is that a more accurate means of counting LOC for SQL and graphics-generated code should be investigated.

Measures of Productivity

When determining the productivity of a maintenance organization, the following are commonly viewed as measures of productivity: the number of problem reports and enhancement requests completed and fielded, the number of software releases installed, and the technical assistance provided. The following subsections discuss these metrics as they relate to support of systems A and B for their full maintenance cycle.

- *Problem Reports*. The maturity of a system is often measured by the number of defects that are seen over the life cycle of a system. After a period of years, the defects should stabilize. When analyzing corrective type actions, such as problem reports, the preponderance of problem reports are latent defects. This means that the defects occurred as a result of the software development effort. The role of the maintainers is to resolve these as they are reported by operations or user personnel. Thus, the total number of problem reports submitted for any system is not a reflection on the performance of a maintenance organization. The maintenance organization should be measured as to how many problem reports it completes, and the timeliness of its solutions.

  The number of problem reports submitted over the life of systems A and B while they were supported by the maintenance organization are reflected in Figure 15.4.

  Initial data were collected from the software developer and placed into the metrics database. Prior to assuming support for system A and system B, the total problem report backlog was 11, which is included in the 1988 figures in Figure 15.4. With the first production delivery of system A and assumption of the maintenance role, a significant number of problem reports were submitted. Figure 15.4 shows the submission of problem reports decreased year by year such that by 1993, almost no activity occurred. The majority of the problem reports were submitted by the end of 1991, or after three full years of operation. The incoming defects stabilized after three years.

  Figure 15.4 also provides the problem report history of system B. The pattern is very similar to that of system A; after three years the system stabilized.

- *Enhancement Requests*: The majority of maintenance work is providing system enhancements. Prior to assuming software support responsibilities for system A from the developer, the backlog of enhancement requests numbered over 20, and for system B the enhancement request backlog was 11. These data were also collected by the maintenance organization and reported to the customers and users to let them know that even prior to initial delivery, there was a significant backlog (not attributable to the maintenance organization) of user-requested enhancements. These data were very useful in controlling perceptions. They let the customer, who provided funding for the maintenance effort know what

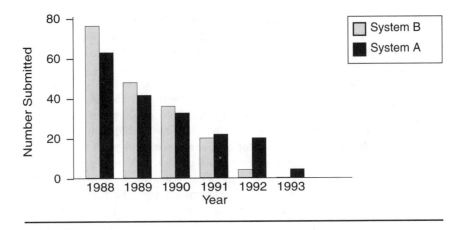

FIGURE 15.4 Problem report activity by years.

the challenges were. As one of the goals was timeliness, it was important to let everyone know how extensive the backlog was, because it impacted overall timeliness. The historical view of enhancement request submissions for system A is depicted in Figure 15.5. As with the problem report activity chart, the figures for 1988 (in Figure 15.5), include the unresolved enhancement requests (11 for system B and 22 for system A) that were transferred to the maintenance organization with the systems.

With the initial production delivery in 1988, a large number of enhancement requests were submitted in 1988 and 1989. This is due to the usage of the system in a high volume operational environment. The number of enhancement request submissions stabilized. However, the total enhancement request and problem report backlog must be looked at to fully appreciate the scope of the software support effort.

The enhancement request activity by years for system B is also depicted in Figure 15.5. These data indicate a similar influx of enhancements submitted during the first year, which dropped off much more dramatically than for system A, but also essentially stabilized.

■ *Backlog*: Figure 15.6 shows problem reports submitted and completed for system A. In essence, it shows the problem report backlog over the entire maintenance phase of the system. "Completed" is the date that the problem report was installed in an official release at a user location. "Open" defines the backlog at the end of the year.

The overall problem report backlog remained fairly constant,

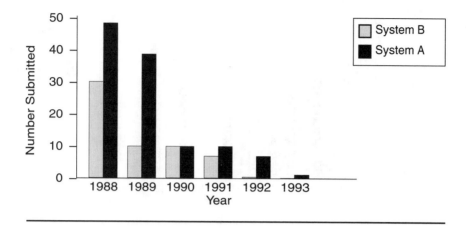

FIGURE 15.5   Enhancement request activity by years.

with some minor growth up until 1991. At that point the staffing levels had peaked, which (coupled with a decline in new problem reports received) enabled the maintenance organization to start bringing the backlog down significantly.

Figure 15.7 shows problem reports submitted and completed for system B. The system experienced a high level of corrective effort during the initial two years of its delivery. This can be anticipated as typical of most systems, and was expected.

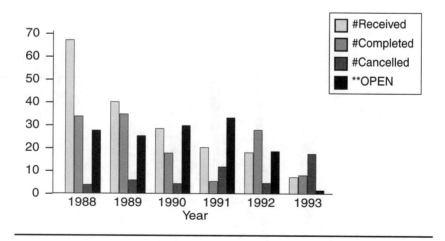

FIGURE 15.6   System A problem reports submitted and completed.

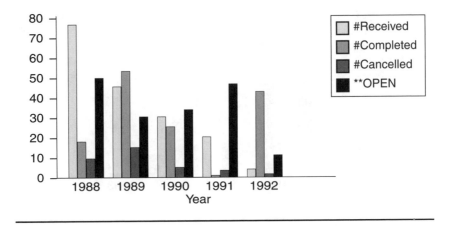

FIGURE 15.7 System B problem reports submitted and completed.

Figure 15.8 shows enhancement requests submitted and completed for system A. It shows the enhancement request backlog over the entire maintenance phase of the system. "Completed" is the date that the enhancement request was installed in an official release at a user location.

Starting with the initial backlog of over 20 enhancement requests, activity increased in 1988 due to operational delivery and by the end of the third year of support, 1991, the backlog denoted by the OPEN category was on its way down.

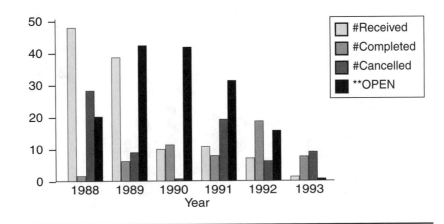

FIGURE 15.8 System A enhancement requests submitted and completed.

Figure 15.9 shows system B enhancement requests submitted and completed over the life cycle. As with system A, the system stabilized after three years of operation or by the end of 1991.

■ *Annual Change Traffic (ACT)*. As defined by Boehm (1981), ACT is "The fraction of the software product's source instructions which undergo change during a (typical) year, either through addition or modification." It is one of the most important parameters used when determining software support staffing levels. It is a major input to the COCOMO model for estimating software resources (see Chapter 8). Starting in 1988, ACT data for system A and system B problem reports/enhancement requests was collected.

Over the life cycle of system A, the average percentage of ACT was 8.38%. The industry range is 10% to 15% and thus this number is consistent with industry norms. Over the life cycle, the ACT percentage for System B was 14.29%. This is somewhat higher but generally comparable with system A. The combined ACT for both systems over their life cycles is 11.34%, which again is consistent with industry standards. Initial staffing, determined by an educated guess, was provided to the maintenance organization in 1987 for system A and system B. The staffing numbers were not based on empirical data, nor had a model been used. In 1990 the maintenance organization revalidated the staffing with two studies and used industry averages for ACT. As a result of the analysis of six years of metric data, there are empirical data for ACT. Those data can be used to estimate staffing for all future systems coming to the maintenance organization. It is interesting to note that

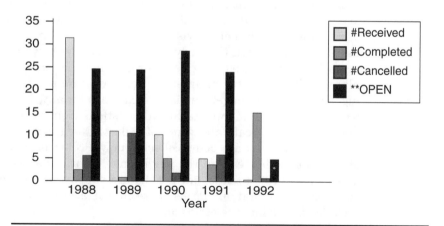

FIGURE 15.9 System B enhancement requests submitted and completed.

these data later validated that the industry averages are applicable to U.S. Navy systems.

Empirical data of 11.34% for ACT can and will be used for future staffing estimates by the Navy maintenance organization. The customer did not believe that its system would have high ACTs. The customer did not believe that after a costly, five-year development, over 10% of the code would be "touched" on an annual basis. Metric data solidified the point that over 10% of the code was touched!

■ *Releases*: Over the life cycle of system A, 18 releases were provided to operational user locations. For system B, a total of 17 releases were provided.

Based on CCB considerations, normally one or two releases are authorized per year. For system A, a total of 18 releases were fielded over the maintenance phase of the system. The average time between releases was 3.4 months. For system B it was 2.7 months. This is far better than for most systems, but was done to support the goal of timeliness.

Each system A release averaged 4.22 problem reports and 2.33 enhancement requests. Each system B release averaged 6.53 problem reports and 1.29 enhancement requests. Releases were fielded very often, but each had very few problem reports and enhancement requests. It was better for the maintenance organization to field small releases more often, because it was trying to dispel the perception that maintenance organizations are slow.

■ *Technical Assistance and Training*. The third part of productivity is technical assistance and training. Whereas the maintenance organization collected large amounts of data regarding problem reports/enhancement requests and releases, very little data were available regarding technical assistance provided to supported users' locations. Numerous visits were made to all the supported users (particularly in the early years) to assist with system management functions, as a formal course of instruction was not in place. Additionally, the maintenance organization provided training for system managers at user locations. Finally, help desks were instituted to answer technical questions from user location personnel. Empirical data were not collected for these areas, but those types of data are being collected now. Preliminary analysis of that data indicates that the provision of technical assistance is a large part (10% to 20%) of the software support effort. The lesson learned is that all forms of technical assistance must be included in the metrics program.

■ *Staffing*. Figure 15.10 shows the staffing for system A and system B over the life cycle. Staffing for each system consisted of govern-

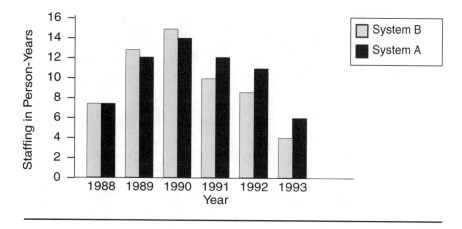

FIGURE 15.10 Staffing over the life cycle.

ment civilians, U.S. Navy officer and enlisted personnel, and civilian contractors.

Staffing for both systems decreased as the systems stabilized. As staffing levels were provided by systems, the maintenance organization reallocated the staffing to satisfy other maintenance requirements.

Figure 15.11 shows system A backlog versus actual staffing. It depicts modification requests (MRs), which are open problem reports/enhancement requests, for the maintenance phase. The staffing was reduced by the maintenance organization over the maintenance phase as the backlog decreased. Full system A staffing was not in place until 1990. Thus, the backlog kept increasing. The maintenance organization always starts with a backlog from the developer and thus staffing needs to be front-loaded.

Figure 15.12 shows similar empirical data for system B.

As with system A, system B staffing decreased with the backlog. System B started with a significant influx of problem reports in the initial year of operation (1988). Proper staffing was not attained until 1990. Staffing was prematurely reduced in 1991. Only because there were no enhancement requests and a minimal number (6) of problem reports submitted in 1992 did the backlog decrease.

Analysis of these data provides good insight into the support process and provides valuable data for planning purposes. Based on the data presented herein, the staffing for other systems should be decreased after the system is in operation for three years, or in this case at the end of 1991.

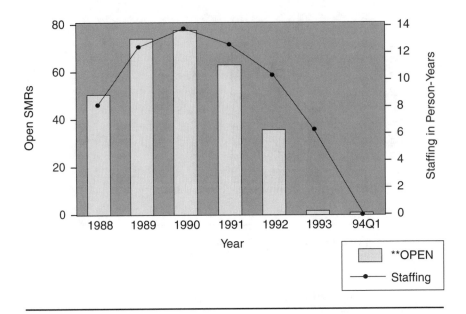

FIGURE 15.11 Backlog of system A MRs (enhancement request and problem report) versus staffing.

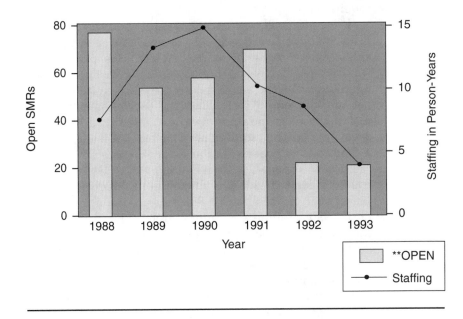

FIGURE 15.12 Backlog of system B MRs (enhancement request and problem report) versus staffing.

■ *Staffing versus LOC*: One of the most important issues for a maintenance organization is staffing for new systems. Metric data like the data just discussed are essential to satisfy the goal of letting the customers know what they are getting for their money. There is always a battle to get resources for maintenance, and staffing estimates are always suspect. Acquisition and user people still tend to believe that maintenance is merely fixing bugs. Vendors state that CASE tools will let a maintenance person organization maintain 200K LOC or more. The customers do not want to staff for maintenance at all. Practitioners cannot get caught up in the vendor hype. They must deal in realities. It was important to determine how many LOC an average maintenance person could maintain. Table 15.1 provides the listing of the various systems supported and the staffing for each. Bacause the maintainers were interested in determining how much code a person could maintain, the figures for system A and system B reflect maximum system size and peak staffing. Looking at the data on an annual basis (Figure 15.2) reveals that system B staffing declined sharply in 1991, which contributed to the large backlog in 1991. System B was clearly understaffed, as the system kept growing in size. System A presented a fairly nice pattern across the maintenance phase, with an average of about 23K LOC per person (Figure 15.1). For system B, the average was close to 45K LOC per person.

For some of the newer systems now at the maintenance organization, these data provide significant insight. For systems F and G, staffing is far too low and the maintenance organization will face some hard times in supporting these systems. The metric data, and analysis of data from the other systems, at least gives the maintainers some empirical data with which to fight the resource battles. Without the data, they would not stand a chance of getting additional resources.

TABLE 15.1　LOC/FSP

System	Total LOC	Staffing	KLOC/FSP
System A	244,889	13.00	23.3 (Avg)
System B	515,315	14.50	45.0 (Avg)
System C	251,804	8.67	29.0
System D	302,604	12.66	23.9
System E	449,653	19.66	22.9
System F	196,457	3.00	65.5
System G	2,300,000	31.00	74.2

Of note is that the LOC data is specific to the Navy maintenance organization. The military duties of the maintainers typically take about one third of their time. Thus, actual LOC per person is higher. Also, these were new systems and in the first few years ACT is much higher. Systems that are 10–15 years old are very stable (Row ACT); LOC per person can be much higher.

Maintenance Categories

Swanson (1976) defined the three maintenance categories as corrective, perfective, and adaptive. Problem reports are corrective in nature, and enhancement requests can be either perfective or adaptive. When software maintenance started for system A and system B, the maintenance organization commenced collecting maintenance category information. The maintenance organization published two reports which indicated that enhancement requests consumed over 80% of the software maintenance effort. The empirical data were consistent with other data that indicate that enhancements consume most of the maintenance effort. Those data were provided to the customer and users in order to show them what they were getting for their money.

Timeliness

One of the ways that the maintenance organization measured customer satisfaction was by tracking the time from an initial request for maintenance (problem report/enhancement request) to delivery at user locations in the form of a new software release.

The average time to complete problem reports and enhancement requests for system A is shown in Figure 15.13. With some inaccurate start data, problem reports typically took about 10 months to field, and enhancement requests took almost 18 months. This seemingly rather excessive timeframe is due to the philosophy of scheduled releases. For a worldwide system, high quality is more important than pushing out insignificant, minor corrections or low-priority new enhancements. It was important to know how long it took for new releases and how things looked from the perspective of the user. All the users care about is how long it takes to get their individual request fielded. For the maintenance organization, it was important to track timeliness and try to improve upon it.

For system B, Figure 15.14 provides similar data. It took nearly 11 months to field system B problem reports and about 15 months to field enhancement requests.

The differences in the timeframes are easily understood and explained. Problem reports are corrective in nature, involve "touching"

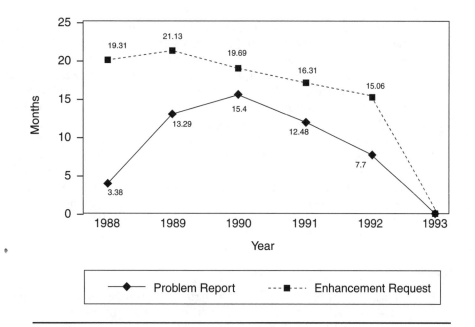

FIGURE 15.13 System A problem report/enhancement request completion times.

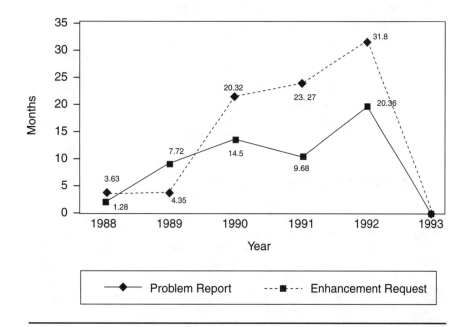

FIGURE 15.14 System B problem report/enhancement request completion times.

relatively few lines of code, and can be acted upon by the maintenance organization without waiting for authorization by the CCB. This is how the Navy SCM process worked. Some organizations need CCB approval for any action. Upon receipt, the maintenance organization performs analysis and then works out a software solution. It is then placed in the next release. Enhancement requests, on the other hand, are enhancements to the system and must be approved by the CCB. Upon receipt of an enhancement request, the maintenance organization performs initial analysis and then must wait until a formal CCB is held. At the CCB, the chairman decides which enhancement requests will be worked and which will go in the next scheduled release. For system A and system B the average delay due to the waiting for the CCB or as a result of prioritization was 4.41 months. Naturally, this information was provided to the users.

Quality

Another goal of the software metrics program is to provide quality software to users. Embedded in the software maintenance process were a number of measures to ensure the quality of the delivered software. For each problem report or corrective action taken, the maintenance organization determined the cause of the error. The majority of problem reports were attributable to the software developer in the form of latent defects and not the maintenance organization.

Using a list offered by Martin and McClure (1983), the maintenance organization analyzed each problem report and determined the cause of the error. To check the quality of their products, there was a code that related to their activity. If a reported problem report was caused by some action that the maintenance organization took, it was flagged. An analysis of system A and system B metric data revealed that errors attributable to the maintenance organization were negligible.

INSIGHTS AND THE LESSONS LEARNED

This case study provided an analysis of six years (1988–1993) of metric data regarding system A and system B over the entire maintenance phase of their life cycles. The primary lessons learned in watching the metrics program evolve over six years is that a practical and reasonable approach to a metrics program is worthwhile. All too often organizations collect too much data. As a result, the programs die. The maintenance organization established a program that is simplistic and practical in nature. The data collected are very mundane. However, without that data, predecessor cryptologic maintenance organizations were not successful in acquiring and retaining resources to perform software maintenance. Having empirical data for a six year period (and more importantly, for the entire maintenance phase of the systems) provided the means to fight the difficult battles to obtain software maintenance resources.

A valuable lessons learned in analyzing the data is that the analysis does not have to be perfect or precise. Trend analysis is important. The metrics program at the maintenance organization has evolved, and certainly might not be the best program in the world. However, the program is still alive (unlike many others that fold after one year) and is providing data valuable to the future of the organization.

Analysis of Metric Data

Analysis of metric data for the two systems provided insight into maintenance operations. The following is a summary of insights gained and the lessons learned from analysis of the metric data.

1. Problem report/enhancement request analysis indicated that the majority of work was enhancements. This well-documented fact in the software engineering and maintenance world is still not generally accepted by customers and users. Most often customers state that industry data does not apply to them; their systems are different. The collection and analysis of six years of data provides the lesson that the Navy systems are not different. Most of the maintenance work for them is in the form of enhancements, just like the rest of the world.
2. The quality of the maintenance work was very good. One of the goals was to provide quality products, and analysis indicated that very few errors were attributable to the maintenance organization.
3. Technical assist visits and the help desk consumed a large portion of the maintenance organization's time. Tracking and reporting of problem reports/enhancement requests and releases did not tell the customers the true scope of the maintenance effort. Maintainers need to track activities such as help desks.
4. Software systems grew considerably in size over a period of years. These types of data were not previously available. The systems do grow, and the maintenance organization has data to document it. This might not be surprising to the software community, but apparently it is to the customers and those who provide the software maintenance resources.
5. The maintenance organization needs to find an accurate means of estimating LOC for code generated by commercial-off-the-shelf products such as relational DBMSs.

6. Studying the timeliness of problem reports versus enhancement requests was very valuable. The customers often lose sight of the fact that enhancements cannot be worked on until the chairman of the CCB authorizes work. Reporting of the CCB time delay to the customers was very valuable in controlling expectations.

7. ACT analysis clearly revealed that Navy systems are very similar to all others. The ACT data substantiated staffing estimates from parametric models.

SUMMARY

This chapter presented two case studies. From the first study, you should appreciate that the metrics program must be supported and must evolve. From the second study, you can appreciate some rather mundane metrics that just happened to work for the maintenance organization. When you get tapped to set up the metrics program for your organization, move cautiously. Do not get consumed and develop a program that is so complex that it fails. If you are supporting the space shuttle or NASA, you might need millions of metrics. Most organizations drown in data—don't make the same mistake.

1. Discuss the goals of your organization.

2. What kind of data would you collect to support these goals?

3. What are the four recommended data to collect?

16

Maintainability

This chapter addresses the topic of maintainability of software systems from the perspective of the maintainer. Maintainability is defined from different points of view, and the ways in which different organizations approach maintainability is mentioned. It discusses maintainability as an attribute of quality and provides an overview of the latest in maintainability research.

WHAT IS THE COST OF MAINTENANCE?

Chapter 3 discussed the overall cost of maintenance and stated that 60% to 80% of software dollars are spent on maintenance. An analysis of what really happens in maintenance indicates that over 80% of the maintenance effort is to provide enhancements or improvements to the software (see Figure 16.1).

Thus, change will occur. Code will be modified in the operations and maintenance phase of the life cycle. Previous discussions on ACT indicated that 10% to 15% of the code will be "touched" (manipulated in some way) on an annual basis. Based on these facts, it is important to ensure that software can be changed easily.

Software maintenance costs have escalated at an alarming rate, and have outstripped development and acquisition costs. As depicted in Figure 16.2 (STSC 1992), finding errors during the operations and maintenance phase of the life cycle is the most costly. Further, the Software Engineering Institute reported that the cost to fix a line of code during

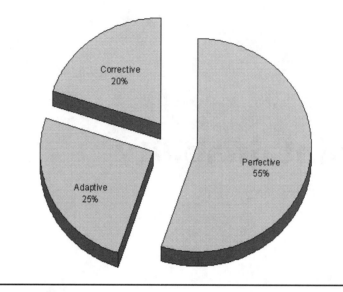

FIGURE 16.1 Percentages of maintenance effort.

the initial development was $50, while the cost to fix it during the maintenance phase is $4,000 (SEI 1991). While these two examples address finding and fixing errors, the same is true for adding enhancements. It is more costly to add enhancements (perfective and adaptive maintenance) during maintenance than during development. Clearly, software maintenance costs can be reduced if better quality systems are developed.

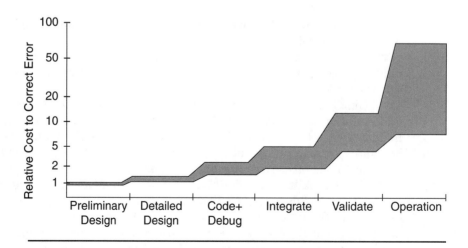

FIGURE 16.2 The penalty of delayed error correction.

Recognizing that quality is defined as "conformance to requirements" (Crosby 1979), one of the primary requirements for software systems should be to have cost-effective maintenance support. In other terms, one attribute of the quality of software systems is its maintainability, where maintainability is the ease with which software can be changed to satisfy user requirements or can be corrected when deficiencies are detected.

WHAT IS SOFTWARE MAINTAINABILITY?

Recognizing that maintainability is the ease with which software can be changed to satisfy user requirements or can be corrected when deficiencies are detected, it is important to determine how the ease can be improved. If it is easy to add, delete, and modify code, costs will decrease. The following sections provide a summary of the definitions of maintainability in circulation today, and discusses some of the issues that impact maintainability.

Software Maintainability Definitions

Government, industry, and academia are all in general agreement concerning the overall definition of maintainability. Their particular definitions include:

- The U.S. Government regards maintainability as the ease with which software can be maintained, enhanced, adapted, or corrected to satisfy specified requirements (FIPS 1984).
- The IEEE Computer Society defines maintainability as: (1) the ease with which a software system or component can be modified to correct faults, improve performance or other attributes, or adapt to a changed environment, or (2) the ease with which a hardware system or component can be retained in, or restored to, a state in which it can perform its required functions (ANSI/IEEE 610.12 1990).
- Martin and McClure (1983) characterize maintainability as the ease with which a software system can be corrected when errors or deficiencies occur and can be expanded or contracted to satisfy new requirements.
- Metrics expert Dave Card and noted software maintenance authority Bob Glass state that maintainability means that changes tend to be confined to localized areas of the system (modules) and are easy to make (Card and Glass 1990).
- The international community defines maintainability as a set of attributes that bear on the effort needed to make specified modifications (ISO/IEC 8402 1986).

■ Academia states that maintainability describes how easy it is to keep a piece of software in operation when modifications to the code become necessary. It is usually stated in terms of the time and effort required to make those changes (Von Mayrhauser 1990).

Even though these definitions differ somewhat, you can get a flavor for what maintainability is; but what things affect maintainability?

ARE ALL SYSTEMS EQUALLY MAINTAINABLE?

If you had the choice of supporting two different systems, both of which were developed in the same language and were the same size, which one would you support? Are all systems equally maintainable? If not, how can software maintenance costs be estimated accurately? If you were an outsourced maintainer, which one would be more cost-effective to maintain?

What criteria would you use to make your determination? The number of comment lines? The complexity of the code? How long would it take to make your choice?

Most organizations do not have a methodology for determining which system they would want to support. One approach is to determine which system is more maintainable. Unfortunately, most organizations do not have a methodology for determining maintainability, either. Getting back to the initial question of which of the two systems would you support, the answer is the one that is more maintainable. Why? Because it will be less costly to maintain.

HOW DOES A MAINTAINER DETERMINE MAINTAINABILITY?

In an era of shrinking resources and escalating maintenance costs, cost-effective maintenance must be performed. The maintainer must be able to determine the relative cost to support each system as it is transitioned. One approach is to determine the relative maintainability of the delivered software system. Currently, no methodology exists for most organizations to do this, and thus all delivered systems are supported using traditional, across-the-board resource estimates with no input as to the maintainability of the system. This is a poor way to approach maintainability, yet there are no standards regarding how to determine maintainability.

Why aren't there any standards for maintainability? Why aren't all systems equally maintainable? Don't developers attempt to develop maintainable systems in order to reduce life-cycle costs? The answer is *no*.

Developers' goals are to deliver a system on time and within budget. (They also strive to satisfy all contractual obligations.) Often systems are delivered that are not maintainable. Why? Because maintainability was not a stated goal of the development effort. Relatedly, a 1990 U.S. Air Force Scientific Advisory Board study (Mosemann 1992) showed that maintainability characteristics ranked somewhere around eighth or ninth out of the top ten items the USAF looks for when building software.

Maintainability must be made a goal of the acquisition effort if software life-cycle costs are to be reduced, and the level of system maintainability must be measured prior to transition.

In order to better determine software maintenance costs, maintainers should measure the maintainability of delivered systems and use the system's maintainability as a factor in determining costs. The next question is how?

IS MAINTAINABILITY POSSIBLE?

Maintainability features must be incorporated into the software development effort and be monitored throughout to reduce software maintenance costs. If this is done, the quality of maintenance of the code can actually improve (NBS 500-130 1985). However, maintainability is not currently a goal of most development efforts, nor is it a goal for most organizations (Mosemann 1992). According to DeMarco, "Rational, competent men and women can work effectively to maximize any single observed indication of success" (DeMarco 1982). Thus, if success is defined by making maintainability a goal, rational, competent people will attain it. This theory is borne out in empirical studies. If maintainability is made a goal of development, developers will produce more maintainable systems.

Currently, there is no incentive for software developers to build maintainable software systems. Cost and schedule drive developers (see the discussion on conflict in Chapter 6). The software development process must be provided incentives and maintainability must be made a goal if software life-cycle costs are to be reduced. Delaying the decision to make maintainability a goal until the operation phase of the life cycle is too late. Product quality will suffer and maintenance costs will increase.

Issues Impacting Maintainability

There are only a few factors that affect maintainability, and if any one of them is not complete, thorough, and of high quality, maintainability will suffer. Some important factors are the development process, documentation, and program comprehension.

- *Development Process.* Maintainability must be an integral part of the software development process. The techniques used must be as unobtrusive to the existing software development process as possible (Lewis and Henry 1989). The problems faced in most software maintenance organization are twofold: improving maintainability and convincing management that the greatest gain will be realized only when maintainability is engineered into software products.
- *Documentation.* In many cases, no documentation or system design specifications are available, and thus software maintenance costs are increased due to the time required for a maintainer to understand the software design prior to being able to modify software. Decisions about documentation to support delivered software are extremely important if responsibility for maintaining or upgrading the system is to be transferred to a new entity (Marciniak and Reifer 1990).
- *Program Comprehension.* Ned Chapin states "The root cause of the costly maintenance of application software is the presence of hindrances in the human understanding of existing programs and systems. These hindrances arise from three major sources: nonunderstandable, inaccurate, or insufficient information available about the program or system; complexity in either the software or the nature of the application or both; and confusion, misunderstanding, or forgetfulness about the program or system." Estimates show that programmers now spend between 47% to 62% of their time attempting to understand the documentation and logic of programs. Human understanding of documentation of programs and systems must be improved if costs are to be controlled.

The goal of maintainability must be established during the requirements, design, and development stages. Maintainability must be built into the software using standards and proven design and development techniques.

WHO IS ADDRESSING MAINTAINABILITY?

Even though there are no standards for maintainability, there are many organizations trying to address maintainability. The following subsections discuss the different approaches of various organizations. These examples can help you determine the maintainability of a system you might be supporting (Pigoski 1993).

The Federal Government

The Federal Information Processing Standard for Software Maintenance, FIPS PUB 106 (FIPS 1984), used by the National Institute of Science and Technology (NIST) and the United States Department of Defense (DoD), provides excellent advice on how to improve the main-tainability of software systems. Most importantly, it states "Maintainability of a system must be taken into consideration throughout the life cycle of the system." It further states that ". . . if the software is designed and developed initially with maintenance in mind, it can more readily be changed without impacting or degrading the effectiveness of the system. This can be accomplished if the software design is flexible, adaptable, and structured in a modular, hierarchical manner."

FIPS PUB 106 presents philosophies, procedures, and techniques to be used throughout the life cycle of a system in order to provide maintainable software. These philosophies, procedures, and techniques are divided into the four categories:

- Source code guidelines.
- Documentation guidelines.
- Coding and review techniques.
- Testing standards and procedures.

Source Code Guidelines. Source code guidelines aid maintainability by providing a structure within which systems can be developed and maintained in a common, more easily understood manner.

Documentation Guidelines. It is important to adopt a documentation standard and to then consistently enforce adherence to it for all software projects. The purpose of the documentation standard is to communicate necessary, critical information, and not to communicate all information. The best form of documentation for the maintainer is on-line documentation that has controlled access and update capabilities.

Coding and Review Techniques. The following techniques should be used when coding and reviewing:

1. Top down/bottom up approach: These approaches for design are used by some organizations to improve maintainability.
2. Peer review: This is a quality assurance method whereby code reviews are performed by programmers on other programmers' work.
3. Inspections: These are formal evaluation techniques to identify discrepancies and to measure quality (error content) of a system. The benefit of inspections is that they produce repeatable results at specified checkpoints.
4. Walk-throughs: These can range from informal to formal, unstructured to structured, and simple to full-scale. They have as their goal open dialogue among all participants.

Testing Standards and Procedures. These standards define the degree and depth of testing to be performed. Test procedures and test data should be developed by someone other than the person who performed the development or maintenance.

Although FIPS discusses many practices which impact maintainability, no clear statement of how to measure implementation of these practices and thus, maintainability, is provided.

Department of Defense (DoD)

The U.S. DoD has a new software development standard, MIL-STD-498. Like its predecessor document, DoD-STD-2167A, it does not address maintainability. However, there are maintainability efforts underway within the U.S. DoD, and these are discussed next.

Air Force (USAF)

The USAF has pursued an aggressive program since 1976 to evaluate software and to determine support requirements. The U.S. Air Force Operational Test and Evaluation Center at Kirtland AFB, New Mexico, is at the forefront of this effort to permit consistent evaluations of software supportability. A series of software supportability guidebooks were developed by the Air Force Operational Test and Evaluation Center to aid in evaluating the life-cycle process, product maintainability, and resources. The guidebooks are in a series of volumes that make up the pamphlet known as AFOTECP 800-2. Currently, there are six volumes with Volume 3, *Software Maintainability—Evaluation Guide*

(AFOTEC V3 1989), of most interest here. Software supportability evaluations focus on computer program code, supporting documentation and its implementation, computer support resources, and life-cycle process planning. Additionally, spare computing capacity is examined because of its impact on software support. Figure 16.3 (AFOTEC V2 1988) provides an overview of software supportability as viewed by the USAF.

Wiltse and McPherson (1990) provide an excellent overview of AFOTEC's software supportability program. The USAF approach is to use a structured questionnaire with optional written comments to assess the software support process. Their concept is to evaluate software support from a management viewpoint, including the "effects of procurement, development, and operational support activities." An overall software support process metric is determined, and then integrated with software product maintainability and support resources.

AFOTEC has developed and verified a software maintainability evaluation method for assessing documentation, source code listings, and their implementation. According to Wiltse and McPherson (1990), "Software maintainability is determined by measuring those characteristics of software products, software documentation and source code that affect the ability of software programmers/analysts to make changes." Standardized questionnaires, one for each piece of software

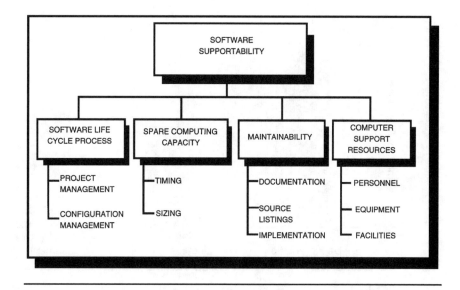

FIGURE 16.3 Elements of software supportability.

documentation, software source listing, and software evaluation are used. Standardized questionnaires are completed on 10% of the software, a representative sample.

Figure 16.4 depicts the number of questions for each type of questionnaire.

The questionnaires are designed to determine the presence or absence of certain desirable attributes in a software product. Figure 16.5 (AFOTEC V3 1989) depicts the software evaluation categories. The hierarchical evaluation structure enables an evaluator to identify potential maintainability problems by category (documentation, source listings, and implementation) or characteristic (modularity, traceability). The following list discusses each category:

■ *Documentation.* Software program documentation is the set of requirements, design specifications, guidelines, operational procedures, test information, problem reports, and other items that provide the written description of a computer program. The primary information source consists of the documents which contain program design specifications, testing information, procedures and maintenance information. The documentation is evaluated at the computer software configuration item (CSCI) level with one documentation evaluation per item. The evaluation is concerned with how well the overall program is documented for maintainability.

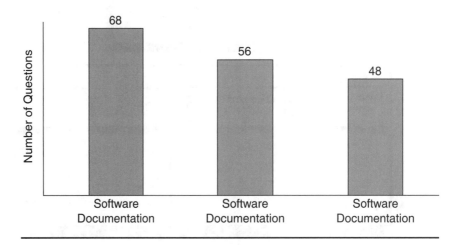

FIGURE 16.4   Summary of software maintainability questions.

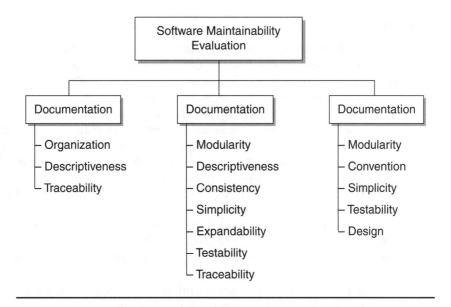

FIGURE 16.5 Software evaluation categories and characteristics.

- *Source Code.* Software source listings are the program code in source language. The listings to be evaluated are the actual compiled, assembled, and linked code. The evaluation focuses on the overall format and content of the source listings.
- *Implementation.* Implementation is the result of representing the design in the documentation and the source listings. The implementation evaluation consists of a separate evaluation after the documentation and source listing evaluation. It is conducted to yield an analysis of the overall design of the software implemented in the documentation and source code.

The AFOTEC 800-2 series is very comprehensive and requires considerable resources.

U.S. Army

Chapter 15 discussed the U.S. Army acquisition metrics program. The metrics discussed there can be used to define maintainability measures. For example, the use of the complexity metric can help maintainability. If complexity is low, maintainability increases.

Industry

Wilma M. Osborne, while at the National Institute of Science and Technology, researched the issue of building maintainable software for industry and government. She was in charge of a NIST program that produced numerous software maintenance guidelines. She states that software quality can be characterized by the attributes shown in Figure 16.6, and that the more these attributes are used in the development process, the more maintainable the system will be. As the number of software quality attributes engineered into the software during development increases, so does its maintainability (Osborne 1989).

Osborne also determined the chief causes of unmaintainable software; these causes are shown in Figure 16.7.

The key to building maintainable software is to develop and implement a program whose sole objective is achieving maintainable software. Osborne (1989) states that the program should include:

1. A plan for ensuring that maintainability requirements are specified as part of the software change design.
2. A measurement procedure to verify that maintainability goals are met.
3. A performance review to advise managers, users, and maintainers on the effectiveness of the maintainability program.

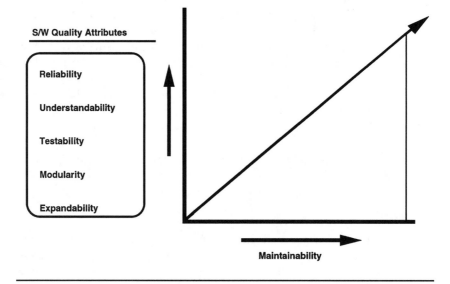

FIGURE 16.6 Osborne software quality attributes.

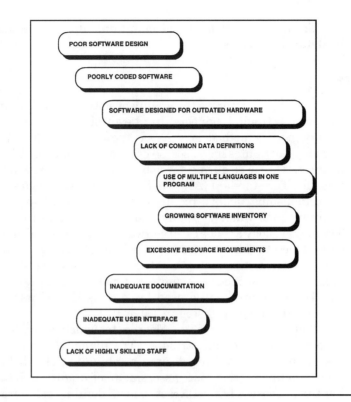

FIGURE 16.7 Chief causes of unmaintainable software.

 Software maintainability characteristics can be measured.

Maintainability must be specified as a goal during the requirements specification phase of the software life cycle. Martin and McClure (1983) state that software must be constructed so that it is:

■ Understandable.
■ Modifiable.
■ Testable.
■ Reliable.
■ Efficient.
■ Usable.
■ Portable.

These are all elements of maintainability and should be considered during delivery.

The IEEE

In an attempt to improve the quality of software, the Institute of Electrical and Electronic Engineers, Inc. developed a standard for a software quality metrics methodology. As we know from Osborne, as the number of quality attributes increases, so does maintainability. Thus, if the quality metrics are used during development, the software will be more maintainable. The standard (ANSI/IEEE 1061 1992) provides a methodology for establishing quality requirements and identifying, implementing, analyzing, and validating process and product software quality metrics. The methodology applies to all software at all phases of any software life-cycle structure. The standard is aimed at those people who are measuring or assessing the quality of software. Although the standard does not prescribe specific metrics, examples of metrics are provided.

The standard can be used by various individuals and organizations for the purposes listed in Table 16.1.

Software quality is the degree to which software possesses a desired combination of attributes. The higher the quality, the greater the maintainability. This desired combination of attributes must be clearly defined; otherwise, assessment of quality is left to intuition. For the purposes of the IEEE standard, defining software quality for a system is equivalent to defining a list of software quality attributes

TABLE 16.1   IEEE Standard Usage

Individual Organization	Use of Standard
Acquisition/ program manager	Identify, define, and prioritize the quality requirements for a system.
System developer	Identify specific traits that should be built into the software in order to meet the quality requirements.
Quality assurance/ control/audit	Evaluate whether the quality requirements are being met.
System maintainer	Assist in change management during a product evolution.
User	Assist in specifying the quality requirements for a system.

required for that system. An appropriate set of software metrics must be identified in order to measure the software quality attributes.

The purpose of software quality metrics is to make assessments throughout the software life cycle as to whether the software quality requirements are being met. The use of software metrics reduces subjectivity in the assessment of software quality by providing a quantitative basis for making decisions about software quality. The use of metrics allows an organization to:

- Achieve quality goals.
- Establish quality requirements for a system at its outset.
- Evaluate the level of quality achieved against the established requirements.
- Detect anomalies or point to potential problems in the system.
- Predict the level of quality when software is modified.
- Monitor for changes of quality when software is modified.
- Assess the ease of change to the system during product evolution.
- Normalize, scale, calibrate, or validate a metric.

The IEEE standard (ANSI/IEEE 1061 1992) defines maintainability as "an attribute that bears on the effort needed for specific modifications," and refers to maintainability as one of the "factors" of software quality. Maintainability has three subfactors, as listed in Table 16.2.

The relationship among factors, subfactors, and some metrics are depicted in Figure 16.8 (ANSI/IEEE 1061 1992). Of note is that many of the metrics are similar to those being used by the U.S. Army.

In sum, the IEEE standard provides valuable information regarding a methodology for software quality metrics and for collection of certain metrics. Use of these metrics increases quality and thereby improves maintainability. Prior to implementing any software quality program, the standard should be considered.

TABLE 16.2 Maintainability Subfactors

Subfactor	Definitions
Correctability	The degree of effort required to correct errors in software and cope with user complaints.
Expandability	The degree of effort required to improve or modify the efficiency of functions of software.
Testability	The effort required to test software.

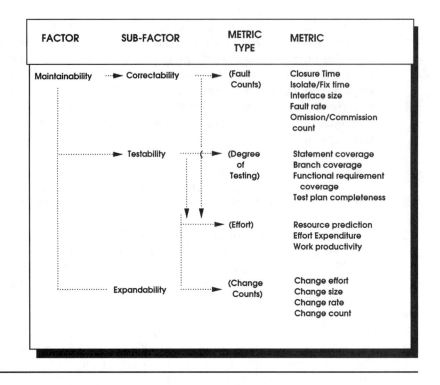

FIGURE 16.8 Relationships.

International Efforts

The international community (IEC/TC56) is working on an international standard that addresses software maintainability and dependability. As this work is still under study and subject to change, it is not referenced. Their current approach, however, is to provide guidance on the maintainability and maintenance of software. They propose to describe the implementation of a maintainability program (throughout the various phases of the life cycle) with the objective of ensuring that the resulting software can be more readily maintained and enhanced.

The basic thrust is to define a software maintainability program with emphasis on:

- The purpose and characteristics of a maintainability program.
- The contents of a maintainability program.
- Participants' responsibilities.

IEC/TC56 is attempting to address maintainability during development and maintenance. It is encouraging to see this type of effort.

Maintainers should follow the IEC/TC56 work on maintainability and use the forthcoming International Standard.

Academic Initiatives

What is academia doing in terms of maintainability? The following discussions give an overview of academia's approach.

Lewis and Henry. Researchers have long attempted to correlate quality and maintainability. Lewis and Henry (1989) state that maintainability must be integrated into the development process, but that it must be unobtrusive. Lewis and Henry describe research in which software metrics were used during multiple phases of the life cycle to monitor maintainability. They reaffirm that software quality metrics have been shown to be valuable indicators in the quantitative evaluation of software. In their research, they chose only metrics that could be automated. They divide software quality metrics into three areas:

1. Code metrics.
2. Structure metrics.
3. Hybrid metrics.

Some conclusions from their research include:

- Software quality metrics identify error-prone software, made so due to a high level of complexity.
- Maintainability is a characteristic that can be integrated into software as it is produced.

This research confirmed earlier research by Kafura and Reedy (1987) that established the link between the use of software quality metrics and the efforts of software maintenance.

Dr. Paul W. Oman at the University of Idaho. This work is primarily sponsored by Hewlett-Packard of Palo Alto, California, and is performed under the direction of Dr. Oman. More recent sponsors include the U. S. Air Force Information Warfare Center and the U. S. Department of Energy. The goal of the research is to determine how best to perform a maintainability assessment of software.

Initially, a definition and taxonomy for software maintainability were developed (Oman 1991). The research deduced that, in order to predict maintainability, either one or both of the following must exist:

1. The history of the maintenance effort must be modeled (if it exists).
2. The individual characteristics affecting that effort must be taken into account.

Oman et al. reasoned that when attempting to assess the maintainability of a software system, the attributes and characteristics of the software system and its surrounding environment must be quantified. Therefore, they defined maintainability as: "The characteristics of the software, its history, and associated environment(s) that affect the maintenance process and are indicative of the amount of effort necessary to perform maintenance changes." (Oman 1991)

Software maintainability was expressed as a hierarchical structure of complex attributes pertaining to the software system. Figure 16.9 depicts the software maintainability hierarchy defined by Oman's research.

The area that is of most interest to maintainers is the target system software. That portion of the hierarchy contains the characteristics of the software system that is to undergo maintenance. It is divided into:

- Maturity attributes.
- Source code.
- Supporting documentation.

Figure 16.10 (Oman 1992) provides the details of the source code subtree.

The University of Idaho research has progressed to the point where a prototype implementation of the software maintainability principles

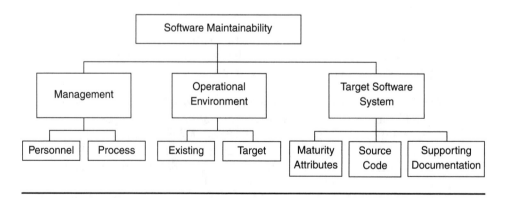

FIGURE 16.9 Software maintainability hierarchy.

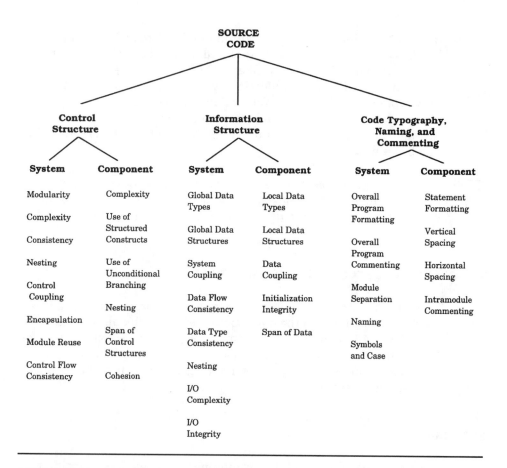

FIGURE 16.10   Source code maintainability attributes.

and metrics previously defined was developed. The prototype, called the HP Maintainability Assessment System (HP-MAS), provides a means of gauging the maintainability of source code. The University of Idaho research acknowledged that many factors influence maintainability, but that all previous research indicated that the predominant factor was the source code itself. Thus, an effort was put forth to build HP-MAS to assess software maintainability based on features of the source program. Currently, prototypes exist for C and Pascal language programs. Future work will concentrate on the maturity attributes and supporting documentation.

This and related efforts at the University of Idaho have pushed to quantify maintainability. Several polynomial regression models were defined that predict software maintainability (Oman 1992; Oman and Hagemeister 1994; Zhu 1993). As stated in one of the more recent articles about maintainability (Welker 1995) these models use some combination of predictor variables in a polynomial equation to define a *maintainability index* (MI). Welker (1995) and Oman applied the models to actual maintenance processes. The models now include a comments-to-code ratio as part of maintainability. This work is continuing and bears watching.

The University of Idaho Software Engineering Test Laboratory research is attempting to quantify maintainability. Maintainers should follow this work closely. This is the most current and comprehensive research in the area of maintainability.

WHAT ARE SOME RECOMMENDED PRACTICES?

There are a number of generally accepted good practices which, when used, will contribute to the development of maintainable software.

Figure 16.11 provides a summary of practices recommended for development and maintenance. These practices, when coupled with an aggressive software quality metrics program, can help bring about more maintainable software.

SUMMARY

Research regarding program comprehension and the transition of large software systems indicates that the source code is the single most important item for the maintenance organization. Areas such as documentation, resources, and support environments are intuitively important, but in many instances they are hard to quantify. Code can be measured. Code can be made more maintainable. It has been proven that maintainers always want current code, in many cases because the documentation is out of date or not available. If the source code can be made maintainable and is measurable, then software maintenance costs can decrease.

Maintainability improves as the number of software quality attributes increase. Software quality can be characterized by many attributes. Martin and McClure use seven different attributes. Oman uses numerous attributes. The USAF uses 192 questions. The U.S. Army boils it down to twelve metrics. The IEEE provides three subfactors for

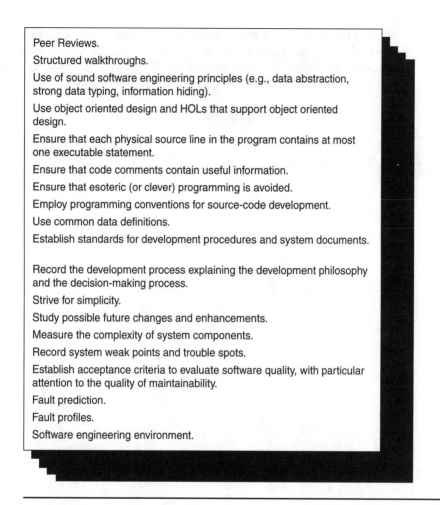

Peer Reviews.

Structured walkthroughs.

Use of sound software engineering principles (e.g., data abstraction, strong data typing, information hiding).

Use object oriented design and HOLs that support object oriented design.

Ensure that each physical source line in the program contains at most one executable statement.

Ensure that code comments contain useful information.

Ensure that esoteric (or clever) programming is avoided.

Employ programming conventions for source-code development.

Use common data definitions.

Establish standards for development procedures and system documents.

Record the development process explaining the development philosophy and the decision-making process.

Strive for simplicity.

Study possible future changes and enhancements.

Measure the complexity of system components.

Record system weak points and trouble spots.

Establish acceptance criteria to evaluate software quality, with particular attention to the quality of maintainability.

Fault prediction.

Fault profiles.

Software engineering environment.

FIGURE 16.11   Recommended practices.

maintainability: correctability, testability, and expandability. Finally, Osborne uses five attributes of software quality: reliability, understand-ability, testability, modularity, and expandability. Many of the attributes overlap; however, there is consensus that as more software quality attributes are engineered into the software during development, so is maintainability. Maintainers need to influence development to ensure that systems are maintainable. Remember *all* the discussions in earlier chapters regarding predelivery involvement? One of the most important things a maintainer can do in predelivery is to influence maintainability The University of Idaho research indicates that the source code is the predominant factor in maintainability. Standards for maintainability are needed and they should be geared to the source code.

1. Why is maintainability difficult to do?

2. How do you address maintainability in your organization?

3. How can you make maintainability easier?

Software Maintenance Management

There are many management issues that relate to software maintenance; they are not unlike those found in other technical organizations. The one primary issue that software maintainers often face is a lack of understanding and support by corporate management. The stories of low morale and feelings of underappreciation are legendary. Maintainers have, for years, felt like second-class citizens. Somehow, the fact that 60% to 80% of life-cycle dollars go to maintenance has not had an impact. The unglamorous support job of maintenance is necessary (even critical) to corporate success, but still there is no recognition of the maintainers. Back in 1983, Nicholas Zvegintzov stated that maintenance soon would be a respectable profession. Unfortunately, it has not happened. Maintenance is still in the background—misunderstood and unappreciated.

Why? Little things like "lumping" problem reports and enhancement requests together (see Chapter 2) foster the notion that maintenance is fixing bugs. The fact is, many people, including corporate management, do not understand that 80% of maintenance is enhancements.

What are the problems in maintenance? This chapter addresses some of the common problems in maintenance and offers some suggestions for attacking the problems.

WHO ARE THE SOFTWARE MAINTENANCE PROFESSIONALS?

Who are the software professionals? They are the ones that carry the weight of the world around on their shoulders. They are us. And what about the software maintenance professional or practitioner? Who is he or she? Unfortunately, we are the ones with the scars. We're the pioneers, the ones out on the front line, we're the ones taking all the heat. The developers are the heroes. The users often say "Look what the developer gave to me—at first I had nothing and look what I've got now. It's wonderful! The maintenance people, they just take so long, and they're so expensive!" That is what we have to contend with, and it sure is not good for our morale.

WHAT DO YOU THINK ARE THE MAJOR PROBLEMS IN MAINTENANCE?

Shouldn't we ask the users what they think the problems are? Certainly. Succinctly, they view maintenance as expensive, slow, and "software for software's sake" (not done for the sake of any corporate good). Hopefully through metrics and the like those issues can be addressed, and users can be educated as to what maintenance really is all about; but what about us? What are our gripes? What are the problems facing you as a maintenance practitioner? Take a few moments and list the top five problems that you face as a software maintenance practitioner (Table 17.1).

Does anyone ask you what your problems are? Does anyone ask us as a group (the software maintenance practitioners of the world) what our problems are? Fortunately, yes.

WHAT ARE THE TOP MAINTENANCE PROBLEMS?

Sasa Deklava (1992) of DePaul University conducted surveys over the past few years at the International Conference on Software Maintenance and at the Annual Meeting and Conference of the Software Management Association. Though the surveys are not statistically significant, the data

TABLE 17.1 Top Five Problems in Software Maintenance

1.

2.

3.

4.

5.

TABLE 17.2 Major Problems in Software Maintenance

Rank	Description of Problem
1	Changing Priorities
2	Inadequate Testing Methods
3	Performance Measurement Difficulties
Tie	System Documentation Incomplete or Nonexistent
5	Adapting to the Rapidly Changing Business Environment
6	Large Backlog
7	Contribution Measurement Difficulties
8	Low Morale Due to the Lack of Recognition and Respect
Tie	Lack of Maintenance Personnel, Particularly Experienced Maintainers
10	Lack of Maintenance Methodology, Standards, Procedures, and Tools
11	Program Code Is Complex and Unstructured
12	Integration of Overlapping and Incompatible Systems or Subsystems
Tie	Maintainers Lack Proper Training
Tie	Strategic Plans
15	Understanding and Responding to Business Needs
16	Lack of Managerial Understanding and Support
17	Antiquated Systems and Technology
18	Lack of Support for Reengineering
19	High Turnover Causing a Loss of Expertise

come from people at maintenance conferences, people that care about maintenance—maintenance practitioners. Dr. Deklava collected data, categorized the major problems in maintenance, and then ranked all of these problems. Table 17.2 provides a rank and a description of the problems.

Take a look at some of the 19 problems and then look at the associated ranking. The number one problem is changing priorities, followed by inadequate testing methods, performance measurement difficulties, contribution measurement difficulties, low morale, lack of experienced people—you have probably encountered all of these. How does this list compare with your top five? Hopefully you addressed the same issues, even if you did not rank them in the same manner. The rank is not nearly as important as the problems. The next few subsections discuss some of the worst problems, and give practical solutions to those problems.

Inexperienced People

One problem identified was the lack of experienced people. I'll start with this problem because of its ripple effect. The perception among those surveyed is that there is a lack of experienced people in the field of software maintenance. Think about your organization. Who's doing the maintenance? What are the demographics? Who are these people in your maintenance organization? This area has been studied by Swanson and Beath (1989). They found that nearly 25% of the people doing maintenance are students! Of the people working in the maintenance industry, up to 61% were new hires.

So why is there a lack of experienced people? We do it to ourselves. We hire students and stick them in maintenance. Recently some maintenance practitioners asked me, "Isn't it a good idea to use students—to grow them?" It certainly is, but why not in development too? Why not a more equitable distribution of the resources? Here is where corporate management must help. They ought to look at this disparity in allocation of resources and correct it. Maybe maintenance is not viewed by corporate management as being that important, and thus it can be staffed with students and new hires? Think about it.

The lack of experienced people is a problem in software maintenance and corporate management needs to address it. Maintenance is staffed primarily by students and new hires. Of course the new hires are inexperienced. Why is it that maintenance has so many new hires? All the good jobs go to the developers. When Sally Software Engineer from Stanford graduates, you say "Sally, how would you like a job? It's in maintenance." Sally naturally says that she will take the job, and to herself says that she'll take it, and after a year try to get out of maintenance and into a real job—like development. The fact is that maintenance is being performed by rookies.

Practical Experience

What about other data? Is there other data to corroborate Swanson and Beath's findings? Although not as scientific as that of Swanson and Beath, I collected random data from my travels teaching, consulting, and interviewing various people. What I have seen is 60% to 80% of the maintenance staff is newly hired software engineers at most organizations.

A Solution to Inexperienced People

What is the solution? What can be done to solve this particular problem? We could have career paths for our software engineering people. A career path might be:

■ Put them at a help desk first.
■ Then do maintenance for a while.
■ Then let them go to development.

Another path might be to perform development before maintenance. Still another alternative is a career path within the maintenance field. You probably need some more incentives to get this to work. Who currently receives the cutting-edge technologies? The developers. Who is the last to get them? The maintainers. Incentives like providing the latest tools and training to the maintainers are nice, but are very hard to implement. They cost money. We need a simpler answer than new career fields or more money.

Why don't we just change the qualifications for people coming into maintenance? Every organization has job descriptions of some kind in an organization or human resources manual. Suppose the job qualifications for a software engineer going into a maintenance position required that he or she have a degree. If the human resource department is doing its job, it hires a new graduate. Your maintenance organization ends up with some 60–80% of its people as new hires. Couldn't the job description be changed to say that for this maintenance position, software development engineers with five years of development experience are required? Or two years software maintenance experience? Or four years in the Army? *Or something?* If 60–80% of the people in maintenance are new hires and the problem is inexperienced people, perhaps the job description should be changed so that maintenance can get experienced people.

Naturally, it is not as simple as that. These increased qualifications must be justified to corporate management, because they directly relate to increased costs. The greater the qualifications, the greater the costs. Again, corporate management must appreciate the need for experienced maintainers.

Maintenance Training

What are the other issues that relate to this lack of experience? Let's talk about these raw recruits some more. They go into the school house, go into the university, and they come to us like babes in the woods. Why? Because they don't know anything about maintenance. They might be great software engineers or developers, but as we talked about before, they are inexperienced. Further, as mentioned at the very beginning of the book, universities do not teach maintenance. DeKlava identified the lack of proper training as a problem for maintainers. The next chapter addresses training in detail but, for now, just recognize that there is a lack of training for maintainers.

Thus far two problems have been addressed. One is the inexperienced people and the other is the lack of training. Guess what happens as a result of those two problems? People leave, and now there is a high turnover problem.

High Turnover

When Sally Software Engineer from Stanford leaves, high turnover and staffing problems result. How are they solved? New recruits are hired fresh out of the university. They don't know anything about maintenance, and the cycle continues. However, there is another factor that also results in high turnover.

When newly graduated software engineers are hired to perform maintenance, they are just pleased to have any kind of a job. They are in maintenance, which is not what they really wanted, but nonetheless it is a job and a start. That's the bad news—they are in maintenance. Then it gets worse. Sally has this nice four-year degree and then what happens? She is told, although she is in maintenance, that she will not analyze, design or code, will not trace problems, and will not design software solutions or enhancements. She is assigned to do software configuration management, where she can track trouble reports, perform version control, and maintain software baselines. Or even better, she is assigned as a tester of somebody else's software. These are some of the things that are done to the new people, and it drives them away. The inexperienced people do not want to be in maintenance, and then things get worse by giving them jobs in software configuration management or testing. We must recognize what their training is in—it is in development. They want to design and code solutions.

The new recruits are inexperienced, and maintenance training is not provided. The problem is compounded further by assigning them to functional areas that for which they are not suited. The wrong type of person is forced into the wrong type of job. Guess what happens? They leave, and again there are turnover and staffing problems.

A Solution to High Turnover

What's the solution? Just like a job description can be changed to make sure experienced people are hired into maintenance, job descriptions for certain fields like software configuration management and testing can be changed to ensure that people who want to perform those functions are hired into them. Maybe all those degrees are not required for certain jobs. Maybe for an area like testing, people with heavy domain knowledge (such as operators and users of the system) can be hired and trained to be testers? For a payroll system, maybe we should get an accountant who is hired and taught the aspects of a computer, as opposed to vice versa? To track problem reports and enhancement requests, people with a master's degree are not needed. Maybe the managers of the world need to find people who want to do those things. Maybe the job descriptions need to be changed. Thus, when people are hired they can be placed in the correct slot, and maybe they won't leave.

Contribution Measurement Difficulties

Another problem is a misunderstanding of what software maintenance practitioners actually do. What do software maintenance practitioners do? How are their contributions to the corporate good measured? How do they contribute to the overall corporate or agency effort? The maintenance practitioners' contribution to the overall effort is not understood. The users think it is fixing bugs. They believe that if better systems are built, there is no need for maintenance; thus the software maintenance practitioners contribution is misunderstood. It's not understood because it is not measured.

Why isn't the contribution measured? Most software maintenance organizations don't have the data. They don't have the metrics. They don't have the empirical data from which to tell the rest of the organization what the maintenance practitioners are contributing. Many software maintenance organizations still do not discriminate among corrective, adaptive, and perfective maintenance (see Chapter 2). They are their own worst enemies. Without the proper data, their contributions can never be measured.

Many organizations track modification requests, problem reports, or enhancement requests. On a pure numbers basis, these modification requests might break down to 50% corrective and 50% enhancement, but on an effort or dollar basis, the corrective changes take 20% of the budget, versus enhancements, which take 80%. Unfortunately, the procedures are set up by the organization to perpetuate the notion that maintenance is merely fixing bugs. It's not a problem unique to maintenance; it is on the developmental side, too. As many systems are being acquired, the software configuration management procedures do not identify the modification requests as corrections or enhancements. That must be changed. Maintainers need to let the other parts of the corporation know what their contributions are. To do that, maintainers must measure contributions and disseminate that data.

A Solution to Contribution Measurement

Maintainers must tell everyone about the new functionality added in a new release, the fact that a reduced inventory is possible because of an information system improvement, and so forth. Maintainers need to tell management that because of the enhancement of the code by maintenance, the latest software release lets the corporation process transactions three times faster than before. Because of the latest software release, the corporation now has on-line banking, giving a competitive edge in the marketplace. Because of the latest software release, system availability is increased some 10%, allowing the corporation to serve more customers. These are the kinds of things that maintainers must ensure that corporate management acknowledges.

Remember Ross Perot in the 1992 U.S. presidential election? He used charts and diagrams to discuss metrics in relation to the state of the U.S. Maintainers need to do the same thing. Metrics for a maintainer are extremely important.

 Maintainers must have maintenance metrics, and they need to share that data with the users and corporate management.

Low Morale

Another problem for software maintenance practitioners is low morale. Maintainers feel that they are not recognized for their contributions.

How should software maintenance practitioners be recognized? How can morale be improved? Joanne Sexton did a study on motivating software maintenance people in the late 1980s. She determined that motivating software maintenance practitioners is no different than motivating other professionals.

A Solution to Low Morale

You need to be creative and spontaneous. Do simple things, like let maintainers go to conferences and seminars. Encourage them to publish. Attendance at conferences and the joy of seeing their practical, job-related experiences published certainly improves morale. Software maintenance practitioners often believe that they do not have anything worthwhile to share in the form of a publication; that is simply not true. For years, the International Conference on Software Maintenance has solicited experience reports from practitioners. Unfortunately, very few submissions result. However, at the critiques of the conference, the attendees constantly ask for more experience reports. A good way to improve morale and self-worth is to help the maintenance practitioners get published.

Large Backlogs

What about the large backlog? Is that a problem at your organization? The backlog never ends. The users always see the maintainer with a backlog and that low priorities somehow never seem to get finished by the maintainer. The software maintenance practitioners view this as a never-ending problem—something they can't solve.

A Solution to Large Backlogs

How can that be changed? What's a good solution? What if there wasn't a backlog? Some maintainers might be out of work, so keep that in mind, but what can be done if there is a backlog of 80 modification requests, and current resources will not eliminate the backlog anytime in the near future?

One way is to deal with modification requests on a release-to-release basis by the use of short-term contracts with maintenance people. The configuration control board (CCB) can help with this. If an active CCB with the users in charge is in operation, the software maintenance practitioners should not be deciding their workload. Typically, the user provides the funding and resources. In the case of an outsource maintenance organization, this arrangement is even more obvious. The user tells the maintainer what to work on, and which items of the large backlog they consider important enough to go in the next release. The users ensure that their highest priority requirements get approved by the CCB and included in the next release. The maintainer is merely a service agency, and uses the short term contract, that is, what goes in the next release, and does not worry about the overall backlog.

The outgrowth of every configuration control board meeting should be marching orders for the next release. All the world-class maintenance organizations, the heroes like Canadian National Railroads, firmly believe in scheduled releases. They work. That's what maintainers need to do. If the CCB says that you need to do these eight enhancements and these three corrections in your next release, go forth and produce. Don't worry about the backlog, that's either the CCB's problem or the software maintenance manager's problem. It should not be a problem for most of the software maintenance practitioners.

Another way to handle the backlog is to use the student population. Use of co-op students and the like can help lessen the backlog. This might seem like heresy, but an approach that works is to bring in some low-cost students and have them work the low-priority items. (Try not to have them be 25% of your workforce.) I've done that, and gotten my wrists slapped a few times for working on items not approved by the CCB, but it did help my training program and did get some low-priority items completed that I would never have resolved.

But wait a minute! What about this term *backlog*? When discussing the large backlog, there are all kinds of negative connotations. Backlog is an inherently negative word. Maybe the word backlog should be changed. Maybe the word backlog needs to be deleted from the maintenance vocabulary.

One of the attendees at my maintenance tutorial (at ICSM-95) said that a big thrust in Europe is to get rid of the term "backlog." Their approach is to use the term "orders," as in "orders received." Users are

---

Practical Experience

At a Navy software maintenance organization, the concept of short-term contracts was used. The maintainers would only be concerned with the 10–15 modification requests to be implemented in the next release. They did not worry about the large backlog. Morale and productivity improved through use of these contracts.

buying something—maintenance, in the form of corrections and enhancements—and the maintainer is satisfying the orders. It is an interesting concept and certainly one that has potential. So please, stop using the term backlog. Say "How many orders have you received?" You can respond, "We have five orders for corrections and seven orders for enhancements."

Consider using "orders" instead of backlog.

The term backlog should be changed. Delete it from the maintenance vocabulary. Please keep in mind that if maintainers had zero backlog (orders), they'd all be out of work, so maybe a backlog (or sizable list of orders) is not such a bad thing after all. This European concept bears watching to see how the software maintenance practitioners respond to it.

Changing Priorities

What can be done about changing priorities? This was the number-one problem identified in Deklava's surveys. Maintainers are working on one thing—and then are told to work on something else. In discussions with other practitioners throughout the world, there is consensus that changing priorities is a problem, but for many it is not the number-one priority.

A Solution to Changing Priorities

The answer to this problem is scheduled releases. There are always real problems that must be addressed almost immediately; you will never totally get away from these. However, organizations without scheduled releases, strong configuration control boards, and strong configuration control procedures are beset with changing priorities. If the users are firmly in charge of the configuration control board (and they should be) and they are the ones funding the maintenance effort, this should not be a big problem. Strong, effective SCM practices and scheduled releases tend to nullify changing priorities.

No Maintenance Process

Another pet peeve of the software maintenance practitioner is the lack of a software maintenance methodology, standards, procedures, and tools. Some organizations do have these methodologies and procedures. Yet, recent studies have shown that some 50% to 60% of organizations have methodologies and procedures but don't use them. Maybe the practitioners don't know they exist. (That sounds like a management problem.)

A Solution to No Maintenance Process

A documented process is very important. It is important to write down your process, whatever it is (see Chapter 5). Refine it and have lots of involvement. If maintainers want to facilitate the training of new, inexperienced hires, introduce them to the maintenance process. If it is not documented, document it and use it as a training aid.

SUMMARY

It must be recognized that maintenance is a part of software engineering. Software engineering does not have the history of civil engineers, but it is an engineering discipline. In order to be successful, software engineering (including maintenance) must address the process of engineering just like manufacturers address their process. Plus, the particular problems of the software maintenance practitioners must be addressed, as well as how maintenance practitioners are viewed by the users and customers. Very often I use the analogy of how the Japanese view the American baseball players: They are expensive, cumbersome, and they break down. That's how the users and customers view software, and by extension the software maintenance practitioners. Look over Deklava's list. How many of these issues can you solve in your organization? The list is a good place to start.

1. What are three of your pet peeves about software maintenance and where do they rank on Deklava's list?

2. Think about solutions to the three pet peeves you list.

3. Where would you put a software engineering new hire in your organization? Why?

Education
and Training

18

Software maintenance is an important aspect of software engineering, and the education of a software engineer is not complete without education and training in software maintenance. However, neither industry nor academia are addressing this issue adequately. Industry does not teach maintenance to its new recruits or new hires; industry relies on academia. Except for a few isolated cases, academia is not teaching maintenance. The burden rests on the maintainer.

This chapter provides a summary of what is happening (or not happening) in the area of maintenance education and training. It also provides suggestions on how and what to include in a maintenance education program. Practical experiences in the teaching of maintenance at the university level are also provided. Finally, some suggestions regarding training are provided.

In this chapter, education refers to providing the concepts, background information, and general knowledge needed by a maintainer to function in maintenance. Normally education would be provided by a university or formal corporate education program. Training is the providing of specialized instruction in fairly specific maintenance skills. As examples, training would be provided:

- To become familiar with a new system, software product, or software.
- To introduce a maintainer's process.
- To learn to use a specific CASE tool.

WHERE DO MAINTAINERS TRADITIONALLY GET EDUCATED AND TRAINED?

How are maintenance people educated and trained? How are they educated and trained at your organization? There are only a few ways to educate and train people to perform software maintenance:

- College or university.
- Corporate education.
- Seminars/tutorials.
- On-the-job training.

What about college or university education? It doesn't exist for maintenance. Except for a few isolated places, like the University of Durham in the United Kingdom or the University of West Florida in Pensacola, software maintenance is not taught. Universities offering a software engineering curriculum emphasize software development. If maintenance is taught, it is usually only as a one-semester course. When you consider how much money is spent on maintenance, and how many of the new hires go into maintenance, it is a crime that the primary resource for software maintenance does not educate for software maintenance. However, within the past year some progress has been made. The University of Maryland and the University of Montreal are now teaching maintenance. There seems to be much greater interest in teaching maintenance at the university level than ever before.

What about software maintenance education at the corporate level? There are many companies with extensive software engineering education programs. Some of the larger U.S. companies have up to 12-week programs. However, a review of the curriculum reveals that they do not teach maintenance; they teach development. They build on the development training provided at the university level and tailor it to their corporate needs. They don't teach new hires how to find an error, or understand a 1M LOC system. Clearly 60% to 80% of the new hires go into maintenance—but corporations don't teach them maintenance. Maintenance is where all the money and people need to go, and corporations don't have any kind of corporate maintenance education or training program.

If the universities do not teach maintenance and corporations do not teach it, what's left? The only other avenue is a seminar or tutorial. Over the years Nicholas Zvegintzov, Norm Schneidewind, Ned Chapin, and I have taught software maintenance at the International Conference on Software Maintenance (ICSM) and other venues. For years, Zvegintzov taught two seminars a year for Technology Trans-

fer, Inc. If you look at the catalogs of the companies providing general computer education, there is nothing on maintenance. For now the best bet is a tutorial at ICSM, although neither those tutorials nor a few two–three day seminars are sufficient to provide the needed maintenance education.

So how do maintainers get educated in maintenance? Typically, maintenance education is not provided, but maintenance training *is* provided through on-the-job training. Even organizations at CMM Level 5 (see Chapter 4) use on-the-job training as the primary training means; these organizations pair up new people with a mentor. At U.S. Navy maintenance organizations, it is accomplished the same way; just place someone on the job and have him or her learn from the others on the job.

HOW DOES INDUSTRY TRAIN ITS SOFTWARE PROFESSIONALS?

Today's software maintenance people typically come from a traditional computer science curriculum but, in some cases, with a software engineering specialization. As a result, the typical graduate has not been introduced to team efforts, presentation making, technical writing, and interpersonal skills. Some large companies are addressing these issues by development of company-wide, specialized training for new software hires. At the Software Engineering Research Forum in 1991 (Rodriguez 1991), a representative of a large communications company stated that there was a training plan for each new hire. All the items mentioned above were taught; however, maintenance was barely touched in the corporate curriculum. The representative also stated that 70–75% of the new hires go into maintenance. A large data services organization also discussed a lengthy indoctrination program for new hires. Again, maintenance was not taught, and 80–85% of their new hires go into maintenance.

Although a majority of new hires go into maintenance and not development, corporate training programs do not address software maintenance.

WHO IS TEACHING THE SOFTWARE PROFESSIONALS?

The typical computer science curriculum with a major in software engineering teaches software engineering concepts, but does not require a class in maintenance. Further, very few universities even offer a course in maintenance. Although the Software Engineering Institute (SEI) at Carnegie Mellon does teach maintenance as part of the graduate software engineering curriculum (Ford 1991), only four hours are devoted to the topic.

Girish Parikh (1986) first addressed this deficiency by stating that he was yet to find a Computer Science, Software Engineering, or Management of Information Systems/Data Processing curriculum that includes software maintenance as a required course. Bob Glass, as the keynote speaker of the Conference on Software Maintenance-1988, chastised computer science professors when he stated that academia teaches compilers and software engineering but nothing about maintaining software.

Unfortunately, not much has changed in the 1990s. Capers Jones (1994) states that poor software training results in canceled projects, long schedules, low productivity, low quality, missed schedules, and technical staff malpractice. In addition, Jones states that inadequate software engineering curricula itself can be traced to the problems of inadequate measurement, inaccurate metrics, and slow technology transfer. The fact that few universities teach appropriate courses to solve these problems perpetuates the problem of inexperienced people and high maintenance costs.

There are a few individuals who have taught maintenance. Parikh first taught maintenance at DePaul University in the mid-1980s. Later, the SEI developed an Ada artifact and materials useful for teaching maintenance (Engel 1989). A review of this very valuable teaching package for maintenance was provided by Zvegintzov (1990). Linda Rising taught a course at Purdue, and successfully implemented the Ada artifact using the SEI materials (Zvegintzov 1990a). Chuck Engel, who was instrumental in developing the Ada artifact and related software maintenance exercises, taught maintenance as part of the Florida Institute of Technology's undergraduate software engineering curriculum (Newman 1991).

Where is maintenance taught? The University of Durham (U. K. collocated with the Centre for Software Maintenance) has been at the forefront of maintenance education and research for years. Dr. Norman Wilde of the University of West Florida has been teaching maintenance since 1990. Lately, the University of Maryland (University College) and the University of Montreal have started teaching maintenance.

The U.S. Air Force (USAF) has recognized this deficiency and addressed it by establishing a course called "Software Generation and Maintenance (SGM)" at the Air Force Institute of Technology at Wright Patterson AFB, Dayton, Ohio (Cardow 1992). The USAF found that it was necessary to teach maintenance, as it was not taught by academia to any large degree. Topics taught in the SGM course include

Introduction to Maintenance, Change Process, Maintainability Analysis, Re-engineering, Maintenance Management, Preventive Maintenance, Software Development Environments (maintenance), and there is a course project.

Howerton (1992) provides details of the activities of four major professional societies that promote curricula development. These societies (the Association for Computing Machinery (ACM), the Data Processing Management Association, the Software Engineering Institute, and the ACM-IEEE curriculum advisory boards) are responsible for the creation of the modern computing curricula. Howerton's analysis of the curriculum recommendations from these organizations concludes that software maintenance is not a primary topic in the principal computing curricula.

That essentially is the state of software maintenance education: There's not much. There is a lack of materials (text books and artifacts) at the university level, and corporate education does not address maintenance.

HOW DO YOU SOLVE THE LACK OF SOFTWARE MAINTENANCE EDUCATION PROBLEM?

How can the problem of a lack of software maintenance education be solved? What is the solution? What do we as software maintenance practitioners do about the problem? We can influence the universities to teach software maintenance in their software engineering curriculum. We can send research funding to the universities and guide their research and teaching in the area of maintenance. We need to be the solution to the problem. What if we cannot get the universities to respond? What if we cannot find a research-minded professor who wants to teach maintenance? *Go teach it yourself.* For now, suffice it to say that there is a problem and we, the software maintenance practitioners, are part of the solution.

If you can't influence a university, or you don't have one nearby, influence corporate education from within. Start a corporate program. What would you teach?

- The history of maintenance.
- How much maintenance costs.
- How users perceive maintenance.
- How to collect empirical data.
- What maintenance process to use.
- Introduction to maintenance metrics.
- How to do maintenance.

Practical Experience

Software maintenance practitioners need to teach maintenance. I wanted the people working with me to be trained before they came to work; I wanted to set up a pipeline of educated maintenance people.

So what did I do? I taught maintenance at the university level. I did it twice, first with C and then with Ada. I set up teams of programmers, testers, SCM people, and documentation groups. I provided large segments of C and Ada code for them to search for problems. I made them write test plans. I made them set up the software maintenance process. I made them work in groups. They didn't like performing in groups very much. Gee, that's too bad, guess what happens when they graduate—60% to 80% go into maintenance groups. Those who came to work with me were knowledgeable about maintenance *before* they came to work with me, and are among the small percentage of new hires with an understanding of maintenance.

Calliss and Calliss (1992) has a good paper on how to set up a corporate maintenance education program.

Software maintenance practitioners should teach maintenance.

Practical Experience

When I set up the U.S. Navy software maintenance organization in Pensacola, I set up a type of corporate education program (Pigoski and Looney 1993) for maintenance. All we did was maintenance. Our people didn't have the experience, and existing Navy education training did not provide maintenance education and training. The program consisted of lectures on what maintenance is, its history, activities, etc. We executed the process, did sample tasks, did code comprehension, did code analysis, and fixed low-priority items. All of these were part of our corporate education and training program.

What Do You Teach for Maintenance?

What do you teach? It depends on your goals. Teaching in a university setting is a little different than teaching for corporate education, but not much. If you assume that the audience for maintenance education is basically inexperienced software engineers, and you know that they are the ones performing maintenance, three primary goals come to mind:

- Teach maintenance concepts.
- Foster the team concept.
- Prepare the students to enter the maintenance workforce.

Topics to be taught by way of lectures include:

- Overview of software maintenance.
- Why maintenance is expensive.
- Evolution of software processes and models.
- Life-cycle models.
- Overview of a maintenance model.
- Predelivery maintenance.
- Maintenance planning.
- Transition.
- Detailed maintenance processes.
- Maintenance organization: roles, responsibilities, functions.
- Maintenance tools and environment.
- Maintenance metrics.
- Maintainability.

If you teach the above, you will provide comprehensive coverage of the topic of maintenance and will provide maintenance education. However, most often when maintenance is taught, the focus is on the code and code fixing. This is really training. A better approach if time is a consideration is to discuss the maintenance process without any discussion of how maintenance fits into the life cycle. Thus, the short version would focus on:

- Definition of maintenance.
- Maintenance organization: roles, responsibilities, functions.
- Detailed maintenance processes.

Capers Jones (1994) discusses the problem of inadequate curricula for software engineering and provides his views on what a modern software engineering curriculum at the university level should include. He recommends that the "Maintenance and Enhancement of Aging Software" be taught. He argues that more than half of the programmers and software engineers (in the United States) work in maintenance, and that university courses are seldom offered. Jones states that students should be taught software entropy, and the specialized tools and methods needed to keep aging software working. These methods include complexity analysis, restructuring, reverse engineering, and re-engineering. Jones' requirements could be satisfied under the lab exercises for detailed maintenance processes mentioned above.

How Do You Teach Maintenance?

Regardless of which list of topics is used, it is very important to have a large chunk of code for the students to work on. This is often a problem. The Software Engineering Institute's (SEI) artifact, "Software Maintenance Exercises for a Software Engineering Project Course" (Engle 1989) provides 10K LOC and software maintenance exercises. The exercises even include modification of a sample software configuration management plan! Even if your organization does not use Ada extensively, you can still use it to teach maintenance. The language might be different from the ones you use, but the concepts are the same. The other approach is to get over 10K LOC and develop the exercises yourself.

What kinds of exercises do you need? According the Zvegintzov (1990), SEI uses three types of exercises:

1. *Bring the system up*. Load and edit documentation, develop the SCM plan (what the source will be named, where it will be kept, and who may change it), load and compile the software, run it on the test suite, make the documentation reflect the current platform, and comply with standards.
2. *Error correction*. A total of six exercises are provided. They address three corrective maintenance actions, a compile error, dead code, and code review.
3. *Functional enhancement*. Seven exercises for enhancements and improving the user interface are provided.

If you develop your own exercises, you need to address all aspects of maintenance. Documentation must be generated and maintained. Code must be corrected and improved. The SEI artifact and exercises provide good samples and are worth looking at even if you develop your own material.

Review the SEI teaching package for maintenance.

How Do You Conduct the Maintenance Class?

Once you have the artifact and exercises taken care of, attention must turn to how the class will be conducted. What do you do on day one? Do you start the lectures? Do you start exercising the process? How long will it take to get to the code modification section? How can you start exercising the process when the students do not know the process? What are the test people doing while the programmers are performing impact analysis?

As with a real maintenance organization, the scheduling is difficult. How do you account for the inherent time delays in the process? What do some of the students do (like the testers) while they wait for code to test? Have the students write term or technical papers that relate to maintenance. Further, the papers should relate to the functional area that they are working in for the maintenance class.

Have students write papers on maintenance topics.

In What Order Should You Teach Things? A suggested chronology of events is:

- Organize the team.
- Teach maintenance concepts.
- Have students present papers to reinforce concepts.
- Start exercising group functions, including SCM, test, QA and programming.
- Exercise the maintenance process.

Organize the team. The first action is to divide the class into functional groups as follows:

- Programming.
- Testing.
- Quality assurance
- Software configuration management.

The instructor should serve as the head of the software maintenance group and coordinate all maintenance efforts. It is difficult to

TABLE 18.1 Organization of a Maintenance Class

Group	Number of People
Programming	5
Quality Assurance	1
Configuration Management	3
Test	3
Class Size	12

determine who should go into which functional area. Develop an organizational chart. Ten to twelve students is an ideal number for teaching maintenance. With larger numbers, it gets difficult to allocate work to all the students. Table 18.1 provides the organization chart and a suggested allocation of people for a class of 12. That number is not realistic

Practical Experience

To determine which area each student should go into, I normally provide an overview of the maintenance organization on the first day and some generalities regarding maintenance functions. I have the students fill out questionnaires regarding their backgrounds with particular emphasis and ask them to consider which area they want to be assigned. On the next class they chose their areas, and I "help" the remainder find their area.

To identify with the real world, I normally have the heads of the various groups (programming, SCM, etc.) provide status presentations to the head of software maintenance (the instructor) and the class each week. These actions foster the team concept, which students do not get enough of in typical university settings.

When I taught maintenance at the University of West Florida, I used the SEI Ada artifact. Many of the students were concerned that the class could not perform maintenance functions because they did not know Ada. I assured them that the primary thrust was the maintenance process, and that having a handful of Ada people would be sufficient. The most critical assignments were to find some Ada people for the programming group and to find someone knowledgeable in UNIX for SCM. Because we had a limited number of Ada people, they were spread around the organization.

for 10K LOC but, for the sake of the class, it does demonstrate that there are other functions in maintenance besides programming.

Teach Maintenance Concepts. Once the organization is in place, lecture. The difficult decision here is to sequence the lectures so that the right information is provided in a timely manner.

Have Students Present Papers. Next in the chronology of events is to have each student write a paper on some aspect of maintenance. A

good length is from 15–25 pages, and the topic must relate to the functional group they are assigned. This is done to reinforce the topic and to help them understand the role of their group in the overall maintenance effort. This is very valuable in the early stages of the class. For example, the head of the software configuration management group should prepare a paper on SCM describing the roles and tasks of SCM. Typically, the head of a group should provide her discussion of the functional area to the class. As another example, the software librarian in the SCM group could write a paper on how the code manager tool used in the project worked. Another member of SCM could write about some of the commercial-off-the-shelf SCM tools.

Practical Experience

Here is a sampling of some of the papers my students developed:

- "The State of Software Maintenance in the United States."
- "Roles and Responsibilities of the Maintenance Organization."
- "Software Maintenance and Modification."
- "The Maintenance Process."
- "Software Maintenance Through the Use of Software Tools."
- "Survey of Analysis and Design Tools."
- "An Overview of Testing."
- "Regression Testing."
- "An Analysis of Unit, System, and Path Testing."
- "An Overview of Software Configuration Management."
- "Tracking Database for Trouble Report/Change Request Report."
- "Use of SCCS for Maintenance."
- "Survey of COTS SCM products."
- "An Overview of Quality Assurance."

Start Exercising Group Functions. Once the organization is in place, the instructor is lecturing about maintenance, and the students are working on their papers, it is time to exercise group functions. At this point the class is not yet ready to exercise the maintenance process—the maintenance organization is not in place, and a system is transitioning for support. There are a number of things that the new maintenance team must do before fixing a correction or implementing an enhancement. These things include:

Software Configuration Management Functions. The SCM group should perform the following:

- Place the code under code control.
- Place test data under SCM.
- Design a trouble report form.
- Set up a tracking database for trouble reports.
- Update and tailor the SEI SCM plan.
- Establish procedures for checking code in and out.
- Perform a software build to ensure that the students can regenerate it.

Have the code under automated code control before starting the class.

Practical Experience

The SEI software artifact, the "DASC - Ada Style Checker," came to us in a VAX/VMS environment. The students had to put it in a UNIX environment and use SCCS for code management. Thus, one of the first actions for the SCM group was to put the system under their SCM tool, SCCS, be able to check code in and out, and, most importantly, be able to rebuild the system and establish controls.

This effort is a very real maintenance issue and takes an inordinate amount of time for students to accomplish. One way to handle this is to place the code under SCM before the students come in. It is better to have them learn only how to rebuild. The transition issue of taking a new system and placing it under code control is too much for a short maintenance class.

Test Functions. The test group should:

- Develop test plan.
- Develop test procedures.
- Develop test database.
- Perform initial testing of the system that was delivered.
- Perform testing of the system rebuilt by SCM.

Quality Assurance Functions. The QA people should:

- Write the QA Plan, including forms and checklists.

Programming Functions. The programmers should:

- Understand the system.
- Perform code comprehension.
- Provide oral presentations to the class about the structure of the system.

Exercise the Maintenance Process. The final event in the chronology is to exercise the maintenance process. Topics suggested by Jones (1994), such as complexity analysis, reverse engineering, and re-engineering can be included here. At this juncture, all code and documentation are under SCM, the guiding documentation is in place, the students are familiar with the code, and it is time to process a modification request. It is worthwhile to have a corrective as well as a perfective maintenance action going through the process. The instructor provides the class with the overview of the process, and one of the term papers documents the process. Thus, you have a documented process for everyone to use.

Practical Experience

The oral presentations were very beneficial. The students were forced to learn the code for this new system and then share that information with the testers, SCM people, etc. They appreciated how code was put together and how it was (or was not) documented.

Practical Experience

With the students not having a maintenance background, lots of lectures must be provided. The students must absorb this material and at the same time start writing papers and get ready to perform their group functions. Coupled with the fact that classes meet only one to three times a week, it is difficult to have all the design and code reviews in class and continue to make progress. Realistically, only a few actual corrective or enhancement fixes can be completed in a semester class. However, that is sufficient to demonstrate what maintenance is. If the instructor does some up-front work, such as putting the code under SCM and having all the test plans and procedures prepared, the students can concentrate on the code portions. It depends on your goals. For me it was to teach the entire maintenance process, and thus I had the students write the plans and develop tracking databases for modification requests.

How Do You Grade a Maintenance Class?   How would the students be graded? For a group project like this, the grading is very complicated. The instructor must provide the guidelines for evaluating and finally grading the students. Evaluating groups working on a project is difficult at best. The students are not comfortable in working in groups. One of your goals of the class should be to teach them how to do this, because that is what happens in the real world.

A suggested grading approach is to provide grades based on individual and group evaluations. Each individual would get a grade. That grade would be based on examination results (a mid-term and final), quiz results, a term paper on a maintenance topic, an oral presentation of the term paper, and oral presentations for technical topics relating to the class that exercise group functions or the maintenance process.

Each individual should provide an evaluation for the members of his group. That becomes a portion of the individual's grade. Then the head of each group (e.g., SCM) provides an evaluation of how the other groups performed (e.g., programming, testing, etc.). That factors into the grade. Finally, the instructor should provide a subjective evaluation, worth about 10% of the overall grade, based on perceptions, effort expended, and knowledge of the topic.

Practical Experience

The students do not like a grading scheme like the above. They are more comfortable in working on their own and getting the grades that they work for and deserve. They do not like being evaluated on the performance of the overall group. However, this approach is the real world, and that is how they will be evaluated later—how they perform in a group setting.

Education Summary The above provides some information on how to teach a maintenance course. It is important for the instructor to have a detailed list of actions, week by week, to account for the potential time delays and to ensure that all students are involved. The smaller the group, the better it is. Do not try to teach to 30 or 40 students; it will not work.

The above provided details on how to educate maintainers. What about training? What are the specific training things that should be provided after maintenance education is provided? The next section discusses maintenance training.

HOW DO YOU START TRAINING?

Every maintenance organization must have a general maintenance training plan to provide for indoctrination and general maintenance training. Additionally, each maintenance organization needs to have a standard list of training requirements for new systems that will be transitioned for maintenance.

The SEI addresses the issue of needing a training plan (Carpenter and Hallman 1995) and provides guidance for an organization to prepare a training plan for the first time. The SEI focus is not maintenance but for those organizations who need a sample and some general guidance, the SEI reference is a good place to start.

An outline for a typical software maintenance training plan is:

1. Purpose.
2. Scope.
3. Objectives.
4. Introduction.
5. General training requirements.
6. Commercial-off-the-shelf products.

7. Software maintenance concepts, process, and environment.
8. System specific applications.

The following discusses each area of the plan.

Purpose. A sample purpose might be as follows: To establish the maintenance training plan for the maintenance organization. The training plan sets forth functional training pipelines and provides central guidance for all aspects of training, as well as identifying specific training requirements for all functional positions.

Scope. A sample scope might be as follows: The maintenance training plan sets forth the training requirements for each functional position within the maintenance organization. All personnel assigned to the maintenance organization fall within the purview of the maintenance training plan.

Objectives. Sample objectives might be: The objectives of the maintenance training plan are:

- To establish central guidance and reference point for all training within the maintenance organization.
- To establish a training program responsive to the needs of the maintenance organization.
- To establish procedures and provide guidance to ensure all that maintenance organization personnel are adequately trained in order to carry out the functions of the maintenance organization.

Introduction. The Introduction should discuss the functions of the maintenance organization. Additionally, it should discuss the maintenance education that personnel should have as a prerequisite to this training. For example, education should include the topics discussed previously under education. Many maintenance organizations will have to include these education topics in the maintenance training plan, as they will not have been taught elsewhere.

General Training Requirements. This section should identify the basic training requirements in the form of categories of training. Sample categories and requirements might be:

- *System Engineering.* Fault isolation and performance analysis.
- *Applications Programming.* Analysis, design, and system-specific knowledge.

- *Systems Programming.* Networks, system administration.
- *Software Testing.* Unit, integration, and system testing.
- *SCM.* Identification, change control, status accounting, auditing, automated software libraries, MR tracking, and version control.
- *Quality Assurance.* IV&V, standards, software inspections, software quality metrics, and maintainability assessments.
- *Software Performance Analysis.* Throughput.

Commercial-off-the-shelf Products. Maintainers require extensive training in the commercial products used to support the organization and specific systems that are maintained by the organization. It is imperative that training be provided in CASE tools, as most CASE programs fail if proper training is not provided (see Chapter 13). Specific CASE tools used in the SEE or STE are included in this section. This training is needed prior to learning the software of a particular system. Sample requirements include:

1. Operating systems.
2. Database management systems.
3. Design tools.
4. Source code analysis tools.
5. Compilers, editors, and linkers.
6. SCM tools.
7. Test tools.
8. Requirements traceability tools.
9. Networks.

The actual list is dependent upon the SEE and STE in use at the maintenance organization.

Software Maintenance Concepts, Process, and Environment. This course is intended to provide maintenance personnel with an introduction to the concepts, process, and environment in use at the maintenance organization. Sample topics might be:

- An overview of the maintenance process.
- A detailed discussion of the maintenance process.
- An overview of the software standards and practices.
- An overview of SCM.
- An overview of testing.
- An overview of software quality metrics.
- An overview of software process improvement.

- A discussion of peer reviews.
- Use of the SEE to support the process.
- Use of the STE to support the process.

System-Specific Applications. For each system or software product, there should be specific training if the application is large or will have a long life cycle. This training can be used to train the initial cadre of maintainers, and then as turnover occurs it can be used to train new personnel. Sample topics might be:

- Theory of operations of the application.
- General description of components.
- Detailed description of subsystem functionality (if appropriate).
- Code structure.
- Control flow.
- Data flow.
- Use of common routines.
- Libraries used.
- Call trees.
- Cyclomatic complexity.

SUMMARY

The state of maintenance education is not good. However, the tide seems to be turning and more and more universities appear to be addressing the issues. Corporate education must pick up the slack and put more emphasis on teaching maintenance the same way that they teach development to software engineers. In addition, after maintainers get their education, there are a number of things they need to be trained to do. Thus, maintainers need a maintenance plan.

1. What would you like to see taught at your organization regarding maintenance?

2. If you were teaching maintenance, what else would you include in your syllabus?

3. Discuss the reasons why maintenance isn't taught.

Impact of Object-Oriented Technology on Software Maintenance

19

Object-oriented technology (OOT) is impacting maintainers as well as developers. Developers are using OOT with more frequency. A majority of new systems are being developed in languages like C++ and Smalltalk. What is the impact on the maintainer? Will maintenance be performed the same way? Will object-oriented systems be more maintainable? This chapter introduces some OOT concepts, discusses what maintenance practitioners are saying about OOT, and describes how OOT is affecting software maintenance.

While there has been a lot of talk about OOT recently, it is not really new nor revolutionary; it has its roots in the language Simula-67, which was developed in the late 1960s (Khoshafian 1993). It is really evolutionary, because most of the basic concepts have been around for a long time. The following section provides some definitions and describes some basic concepts.

WHAT ARE SOME OOT TERMS?

The use of OOT is an attempt to model real-world entities with abstractions called *objects*. These abstractions identify the relevant attributes and relationships of an object, and include them in a package commonly called a *class*. For many years, systems were developed in a manner that kept the data separate from the procedures that manipulated that data. This separation of data and procedures resulted in different techniques for maintaining either the data or the procedures.

In the beginning this separation made sense, because the procedures were implemented as wires in a plug board, and the data were maintained on punched tape or magnetic drums. However, as computers and programs have evolved, the distinction between procedures and data has become blurred. In fact, it is now possible to store procedures in relational database management systems along with the data with which they are associated.

Combining related data and procedures is called *encapsulation*. This encapsulation allows the development of software units that can be developed and maintained independently of other units. The procedures associated with an object are known as *methods* or *messages*.

An object-oriented approach can be used during any of the life-cycle phases of a system, including analysis, design, implementation, operations, and maintenance. In order to use an object-oriented methodology effectively during the operations and maintenance phase of a system's life cycle, the maintainer must:

- Understand the general system concepts.
- Understand the developmental methodologies used to define precise features and capabilities of the system.
- Know how to use any object-oriented tools used in the development of the system.

The following are some common definitions found in the OO literature.

- *Object*. An abstraction for a real-world entity; implemented as a set of data and associated functions.
- *Attribute*. An abstraction of a characteristic of an entity.
- *Class*. A grouping of objects that share specific attributes.
- *Relationship*. An interaction between objects.
- *Method*. A processing module that performs an operation on a class; the module performs one simple task.
- *Message*. The thing sent to an object to invoke a method.
- *Encapsulation*. The process of combining data and methods to provide a single conceptual object.
- *Information Hiding*. The process of hiding the implementation details from the user of the object.
- *Inheritance*. A special relationship in which a subclass *inherits* some of its characteristics from the parent class.
- *Polymorphism*. The concept which allows a single function at the conceptual level to take on different forms at the implementation level based on the type of the object.

■ *Dynamic Binding.* The process of binding values to variables at run time instead of at compile time.

WHY OOT IS DIFFERENT

Other approaches focus on the functions or procedures that must be performed without regard to the data they work with. However, over time, these functions change as the requirements evolve; and, because these procedures are usually interdependent, the changes often require rework.

On the other hand, objects in a system are relatively static over time because the procedures are directly associated with the data which they manipulate, allowing the system to be more resilient to change. This resiliency allows the system to be more easily maintained and reused.

The essential maintenance tasks for an object-oriented approach are the same as for traditional approaches. These include analysis, design, and programming. They are most commonly referred to as:

■ Object-Oriented Analysis (OOA)
■ Object-Oriented Design (OOD)
■ Object-Oriented Programming (OOP)

The following discusses these OO terms and shows how they are used in a maintenance process.

Object-Oriented Analysis (OOA)

The analysis performed in support of a modification request (MR) requires the maintainer to fully understand the request in order to design a solution. The analysis that is performed depends upon whether the request is corrective, adaptive, or perfective. If the MR is corrective, the maintainer must first replicate the problem in order to begin to understand it. If the MR is adaptive, the maintainer must understand the changes in the environment that require the software to adapt. If the MR is perfective, then the maintenance effort might be a small development project that adds a new capability. In each of these cases, it is incumbent upon the maintainer to fully understand the implications of the request. Furthermore, an object-oriented analysis approach requires the maintainer to:

- Understand the conceptual entities in the system.
- Understand the behavior and operations of the conceptual entities.
- Expose information related to the request.

Additionally, the maintainer needs to know:

- What the software is doing.
- What the software is doing it to.
- When it is being done.

It is essential that the maintainer have a thorough understanding of the problem being addressed and the current system design, so that the solution preserves the existing system design logic. Maintainers understand the problem when they can specify the modification requirements in a manner that is:

- Complete.
- Consistent.
- Reviewable.
- Verifiable.

Currently, there are several different methodologies to perform OOA:

- Coad-Yourdon.
- Firesmith.
- Rumbaugh (OMT).
- Seidewitz-Stark.
- Shlaer-Mellor.
- Wirfs-Brock.
- Booch.

Each of these methodologies has it strong points that make it more or less suitable for particular applications. Familiarity with one approach does not guarantee an expertise in another. In a maintenance environment, it is important to have a thorough understanding of the OOA methodology used for the system being maintained, so that the same type of considerations can be used when evaluating a maintenance change. A comparison of the first six methods can be found in the *Encyclopedia of Software Engineering* (Bailin 1994). The Booch, Coad-Yourdon, and OMT methodologies are the ones with which most people are familiar.

Maintainers must understand the OO methodology before performing maintenance on an OO system.

Object-Oriented Design (OOD)

The design of the solution to a modification request (MR) is totally dependent upon the analysis performed. For a corrective MR, the design may occur at the same time as the analysis, depending upon how simple the problem is. For an adaptive MR, the design may be as simple as rebuilding using new tools, including compilers, linkers, etc. For a perfective MR, the level of effort may be significantly greater than for an adaptive MR and depends on whether or not the maintainer is required to:

- Identify new classes and associated methods.
- Determine the classes affected in modifying the system.
- Ensure that encapsulation, inheritance, and polymorphism are preserved.
- Ensure that information is hidden to promote system modularity.

A design solution is defined when the changes to system components used to construct the system have been modified in accordance with the implementation technology used to develop and maintain the system. The modifications to the design should make the following issues clear:

- How new conceptual entities identified in the analysis will be realized.
- How they will be packaged in the given implementation technology.
- How the system performance will be affected.

The resulting solution will modify the code in some fashion. The types of changes for an object-oriented system are summarized by Kung (1994) as follows:

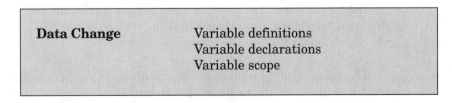

Data Change	Variable definitions
	Variable declarations
	Variable scope

	Variable access mode
	Variable access
	Variable initialization
Method Change	Adding, deleting, or changing a predicate
	Adding or deleting local variables
	Changing the logic of a code segment
Class Change	Component changes
	Interface changes
	Relationship changes
Class Library Change	Changing the defined members of a class
	Adding or deleting a class and its relationships with other classes
	Adding or deleting a relationship between two existing classes
	Adding or deleting an independent class

Once these issues are resolved, the maintainer identifies the components needed to implement the design. Functions are aggregated together with the data they access into a *class* or by indicating how to modify an existing class. Classes are used in OO methodology to encapsulate data and operations, and to provide inheritance of data and operations. As previously defined, inheritance permits the use of class characteristics in subclasses.

Object-Oriented Programming

Once the design is complete, the solution is turned over to the programmer for implementation. The design solution requires the maintainer to:

- Define the data structures and algorithms for the classes.
- Apply available language constructs.
- Hide information.

The solution is implemented by creating or modifying the data structures and algorithms necessary to build the design components.

While procedural languages can be used to implement an object-oriented design, they do not provide the software engineering capabilities available in object-oriented languages such as Smalltalk. Object-oriented programming (OOP) is characterized by hiding the information in components to promote modularity. In order to correctly implement the solution, the maintainer needs to know:

- How information is represented in data.
- How the data is accessed.

OOP implements the solution by utilizing the constructs of the chosen language to provide for the important object-oriented characteristics as listed here:

Language	Encapsulation	Inheritance	Polymorphism
C++	Class	Derived Class	Virtual Function
Smalltalk	Class	Subclass	Message Selector
Ada	Package	Extended Type	Class Wide Types

Object-Oriented Testing

From a maintainer's perspective, the same testing methods that apply to structured programs apply to object-oriented programs. By definition, black-box testing does not care about the internals of the system; 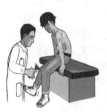 it requires the tester to generate test cases based primarily on the requirements at the system level. The fact that the requirements are satisfied by an object-oriented system is of no consequence. Much of the actual code in an object-oriented system is still structured, procedural code using typical constructs and logic. In fact, in a survey conducted by Wilde and Huitt (1992), 50% of the modules in a typical object-oriented system comprise less than five lines of code. Therefore, the effort that goes into white box testing (which validates the actual logic) will also remain virtually unchanged, if not simplified. The decrease in lines of code per module is offset by the fact that there are typically more modules to test, which may cause the *integration complexity* to increase and the overall comprehension of the program to be more difficult. Maintainers will have to place a greater emphasis on the integration level tests to make sure that all the interfaces are thoroughly tested.

Integration testing for OO systems is even more critical than for traditional systems.

The only completely new challenge for maintainers will result from the use of the polymorphism, dynamic binding, and private data capabilities offered by object-oriented methods. Test personnel must have an above-average grasp of these concepts and how they are implemented specifically in the system under test. Testers must verify not only that the modules work, but that they cannot be forced to work when they should not. Given the general lack of comprehension regarding these capabilities today, adequately testing software that uses these concepts will present the greatest challenge. Over time, as maintainers become more and more familiar with these concepts, ways of testing them will be developed and become as typical as path testing or other methods for structured programming.

A final thought regarding testing: A major advantage of object-oriented programming is the potential for reuse of objects. As mentioned earlier, once an object has been constructed and tested and added to the reuse library, it does not need to be retested if it is used unchanged. If it is modified before being reused, it will still need to be tested; however, the probability of finding errors should be significantly less than in code that was not reused. A prime example of code reuse without retesting are the subprograms contained in the libraries that are typically provided with a programming language. All of these functions and procedures are being reused, yet no one gives any thought to testing them individually each time they are used; only the new code is tested. This is precisely the point that Harmon (1993) was making when he asserted that 90% reuse would yield only 10% as many defects. The reduction in number of defects is probably not exactly inversely proportional to the amount of reuse because there will still be integration defects, but it will reduce the overall testing burden.

Object-Oriented Database (OODB)

Another topic that is germane is the programming of databases. Just as the methodologies for developing code have evolved over the years, the types of databases have also evolved. According to Khoshafian (1993) "... object-oriented databases are an extension of two concepts: *object orientation* and *databases*." The earlier database types were navigational in nature, and did not have a strong theoretical foundation. The relational database as defined by Dr. E. F. Codd was the first step toward providing the missing theoretical foundation. For some applications, the strong theoretical foundation was too restrictive, which led to the development of the semantic data model and the entity-relationship model. These approaches tried to relax the restrictions of the relational model while retaining the theoretical foundation. These models provided for inheritance, object identity, and abstract data typing, and provided the foundation for object-oriented databases as we know them today.

Object-oriented databases are still relatively new, and information about the impact on maintenance is rather skimpy. However, the combination of an object-oriented database with an application developed using object-oriented techniques should be easier to maintain. If an object-oriented system manages its own data using internal data structures or a relational database, the developer is required to manage all the methods and inheritance relationships himself. On the other hand, if an object-oriented database is used, a great deal of the management issues can be incorporated into the database management system itself, making the application software simpler and easier to maintain.

OO databases should be easier to maintain.

WHY OOT IS BEING USED

You now have an appreciation of *how* OOT is used by the maintainer. But why is OOT catching on? Why are organizations using OOT more and more?

The reason many organizations are using object-oriented methods to develop and then maintain software is that they believe that OOT provides:

- Faster development.
- Greater reuse potential.
- Increased quality.
- Easier maintenance.
- Enhanced modifiability.

All of these result in reduced life-cycle costs, which is everyone's consideration. These are the reasons why organizations are using OO— but has OO lived up to it promise? According to Harmon and Taylor

(1993), object-oriented technology has proven itself capable of improving development speed from one hundred to over one thousand percent. They state that the speed comes not from programming faster, but from programming less. By creating reusable classes, productivity gains are realized on subsequent projects by recombining the existing classes.

While this productivity gain is significant for development, it would only apply to maintenance in the case of adding a significant new capability, where the maintenance is really a mini-development effort and can employ reuse. Part of the faster development also attributable to reuse is that the testing effort can be reduced. Once a class has been thoroughly tested and added to the library, it is not necessary to completely retest it each time it is reused. Harmon and Taylor observe that only the new code in a development has to be tested from scratch. Therefore, the number of anticipated defects should be directly proportional to the amount of new code; so a system built with 90% reused code only contains 10% new code, and consequently 10% as many defects. Thus, there is increased quality.

Quality is improved with OO systems—but class libraries are needed first.

Are OO systems easier to maintain? Harmon and Taylor (1993) state that they are, and:

> The increased ease of maintenance comes from several sources. First, if you only have 10% as many defects to begin with, you have a lot fewer bugs to chase down after the software is in the field. Second, the encapsulation and information hiding provided by objects serves to eliminate many kinds of defects and make others easier to find. . . Finally any repairs you do make have less of a ripple effect because they are isolated by the affected objects. This means you no longer create ten new bugs for each one you eliminate. . . [Furthermore] because changes are neatly encapsulated, you can alter a system in rather fundamental ways without ever breaking it. Polymorphism and dynamic binding . . . are particularly valuable here. It is actually possible to make old software handle requirements that did not even exist at the time the system was conceived simply by adding new objects.

However, these statements directly contradict some of the statements made by Daly (1995) and Hsia (1995), where they indicate that the maintenance of OO systems is more difficult. The following section shows what software maintenance practitioners are saying regarding the promised and realized benefits of OOT.

WHAT MAINTENANCE PRACTITIONERS ARE SAYING

So what has the impact been on maintenance? What are practitioners saying about OOT?

Faster Development

There are those who believe that customers will see the benefits of OOT development through the faster availability of functionalities. There are others (Leung 1994) who state that is not necessarily true. He and others state that increased design time increases development time for OOT. Libraries often do not exist. There are no short-term benefits to OOT. Faster development does not occur until the libraries exist and are reused. How does this impact maintenance? Maintenance may be faster if libraries exist. However, there are no empirical data available that prove that maintenance is faster in OOT systems.

OOT development is slower due to increased design time. Productivity goes down in the first two years of development.

Reuse

The NASA Software Engineering Laboratory (SEL) states that reuse is up from 20%–30% to 80% in OO applications. It takes 3–4 projects to get that level of reuse. Of interest is that reuse will only come about *after* the development of a class library. Reuse takes time: reuse is not instantaneous. Maintainers need to develop class libraries to achieve any economic benefits.

There is no economic benefit to using OO in the early years. The benefits come later.

Only now are empirical data regarding reuse becoming available. The impact of reuse on maintenance is yet to be determined. Intuitively, it should help.

Quality

Quality only goes up once class libraries are developed. Practitioners state that quality is improved but remember: While quality is being improved in the early stages, productivity goes down.

Easier Maintenance and Enhanced Modifiability

Glass (1994) states that there is no data on maintainability. NASA SEL states that although there is considerable reuse, there is no data yet on maintainability at this point. Slonim (1994) at the International Conference on Software Maintenance stated that since the time OOT was introduced in 1967, there is no evidence to show that an OOT product is easier to maintain! Leung (1994) provided some insights into OOT at the same conference. He stated that rework increases with OOT when new applications are built (like adding adaptive or perfective changes). The OOT framework needs to be evolved, and some existing classes need to be modified.

OO MAINTAINABILITY

As maintainability is crucial to reducing life-cycle costs, it is worth spending more time on this topic. The following discusses maintainability in more detail.

One of the main arguments for using OO methods is that it should reduce the amount of maintenance required on the software developed. Several studies have been conducted to determine the impact of OO methods on maintainability. According to Henry (1990), individual maintenance tasks are more difficult when using object-oriented software compared to procedural software. On the other hand, data collected supports the premise that object-oriented techniques resulted in fewer maintenance changes and reduced maintenance effort overall.

However, there is not much empirical data upon which to base claims about the effectiveness of OO. According to Daly (1995), inheritance makes dependencies among objects harder to find and analyze. Additionally, the greater the depth of inheritance, the greater the level of difficulty associated with understanding and maintaining the software.

Inheritance is one of the key factors in determining maintainability. Greater levels of inheritance help reuse, but decrease maintainability.

Some of the difficulties associated with inheritance can be mitigated with better data encapsulation (Mancl and Havana 1990). Daly's study indicated that object-oriented software with a hierarchy of only three levels of inheritance depth has been shown to be on average 20% quicker to maintain than equivalent object-base software with no inheritance.

However, Daly also states that software with deeper levels of inheritance did not do as well as code with fewer levels. Presumably this is a result of greater complexity and increasing comprehension difficulties as the levels of inheritance increase.

While most of the current research has focused on the inheritance characteristic of OOT, the other characteristics also have an impact and might actually be the real reason for some of the difficulties associated with maintaining OOT software.

If the system was developed correctly, most of the maintenance issues related to OOT software should depend upon the structure of the system. Most of the changes would involve the modification or deletion of existing classes, or the creation of new classes and relationships between classes (Hsia 1995).

In most of the OOT systems being developed today, the class relationships are complicated and difficult to understand, and changing a class might have unexpected side effects (Hsia 1995). The use of dynamic binding complicates the maintenance process by making it more difficult to trace dependencies using tools that are currently available (Wilde 1992). In sum, maintainability is not a given for OOT systems. These systems are not inherently more maintainable. More data must come forth, and more research is needed by authorities such as Henry and Wilde.

RELATED OO ISSUES

There are other related issues that need to be discussed. The following provides discussion of some of those issues.

Training

The increased training required is one of the more important aspects of OOT. Typically development is not as fast as one might think, because of the need for training. The OOT staff needs training in the OOT methodology used, and the SEE needs to be retooled. Leung (1994) states that there is a loss of productivity. Of note is that many maintainers are making a huge mistake in the way they are addressing training for OO. Many are merely sending personnel to a programming course (e.g., for C++). This not a good approach. People need to understand the underlying OO methodology, which takes considerable time, training, and money. This must be done *before* people go off to the programming classes.

Maintainers need training in the OO methodology before learning OO programming.

Development Methodologies

The emergence of OOT has caused much discussion about the development models used and the need for a new model for OOT. Henderson-Sellers and Edwards (1990) put forth that a whole new life cycle must be used for OOT. The water fountain life cycle is one that is most often put forth for OOT development. More information on the fountain model can be found in the *Encyclopedia of Software Engineering* (1994) and Henderson-Sellers (1996).

Methodologies

Booch, Rumbach, and Code/Yourdon are the methodologies that seem to be getting the most play. Each has different advantages. Of interest now is that Rumbach has joined Booch at Rational Corporation, and they are merging the best of the two different methodologies. This might result in more of a standard methodology.

METRICS

Are metrics impacted with OOT systems? Do maintainers use the same metrics? The following addresses these issues.

In order to effectively manage a software development or maintenance effort, it is necessary to measure the characteristics of the code. For a development effort, the metrics are used to predict either the quality of the software or the productivity of the development staff. For a maintenance effort, the metrics are used to identify potential problem areas against which resources must be applied.

There are many metrics which have existed for quite some time to evaluate procedural code:

- Lines of code.
- Function points.
- Halstead metrics (Halstead 1977).
- McCabe's Cyclomatic Complexity (McCabe 1976).
- Henry and Kafura's Information Flow Metric (Henry and Kafura 1981).
- Adamov and Richter's Hybrid Metrics (Adamov and Richter 1990).

While these metrics may still be meaningful for the development of object-oriented software, they tend to concentrate on the procedural aspects of code. Kolewe (1993) states that, "Cyclomatic complexity, for example, is particularly misleading when applied to object-oriented C++ code."

Kolewe (1993) as well as Li and Henry (1993) both identify six metrics that can be used to measure the complexity of the object interactions in the design. They include:

- Weighted methods per class.
- Depth of inheritance tree.
- Class coupling.
- Response for a class.
- Lack of method cohesion.
- Number of children.

These are important for OOT developments, and they are important for maintainers. Different metrics are needed for OOT. The following are of prime interest to maintainers.

Weighted Methods Per Class

The weighted methods per class metric measures the complexity of the behavior of a class. It can basically be thought of as the sum of the cyclomatic complexities of the methods in the class. The rationale is that a class with a lot of small methods might be as difficult to maintain as a class with only a few complex methods.

Depth of Inheritance Tree

The depth of inheritance tree metric measures the number of classes needed to understand how to use a method in a particular class. In essence, it counts the number of ancestors for a specific class.

Class Coupling

The class coupling metric measures the number of classes needed to understand how to use a specific class. It depends on the use and association relationships with other classes. In general, if the classes within a system have a high class coupling measure, the system has probably been over-abstracted. This over-abstraction usually occurs as a result of breaking up atomic classes in order to reuse code.

Response for a Class

The response for a class metric measures the number of other classes called by the methods of this class. This metric is the count of all the methods contained in the class, plus the count of all the unique methods called by the methods of the class; consequently, the complexity of the class is directly proportional to this metric.

Lack of Method Cohesion

The lack of method cohesion metric measures the cohesiveness of a class. This metric indicates the degree to which the class variables are not used by the class methods.

Number of Children

The Number of Children metric measures the scope of the properties of a class. Chidamber and Kemerer (1991) proposed this metric as a measure of the scope of the properties of a class, noting that "generally it is better to have depth rather than breadth in the class hierarchy." While there are other metrics applicable to OOT systems, those listed above are considered to be the most useful at this time.

LESSONS LEARNED

OOT is not the panacea that OOT proponents would have you believe. On the other hand, it is not just a fad, as OOT opponents claim. The theory behind OOT is sound. However, many of the concepts embraced by the object-oriented approach are new, and (contrary to what some people say) not easy to learn and understand. For the object-oriented approach to be effective, the organization must select a specific methodology and procure an appropriate amount of training to ensure that key individuals are well versed in its application. Training only one person is not sufficient. Furthermore, this training should focus on the methodology and not the programming language. Teaching a programmer C++ does not make the programmer understand the concepts behind the object-oriented design methodology used.

Based on experience and research, the problems that have been experienced with OOT have more to do with a lack of training. Shifting to a new paradigm takes time and training. As with maintenance, OOT is not taught well. It is only now entering university curricula.

When the schools start incorporating OOT into the entire curriculum, many of the problems will be reduced or disappear. Over time OOT will be accepted in the same way that the reluctance to accept structured programming was overcome. Today, almost everyone agrees on the benefits of structured programming. In fact, most of the newer, more widely accepted programming languages have constructs that support this concept. The same thing will happen with OOT. And, just as structured programming did not solve all the software engineering problems, neither will OOT.

Nevertheless, if the objects are created correctly, and properly encapsulate all the information related to the object, maintenance will be easier because the maintainer only has to understand the object, not the whole system. It is true that polymorphism and dynamic binding cause problems at first, but once understood and used correctly, they can be a powerful tools. An analogy can be drawn between these two concepts and recursion. Recursion is also a difficult concept for beginning programmers to deal with when they first encounter it. However, after some exposure and training, they can learn its strengths and weaknesses. When used correctly, recursion can greatly improve the performance of an application; however, if used incorrectly, it can bring a computer to its knees. The same can be said for polymorphism and dynamic binding.

SUMMARY

What is the future of OOT? It's here to stay; there is no going back. OOT embraces the concepts of information hiding and data abstraction in a way that is not possible with earlier conventional methods. These concepts have long been accepted as good software engineering practices. Will it solve all the development problems experienced by software developers? Probably not, but it does put in place some very powerful tools to move in the right direction. Most of the benefits to be realized by OOT are in the development phase. The greatest benefits that can be realized now have to do with reusability and the way it can improve productivity. The difficulties with object-oriented development have to do with the fact the defining and implementing objects is not intuitive, and there is an expensive initial training cost.

The benefits for maintenance are not so obvious, and might not be for some time. OOT can make maintenance easier. However, it requires that maintainability be built in from the beginning and that both the designers and programmers be well versed in the capabilities of the methodology.

1. Describe how OOT supports reuse.

2. Describe why object-oriented metrics are different from conventional metrics.

3. Conduct a literature search for empirical data regarding OO reducing life cycle costs. Report the results.

Software
Maintenance
Resources

The previous nineteen chapters provided significant information on the topic of software maintenance. The references cited contain more details on various topics and are a natural resource for software maintenance practitioners; but what other resources are available? This chapter summarizes the few resources that are available and discusses the resource of research.

WHAT RESOURCES ARE AVAILABLE?

Maintenance organizations need access to the proper resources in order to be successful. The bibliography at the end of the book provides some necessary reference material. Additionally, there are organizations, conferences, and periodicals that focus on software maintenance. Zvegintzov's *Software Maintenance Technology—A Reference Guide* (1994) provides a detailed directory, guide, and index to resources on software maintenance. Hagemeister and co-authors (1992) also provide an annotated bibliography on software maintenance.

WHAT ARE SOME HELPFUL ORGANIZATIONS?

The University of Durham Centre for Software Maintenance (CSM) was established in April 1987 at the University of Durham, U.K. It is the first such center worldwide. The CSM mission is to achieve and maintain excellence in research in the field of maintenance. The CSM mission statement is broken down further as follows:

- To undertake both basic and applied research in software maintenance.
- To collaborate closely with industry and public institutions in their enhancement of their software activities.
- To provide a stimulating and high quality environment for postgraduate education and research.
- To communicate and transfer the CSM technology to the science, engineering, and industrial communities as widely as possible.
- To promote the cause of software maintenance within the scientific and engineering community.

The CSM is a vital source of information that can be reached on the Internet at http://www.dur.ac.uk.

WHAT ARE SOME CONFERENCES AND WORKSHOPS?

There are only a few conferences and workshops that focus on maintenance. The IEEE Computer Society sponsors the International Conference on Software Maintenance (ICSM) in the fall of each year. ICSM's first event was held as a workshop in Monterey, California in 1983, and has evolved into an annual international conference.

The U.S. Professional Development Institute (USPDI) of Silver Spring, Maryland, sponsors the Conference on Software Maintenance and Management in the spring. The University of Durham hosts an annual workshop on maintenance, normally in the fall. Durham's conference is the main European conference dealing with software maintenance. Both USPDI and Durham's 1996 events had the Year 2000 Conversion as their main themes.

WHAT PERIODICALS ARE AVAILABLE?

There is only one periodical that concentrates on software maintenance. *The Journal of Software Maintenance: Research and Practice,* published by John Wiley & Sons, Ltd., commenced publication in 1989. It comes out bimonthly and publishes referred papers on topics in software maintenance that are of interest to both practitioners and academics. The editors are Keith Bennett (of the CSM) and Ned Chapin (of InfoSci, Inc.). In addition to research papers, articles from practitioners working in the field are published. Some of these are in the form of case studies that describe the maintenance or management of practical systems, surveys of the state-of-the-art in a specific area of software maintenance, or tutorials on topics of relevance to practitioners. The journal also publishes summaries of conferences.

Unfortunately, *Software Management News*, formerly *Software Maintenance News*, ceased publishing in December 1994. Nicholas Zvegintzov started it in November 1983, and for many years provided a forum for software maintenance practitioners. The publication is missed, as there is a great void in the area of practical applications. Past issues can be obtained from Software Management Network, B10-Suite 237, 4546 El Camino Real, Los Altos, California 94022, or by phone at (415) 969-5522.

One of the best places for maintenance information is the *Journal of Systems and Software*. Bob Glass is the editor, and in his Editor's Corner he often discusses his very practical views on maintenance. There is an occasional article on maintenance in *IEEE Computer*, *IEEE Software*, and other software engineering journals. The periodical *Software Development* normally devotes its August issue to maintenance.

WHAT ARE SOME INTERNET RESOURCES?

How about the Internet? What can maintainers learn from surfing the net? Can maintainers find valuable resources? The answer is no—not yet. If you search the net, you find very little regarding maintenance. You will find the Centre for Software Maintenance, a worthwhile resource. In general you find that there are a number of home pages, but there are no repositories of articles nor central locations for available services. Even so, it is still fertile territory, and maintainers might wish to advertise their software maintenance wares on the net.

WHAT IS THE LATEST RESEARCH AVAILABLE?

Unfortunately, research for software maintenance is currently not a high priority. Seemingly, most research is in software development. Parikh (1986) bemoaned the lack of a national laboratory or a concentrated effort; not much has changed since 1986. Some organizations are conducting software research under the banner of software engineering. The combined University of Florida/Purdue University Software Engineering Research Center and its University of West Florida extension do conduct some maintenance research. The majority of this work is in the area of program comprehension and tools development.

Significant research in maintenance is performed at the Centre for Software Maintenance at the University of Durham, U.K. A newsletter with recent results is published on a regular basis. Additionally, the Centre routinely publishes research material in the *Journal of Software Maintenance* and the *Proceedings of the International Conference on Software Maintenance*. Current research includes the following topics:

- Application management environments and support.
- Software visualization.
- Reverse engineering.
- Program comprehension.

Malcolm Munro and Keith Bennett (co-editor of the *Journal of Software Maintenance)* continue to conduct research in all areas of maintenance and have done so for many years. Recent work by Munro is found in Capretz and Munro (1994), Cimitile (1995) for program slicing, and Boldyref (1995) for program comprehension. Bennett's most recent research work is found in Yang and Bennett (1994) on reverse engineering, Yang and Bennett (1995) on reverse engineering, Bull (1995), and Smith (1995) on the future strategy for maintenance.

Metrics research is performed by Norm Schneidewind (1992, 1995) at the Naval Post Graduate School and by John Munson (1992) at the University of Idaho. Both are currently working on software metrics and reliability of the space shuttle software. Khoshgoftaar (1995) at Florida Atlantic University is currently researching error-prone modules. Paul Oman (1992) continues his maintainability metrics research at the University of Idaho (Oman 1994; Pearse and Oman 1995; Welker and Oman 1995).

Testing research is done by Lee White (1992) at Case Western Reserve University. Recent firewall testing work is contained in Abdullah (1995). Mary Jean Harrold, formerly at Clemson and now at Ohio State University, specializes in testing. Some of her recent research is found in Harrold (1992) and Harrold and Soffa (1994).

Hausi Muller (1992, 1994) at the University of Victoria is researching reverse-engineering topics, including the building of reverse-engineering toolsets for program understanding.

The University of Naples is also well respected for its maintenance research. Cimitile and De Carlini continue to conduct extensive research, and have joint research projects with the University of

Salerno, University of Bari, and the University of Durham. Recent research is found in Cimitile (1993) on reengineering, Canfora (1994) on reengineering, and Cimitile (1995) on program slicing.

SUMMARY

There are very few resources available to maintainers. There are only a few conferences and fewer periodicals concentrating on maintenance. In spite of a noticeable lack of research funding, there are organizations like the Universities of Durham and Naples conducting excellent maintenance research.

What is the future of maintenance? Where is it going? The next chapter addresses that topic.

1. Conduct a literature search and find recent maintenance publications on costs, software transition, the ISO/IEC 12207 maintenance process, and object-oriented testing for maintenance.

2. Surf the Internet and try to locate software maintenance resources. Identify companies providing services, available standards, information on conferences, and maintenance articles.

3. Review recent periodicals and comment on their approach to maintenance.

4. If appropriate, contact your local university and find out how it is teaching software maintenance. Describe the approach.

The Future
of Software
Maintenance

You now know what maintenance is all about. You know the history, the categories of maintenance, the process, how to use metrics, how to teach maintenance, and what resources are available to help. The practical experiences and case-study data help to clarify and reinforce concepts. I believe that this book provides some practical solutions to maintenance issues and helps protect software investments. But what about the future?

Where is maintenance going? What will maintainers face in the coming years? What are the challenges? The following addresses some areas that I think are important and will impact maintainers in the coming years.

WILL OBJECT-ORIENTED TECHNOLOGY (OOT) STAY?

There is nothing stopping OOT. It is finally getting recognition, and the next few years will bring about a closer coupling of users, developers, and maintainers because of OOT. The concept of objects is one that is understandable—people can relate to it. More and more of the business magazines are discussing objects and OOT. OOT is helping to place more of a business emphasis on computing and thus, maintenance. This closer coupling will also bring about a better understanding of what maintainers do for the corporate good. This will in turn help maintenance finally be viewed as a true corporate asset.

WHAT WILL THE FUTURE ENVIRONMENTS FOR MAINTENANCE BE?

The continued use of CASE tools and integrated CASE tools will evolve into better environments for maintenance. Tools will work better together—integration will be easier. Products that are not easily integrated will lose market share. Only the tools that are integrated easily and work with other tools will survive.

There will be a consolidation of tools. Vendors are buying up other tools and customers can look forward to one-stop shopping for tools. Instead of going to multiple vendors for tools, customers will be able to go to one vendor who will provide fully integrated environments.

Tools will become world-wide assets. The United States has dominated the tool market, but that will no longer be the case. Many tools from Europe are being used in the United States, and this trend will continue.

WHAT WILL HAPPEN WITH PROCESS AUTOMATION?

Fully integrated environments will foster automation of the maintenance process. Once the integrated environments are accepted and in place, there will be a big push to automate the maintenance process. Automation will facilitate training, improve the collection and analysis of metrics, help alleviate turnover problems, and ultimately help to reduce maintenance costs.

WHAT WILL THE SOFTWARE DEVELOPMENT METHODOLOGIES BE?

Widespread use of the incremental, evolutionary, and other software development methodologies (e.g., spiral, water fountain, etc.) will result in dramatic changes to maintenance as it has traditionally been viewed. Use of these methodologies will cause "continuous development." Products will be incrementally delivered and placed in operation. These will need support (maintenance) while other increments are still under development. The new increments will implement requirements not satisfied in the previous increments. The lines between development and maintenance will be blurred even further than they are today. This will impact how development and maintenance are organized, how the process is performed, how costs are determined, and ultimately how maintenance is viewed. There will also be a big impact on software configuration management and how it is performed.

Maintenance is not going away; it is here to stay, and growing. As new increments of software updates are delivered, they need corrections and enhancements. Organizations must decide if the maintainers will perform any of the enhancements, or if they will be developed in the next incremental update. How users relate to development and maintenance will also be impacted. The lines of communication for the users must be made crystal clear if customers are to be satisfied. I expect that, because of the new software development methodologies, maintainers will only work on corrective and adaptive solutions, and developers will work on perfective changes. The users will only see changes to their software through new releases, and they will again perceive that "maintenance is merely fixing bugs." The new features, the user-driven enhancements that I addressed so often in this book, will evolve back to the developers, who will never go away as they "continue to develop" their product.

WHAT WILL HAPPEN WITH COMMERCIAL-OFF-THE-SHELF (COTS) PRODUCTS?

 COTS products are more prevalent than ever. System development as we know it (large-application code development) will not be the same in the future. Organizations will buy off-the-shelf components and integrate them to develop systems. The impact on maintenance is staggering. The current maintenance process does not account for this type of maintenance; neither does cost estimating, nor personnel resource estimating. Maintainers who are effective in maintaining COTS-based systems have a bright future.

WHAT WILL THE IMPACT ON REMOTE SOFTWARE MAINTENANCE BE?

Telecommunications, which is impacting the entire world, will also impact software maintenance. Software updates and diagnostic work will be performed remotely via telecommunications media (such as the Internet). The days of being on-site to diagnose, isolate, and repair software problems will be gone. As an example, maintainers in India will be performing remote maintenance on systems in the United States.

WHAT WILL MAINTENANCE PEOPLE DO?

The maintainers of tomorrow must be smarter, better educated, and better trained. Systems are becoming more complex as tools and environments become more complex. Maintainers will have to have a broader knowledge of more and more topics to be effective maintainers.

WHAT WILL HAPPEN TO OUTSOURCING?

Outsourcing will continue to grow and will become a dominant industry within the software world. However, outsourced maintenance will be for corrective and adaptive actions only, with many companies and agencies retaining the perfective category of maintenance for their own organizations to complete.

WHAT WILL OCCUR WITH STANDARDS?

As everything becomes more global, there will be greater emphasis on standards. ISO/IEC 12207 will drive the world software trade and will impact maintenance.

SUMMARY

Maintainers can expect many changes in the coming years. It will take more than luck to handle the challenges of tomorrow. Remember, "Luck is the product of good planning" (Branch Rickey). Keep in mind that careful planning is the key to meeting challenges. Maintenance must and will change. It will not go away—but it will change. Plan on it. Good luck!

1. Discuss some issues that will confront maintainers in the next few years and in the next 10 years.

2. Discuss how maintainers can cope with the new software development methodologies.

3. Discuss the pros and cons of performing remote software maintenance.

4. Discuss how cost will be impacted by the issues presented in this chapter.

Glossary

acquirer: An organization that acquires or procures a system or software products from a supplier. See **customer**.

acquisition process: One of the primary processes of the ISO/IEC life-cycle model that causes the initiation of the software life cycle. It defines the activities of the acquirer and the organization that acquires a system, software product, or software service. See Chapters 4 and 5.

adaptive maintenance: One of the three categories of maintenance defined by Swanson. Adaptive maintenance consists of any effort that is initiated as a result of changes in the environment in which a software system must operate. See also **corrective maintenance** and **perfective maintenance**. See Chapter 2.

annual change traffic (ACT): The number of source lines of code modified or added (the number of lines "touched") during the year. ACT is a necessary variable for COCOMO. See also **COCOMO**. See Chapter 8.

charter: A document that delineates all responsibilities, authorities, and functions of the maintenance organization; the operations of the software maintenance organization; the need and justification for changes; responsibilities for making the changes; change control and procedures; and the process and procedures for controlling changes to software. Also known as a *software maintenance policy*. See Chapter 12.

COTS: An acronym for commercial-off-the-shelf software products.

computer-aided software engineering (CASE): A set of software tools that automate and contribute to the improvement of the development and maintenance processes of the software life cycle. See Chapter 13.

configuration control board (CCB): A group of people who review the modification requests and determines if work should commence.

COCOMO: An acronym for *constructive cost model*. COCOMO is a parametric model used to determine personnel resources. See Chapter 8.

corrective maintenance: One of three categories of maintenance defined by Swanson. Corrective maintenance refers to changes necessitated by actual errors (induced or residual "bugs" in a system). See **adaptive** and **perfective maintenance**. See Chapter 2.

COSEE: An acronym for *common software engineering environment*, a project that provided an integrated CASE environment. See Chapter 14.

customer: The person or persons for whom the product is intended, and usually (but not necessarily) who decides the requirements. See **acquirer**.

developer: An organization that performs development activities (including requirements analysis, design, and testing through acceptance) during the software life-cycle process. See **supplier**.

development model: A framework used to guide the set of activities performed to translate user needs into software products.

development process: One of the primary processes of the ISO/IEC life-cycle model. It provides guidance for the developer of software. See Chapters 4 and 5.

enhancement: See **perfective maintenance**.

enhancement request: After a modification request (MR) is filed by a user, the maintainer will identify the MR as either a problem report or enhancement request. Enhancement requests are perfective changes requested by the user. See **perfective maintenance**. See also **problem report** and **modification request**. See Chapters 2 and 5.

environment: All of the automated facilities that a software engineer has available to perform the task of software development and maintenance. See Chapter 14.

evolutionary model: A model used to develop a software product. The Evolutionary model develops a system in builds, but differs from the Incremental model in that it acknowledges that the requirements are not fully understood and cannot be defined initially. The requirements are partially defined up front, and then are refined in each successive build. Interim products are available for use. The activities within the model are employed repeatedly in the same sequence through all the builds. See also **Incremental** and **Waterfall model**. See Chapter 2.

GOTS: An acronym for *government-off-the-shelf* software products.

help desk: A service maintained by the maintainers to aid users with the usage of a software product.

ICASE: An acronym for *integrated computer-aided software engineering*. A set of integrated software tools networked through a database that automate and contribute to the improvement of the development and maintenance processes of the software life cycle. See Chapter 13.

Incremental model: A model used to develop a software product. Called the pre-planned product improvement model, it starts with a given set of requirements and performs development in a sequence of builds. All requirements are defined first, there are multiple builds, and there might be some interim product for use. The first build incorporates a part of the requirements, the next build adds more requirements, and so on, until the system is complete. The activities within the model are employed repeatedly in the same sequence through all the builds. See also **Evolutionary model** and **Waterfall model**. See Chapter 2.

logistics group: The people responsible for setting up and planning the hardware and software aspects of a system. They should also be involved in planning for maintenance. See Chapter 6.

Maintainability: The ease in which a software product can be maintained, enhanced, adapted, corrected, expanded, and contracted. See Chapter 16.

Maintainer: An organization that performs maintenance activities.

Maintenance Concept: A document prepared early in the development effort of a software product that addresses the scope of software maintenance, the tailoring of the postdelivery process, the designation of who will provide maintenance, and an estimate of life-cycle costs. The maintenance concept is one part of a three-part planning strategy. See also **maintenance plan** and **resource analysis**. See Chapter 7.

Maintenance Environment: See **environment**.

Maintenance Model: A framework used to guide the set of activities to perform maintenance.

Maintenance Organization: See **maintainer**.

Maintenance Plan: A document prepared after the maintenance concept and during the development of the software product. It specifies why support will be needed, who will do what work, what the roles and responsibilities of everyone involved will be, what the estimated size of the staff for the project will be, how the work will be performed, what resources will be available for support, where support will be performed, and when support will commence. The maintenance plan is one part of a three-part planning strategy. See also **Maintenance Concept** and **Resource Analysis**. See Chapter 7.

Maintenance Process: One of the primary processes of the ISO/IEC life-cycle model. It provides guidance for the maintenance of software. See Chapters 4 and 5.

Maintenance Reviews/Acceptance: An activity of the ISO/IEC 12207 maintenance process. It is used to ensure that the software product is correct. See Chapter 5.

maintenance scope: See **scope of maintenance**.

modification implementation: An activity of the ISO/IEC 12207 maintenance process. It encompasses all the design, implementation, testing, and delivery actions needed to resolve modification requests. See Chapter 5.

modification request: The means by which problems are reported and enhancements are requested. See also **problem report** and **enhancement request**.

operation process: One of the primary processes of the ISO/IEC life-cycle model. It provides guidance for the operation of software. See Chapters 4 and 5.

outsourced maintainer: A maintenance organization that is not a physical part of the development organization that is contracted to do maintenance.

perfective maintenance: One of three categories of maintenance defined by Swanson. Perfective maintenance (also known as enhancements) includes all changes, insertions, deletions, modifications, extensions, and enhancements made to a system to meet the evolving and/or expanding needs of the user. See also **adaptive maintenance** and **corrective maintenance**. See Chapter 2.

postdelivery: The period of time in the software development life cycle after the software product is put into use.

predelivery: The period of time in the software development life cycle before the software product is put into use.

preventive maintenance: In addition to Swanson's three categories of maintenance, the IEEE has a fourth category. Preventive maintenance is performed for the purpose of preventing problems before they occur. See **adaptive maintenance**, **perfective maintenance**, and **corrective maintenance**. See Chapter 2.

problem and modification analysis: An activity of the ISO/IEC 12207 maintenance process. It is the most critical step in the modification resolution process, in which the maintainer evaluates the Modification Request to understand the problem, develop a solution, and obtain approval for implementing a specific solution. See Chapter 5.

problem report: After a modification request (MR) is filed by a user, the maintainer will identify the MR as either a problem report or enhancement request. Problem reports are for corrective and adaptive changes requested by the user. See also **enhancement request** and **modification request**. See Chapters 2 and 5.

process implementation: An activity of the ISO/IEC 12207 maintenance process. It occurs early in the product life cycle, when the maintainer establishes the plans and procedures that are used during the **maintenance process**. See Chapter 5.

process model: A framework to identify, define, and organize data, strategies, rules, and processes needed to support the way an organization wants to do business. See Chapter 4.

program manager: A person who is directly responsible for managing a particular program and who has the authority, responsibility, and accountability for program cost, schedule, performance status, and risk.

quality assurance: A planned and systematic pattern of all actions necessary to provide adequate confidence that the item or product conforms to established technical requirements.

resource analysis: A document that determines how to plan the environment and personnel resources for a software project. This document is often prepared late in the development process. Resource analysis is part of a three-part planning strategy. See also **maintenance concept** and **maintenance plan**. See Chapter 8.

scope of maintenance: A determination of the level of maintenance the maintainer will provide. There are four levels; Level 1—full maintenance, Level; 2—corrective maintenance (not to be confused with the maintenance category *corrective maintenance*); Level 3—limited corrective maintenance; and Level 4—limited configuration management. See also **corrective maintenance**. See Chapter 7.

software configuration management (SCM): The set of activities that is developed to manage change to the software's documentation and code throughout the software life cycle.

software engineering environment: The set of automated tools, firmware devices, and hardware necessary to perform the software engineering effort. The automated tools may include (but are not limited to) compilers, assembles, linkers, loaders, operating systems, debuggers, simulators, emulators, test tools, documentation tools, and database management systems. See Chapter 14.

software maintenance: The totality of activities required to provide cost-effective support to a software system. Activities are performed during the predelivery stage as well as the postdelivery stage. Predelivery activities include planning for postdelivery operations, supportablity, and logistics determination. Postdelivery activities include software modification, training, and operating a help desk. See also **predelivery** and **postdelivery**. See Chapter 4.

software maintenance manager (SMM): This person has overall responsibility and performs the functions of developing organizational documents and conducting general oversight of maintenance activities.

software maintenance policy: See **charter**.

software metrics: A manner in which to measure the processes of software development and maintenance to affect the quality, efficiency, cost, productivity, etc., of a software product. See Chapter 14.

software migration: An activity of the ISO/IEC 12207 maintenance process. It includes the activity of moving an old system to a new operational environment. See Chapter 5.

software modification function: The function that includes: the analysis of problems, the isolation of faults, the analysis of enhancement requests, and the designing, coding, unit testing, and documenting of changes to a software product.

software retirement: An activity of the ISO/IEC 12207 maintenance process. It involves removing a product from service in an orderly manner once it has outlived its usefulness. See Chapter 5.

software test environment: A set of automated tools, firmware devices, and hardware necessary to test software. The automated tools may include (but are not limited to) test tools such as simulation software and code analyzers, and can also include those tools used in the software engineering environment.

supplier: An organization that enters into a contract with the acquirer for the supply of a software product under the terms of the contract. See **developer**.

supply process: One of the primary processes of the ISO/IEC lifecycle model that peforms the development, operation, and/or maintenance process. It provides guidance for the provider of development products, maintenance service, and operation service. See Chapters 4 and 5.

supportability: The elements that the maintainer must know to determine how easy or difficult it will be to perform maintenance on a particular software product. These elements include the structure of the code, how often the code is commented, how many lines of code exist, and the complexity of the modules. See Chapter 7.

transition: The process of transferring the software and the responsibility for the software from the developer to the maintainer. See Chapters 9, 10, 11.

transition plan: A document that states how the transition will occur, who will be responsible for it, when it will happen, and other details. It includes details about the use of a maintenance escort, the maintainer visiting the developer, the funding needed to effect the transition, and the authorization to look at software development folders. See Chapters 9, 10, 11.

turnover process: See **transition**.

user: The person or persons operating or interacting directly with the system. The user often states requirements to the customer, supplier, or maintainer.

user liaison support: See **help desk**.

Waterfall model: A model used to develop a software product. This model is a once-through, do-each-step-once approach model where all requirements are defined first, there is essentially only one build, and the user does not get an interim product. See also **Evolutionary model** and **Incremental model**. See Chapter 2.

Bibliography

Abdullah K., Kimble J., and L. White. 1995. Correcting for Unreliable Regression Integration Testing. *Proceedings of the International Conference on Software Maintenance—1995.* Los Alamitos, CA: IEEE Computer Society Press. 232–41.

Abran A. and H. Nguyenkim. 1991. Analysis of Maintenance Work Categories Through Measurement. *Proceedings of the International Conference on Software Maintenance—1991.* Los Alamitos, CA: IEEE Computer Society Press. 104–13.

Adamov R. and L. Richter. 1990. A Proposal for Measuring the Structural Complexity of Programs. *Journal of Systems Software.*

AFOTECP 800-2, Volume 2, Software Support Life Cycle Process Evaluation Guide, 1 NOV 88.

AFOTECP 800-2, Volume 3, Software Maintainability—Evaluation Guide, 31 OCT 89.

Agresti W. Evolving Measures for Evolving Software. Speech presented at The International Workshop on Software Evolution, Processes, and Measures. September 24, 1994.

American National Standard Institute/IEEE (ANSI/IEEE-STD-610.12). 1990. *Standard Glossary of Software Engineering Terminology.* Los Alamitos, CA: IEEE Computer Society. 7–83.

American National Standard Institute/IEEE (ANSI/IEEE STD 730). 1989. *Standard for Software Quality Assurance Plans.* IEEE Los Alamitos, CA: Computer Society Press.

American National Standard Institute/IEEE (ANSI/IEEE STD 1061). 1992. *IEEE Standard for a Software Quality Metrics Methodology.* Los Alamitos, CA: IEEE Computer Society Press.

American National Standard Institute/IEEE (ANSI/IEEE STD 1209). 1995. *Standard for Software Maintenance*. Los Alamitos, CA: IEEE Computer Society Press.

ARDEC. Software Metrics in Test & Evaluation: AMC Guidance for Implementation of Step Metrics. U.S. Army Armament Research, Development & Engineering Center (ARDEC).

Arthur L.J. 1988. *Software Evolution: The Software Maintenance Challenge*. New York, NY: John Wiley & Sons.

Bailin S.C. 1994. Object-Oriented Requirements Analysis. *Encyclopedia of Software Engineering*. New York, NY: John Wiley & Sons.

Basili V.R. 1985. Quantitative Evaluation of Software Methodology. *Proceedings of the First Pan-Pacific Computer Conference*.

Beizer B. 1992. *Software Testing and Techniques* (2d ed.). New York, NY: Van Nostrand Reinhold Company.

Boehm B.W. 1976. Software Engineering. *IEEE Transactions on Computers*. C-25(12):25–32.

Boehm B.W. 1981. *Software Engineering Economics*. Englewood Cliffs, NJ: Prentice-Hall.

Boehm B.W. 1988. A Spiral Model of Software Development and Enhancement. *IEEE Computer*. 1988 (5):61–72.

Boldyreff C., Burd E., Hather R., Mortimer R., Munro M., and E. Younger. 1995. The AMES Approach to Application Understanding: A Case Study. *Proceedings of the International Conference on Software Maintenance—1995*. Los Alamitos, CA: IEEE Computer Society Press. 182–91.

Booch G. 1996. *Object Solutions: Managing the Object-Oriented Project*. Menlo Park, CA: Addison Wesley.

Bozman J.S. 1993. Grocer Buys Into Open Systems. *Computerworld*. March 22. 27(12):57, 59.

Brooks R. 1983. Towards a Theory of the Comprehension of Computer Programs. *Man-Machine Studies*. 543–54.

Bull T.M., Younger E.J., Bennett K.H., and Z. Luo. 1995. Bylands: Reverse Engineering Safety-Critical Systems. *Proceedings of the International Conference on Software Maintenance–1995*. Los Alamitos, CA: IEEE Computer Society Press. 358–65.

F.W. and D.L. Calliss. 1992. Suggested Scenarios of Software Maintenance Education. Arizona State University Technical Report TR-92-011.

Canfora G., Cimitile A., and M. Munro. 1994. Re^2: Reverse Engineering and Reuse Re-engineering. *Journal of Software Maintenance*. 6(2):53–72.

Capretz M.A. and M. Munro. 1994. Software Configuration Management Issues in the Maintenance of Existing Systems. *Journal of Software Maintenance*. Vol 6(2): 1–14.

Card D.N. and R.L. Glass. 1990. *Measuring Software Design Quality*. Englewood Cliffs, NJ: Prentice Hall.

Cardow J. 1992. You Can't Teach Software Maintenance! *Proceedings of the Sixth Annual Meeting and Conference of the Software Management Association*. 335–62.

Carlton A. et al. 1992. *Software Measurement for DoD Systems: Recommendations for Initial Core Measures* (CMU/SEI-92-TR-19). Pittsburg, PA: Software Engineering Institute, Carnegie Mellon University.

Carpenter M.B. and H.K. Hallman. 1995. *Training Guidelines: Creating a Training Plan for a Software Organization* (CMU/SEI-95-TR-007). Pittsburg, PA: Software Engineering Institute, Carnegie Mellon University.

Chapin N. Attacking Why Maintenance is Costly—A Software Engineering Insight. 1980. *Proceedings of IEEE*. 68(9).

Chapin, N. The Job of Software Maintenance. 1987. *Proceedings of the International Conference on Software Maintenance—1987*. Los Alamitos, CA: IEEE Computer Society Press. 4–12.

Chapin N. Software Maintenance Life Cycle. 1988. *Proceedings of the International Conference on Software Maintenance—1988*. Los Alamitos, CA: IEEE Computer Society Press. 6–13.

Chidamber S. and C. Kemerer. 1991. Towards a Metrics Suite for Object-Oriented Design. *Proceedings of OOPSLA '91*. ACM SIG-PLAN Notices 26 (II).

Chikofsky E. and R. Norman. 1994. CASE. *Encyclopedia of Software Engineering*. New York, NY: John Wiley & Sons.

Cimitile A., Fasolino A., and P. Maresca. 1993. Reuse and Reengineering and Validation via Concept Assignments. *Proceedings of the International Conference on Software Maintenance—1993*. Los Alamitos, CA: IEEE Computer Society Press. 216–25.

Cimitile A., Fasolino A., and M. Munro. 1995. Identifying Reusable Functions Using Specification Driver Program Slicing: A Case Study. *Proceedings of the International Conference on Software Maintenance—1995*. Los Alamitos, CA: IEEE Computer Society Press. 124–33.

Cimitile A. and U. De Carlini. 1989. Maintenance Testing (1). *Software Maintenance News*. 7(1):28.

Cimitile A. and U. De Carlini. 1989. Maintenance Testing (2). *Software Maintenance News*. 7(2):22.

Cimitile A. and U. De Carlini. 1989. Maintenance Testing (3). *Software Maintenance News*. 7(3):34.

Crosby P.B. *Quality is Free*. 1979. New York, NY: McGraw-Hill.

Curtis B. 1985. *Tutorial: Human Factors in Software Development*. Washington, DC: IEEE Society Press.

Daly J. et al. 1995. The Effect on Inheritance on the Maintainability of Object-Oriented Software: An Empirical Study. *Proceedings of the International Conference of Software Maintenance—1995*. Los Alamitos, CA: IEEE Computer Society Press. 20–9.

Deimel L.E. and J.F. Naveda. 1990. *Reading Computer Programs: Instructors Guide and Exercises*. CMU/SEI-90-EM-3. Pittsburg, PA: Software Engineering Institute, Carnegie Mellon University.

Dekleva S.M. 1992. Delphi Study of Software Maintenance Problems. *Proceedings of the International Conference on Software Maintenance—1992*. Los Alamitos, CA: IEEE Computer Society Press.

DeMarco T. 1982. *Controlling Software Projects: Management, Measurement, Estimation*. Englewood Cliffs, NJ: Prentice Hall.

Donnelly R.E. 1992. Software Metrics: Initiating a Program. *Proceedings of the Sixth Annual Meeting and Conference of the Software Management Association*. 2.37–2.50.

Engel C., Ford G., and T. Korson. 1989. *Software Maintenance Exercises for a Software Engineering Project Course*. (CMU/SEI-89-EM-1). Pittsburg, PA: Software Engineering Institute, Carnegie Mellon University.

Fay S. D. and D. G. Holmes. Help! I Have to Update an Undocumented Program. *Proceedings of the International Conference on Software Maintenance—1985*. Los Alamitos, CA: IEEE Computer Society Press, 194–202.

Federal Information Processing Standards Publication (FIPS PUB 106). 1984. *Guideline on Software Maintenance*.

Florac W. 1992. *Software Quality Measurement: A Framework for Counting Problems and Defects* (CMU/SEI-92-TR-22). Pittsburg, PA: Software Engineering Institute, Carnegie Mellon University.

Ford G. 1991. *1991 SEI Report on Graduate Software Engineering Education*. (CMU/SEI-91-TR-2). Pittsburg, PA: Software Engineering Institute, Carnegie Mellon University.

Forte G. and R.J. Norman. 1992. A Self-Assessment by the Software Engineering Community. *Communications of the ACM*. 35(4):26–32.

Foster J.R., Jolly A.E.P., and M.T. Norris. 1989. An Overview of Software Maintenance. *British Telecom Technology Journal*. 7(4):37–46.

Fugetta A. 1993. *A Classification of CASE Technology*. Los Alamitos, CA: IEEE Computer Society Press.

Gallagher K.B. and J.R. Lyle. 1991. Using Program Slicing in Software Maintenance. *IEEE Transactions on Software Engineering*. 17(8): 751–61.

Gamalel-Din S.A. and L.J. Osterweil. 1988. New Perspectives on Software Maintenance Processes. *Proceedings of the International Conference on Software Maintenance—1988*. Los Alamitos, CA,: IEEE Computer Society Press, 14–22.

Glass R.L. 1994. The Software Research Crisis. *IEEE Software*. 11(6): 42–47.

Glass R.L. and R.A. Noiseux. 1981. Software Maintenance Guidebook. Englewood Cliffs, NJ: Prentice Hall.

Goethert W., Bailey E., and M. Busby. 1992. *Software Effort & Schedule Measurement: A Framework for Counting Staff-Hours and Reporting Schedule Information* (CMU/SEI-92-TR-21). Pittsburg, PA: Software Engineering Institute, Carnegie Mellon University.

Grady R.B. and D.L. Caswell. 1987. *Software Metrics: Establishing a Company-wide Program*. Englewood Cliffs, NJ: Prentice-Hall.

Grady R.B. 1992. *Practical Software Metrics for Project Management and Process Improvement*. Englewood Cliffs, NJ: Prentice-Hall.

ISO/IEC. 1995. Information Technology—Guide for ISO/IEC 12207 (Software Life Cycle Processes). Draft Technical Report.

Hagemeister J. et al. 1992. An Annotated Bibliography on Software Maintenance. *ACM SIGSOFT Software Engineering Notes*. 17(2):79–84.

Halstead M.H. 1977. *Elements of Software Science*. New York: Elsevier, North-Nolland.

Harmon P. and D. Taylor. *Objects in Action: Commercial Applications of Object-Oriented Technologies*. Reading, MA: Addison-Wesley.

Harrold M.J., McGregor J.D., and K.J. Fitzpatrick. 1992. Incremental Testing of Object-Oriented Class Structures. *Proceedings of the 14th Software Engineering Conference*. 68–80.

Harrold M.J. and M.L. Soffa. 1994. Efficient Computation of Interprocedural Definition Use Chain. CAM Transitions on Programming Language and Systems. 175–204.

Henderson-Sellers B. 1996. *Object-Oriented Metrics; Measures of Complexity*. Upper Saddle River, NJ: Prentice-Hall PTR.

Henderson-Sellers B. and J.M. Edward. 1990. The Object Oriented System Life Cycle. *ACM*. 143–59.

Henry S., Humphrey, M. and J. Lewis. 1990. Evaluation of the Maintainability of Object-Oriented Software. IEEE Conference on Computer and Communication Systems, September, 1990.

Henry S. and D. Kafura. 1981. Software Structure Metrics Based on Information Flow. *IEEE Transactions on Software Engineering*. Los Alamitos, CA: IEEE Computer Society.

Hetzel B. 1993. *Making Software Measurement Work; Building on Effective Measurement Program*. Wellesley, MA: QED Publishing Group.

Howerton C.P. 1992. Software Maintenance in the Computing Curricula. *Proceedings of the Sixth Annual Meeting and Conference of the Software Management Association*. 364–81.

Hsia P. et al. 1995. A Study on the Effect of Architecture on Maintainability of Object-Oriented Systems. *Proceedings on the International Conference on Software Maintenance—1995*. Los Alamitos, CA: IEEE Computer Society Press. 4–11.

Humphrey, W.S. 1989. *Managing the Software Process*. Reading, MA: Addison-Wesley.

IEEE. 1993. *IEEE std 1219: Standard for Software Maintenance*. Los Alamitos, CA: IEEE Computer Society Press.

IEEE. 1995. *IEEE std 1348: A Recommended Practice for the Adoption of CASE Tools*. Los Alamitos, CA: IEEE Computer Society Press.

International Standard Organization. 1994. *ISO 8402: Quality Management and Quality Assurance Vocabulary*. Geneva, Switzerland.

International Standard Organization. 1991. *ISO 9126: Information Technology-Software Product Evaluation-Quality Characteristics and Guidelines for Their Use*. Geneva, Switzerland.

International Standard Organization. 1995. *ISO 12207: Information Technology—Software Life Cycle Processes*. Geneva, Switzerland.

International Standard Organization. 1995. *ISO 14102: Information Technology—Guideline for the Evaluation and Selection of CASE Tools*. Geneva, Switzerland.

Joint Logistics Commanders Joint Policy Coordinating Group on Computer Resources Management. 1995. *A Practical Software Measurement: A Guide to Objective Program Insight*. Newport, RI: Naval Undersea Warfare Center.

Jones C. *Programming Productivity*. 1996. New York, NY: McGraw-Hill.

Jones C. 1991. *Applied Software Measurement*. New York, NY: McGraw-Hill.

Jones C. 1994. *Assessment and Control of Software Risks*. Englewood Cliffs, NJ: Prentice Hall.

Kafura D. and G.R. Reedy. 1987. The Use of Software Complexity Metrics in Software Maintenance. *IEEE Transactions on Software Engineering*. SE-13(3).

Kellner M.I. and G.A. Hansen. 1988. *Software Process Modeling*. Pittsburg, PA: Software Engineering Institute, Carnegie Mellon University.

Kern L.C. and G.E. Stark. 1992. *Software Sustaining Engineering Metrics Handbook* Version 1.0. Houston: NASA.

Khoshafian S. 1993. *Object-Oriented Databases*. New York, NY: John Wiley & Sons.

Khoshgoftaar T.M., Szabo R.M., and J.M. Voas. 1995. Detecting Program Module with Low Testability. *Proceedings of the International Conference on Software Maintenance—1995*. Los Alamitos, CA: IEEE Computer Society Press. 232–41.

Kolewe R. 1993. Metrics in Object-Oriented Design and Programming. *Software Development*. 53–62.

Kung D. et al. 1994. Change Impact Identification in Object-Oriented Software Maintenance. *Proceedings of the International Conference on Software Maintenance—1994*. IEEE Los Alamitos, CA: Computer Society Press. 202–11.

Lehman M.M. 1980. On Understanding Laws, Evolution, and Conversation in the Large-Program Life Cycle. *The Journal of Systems and Software*. 1:213–21.

Leung H.K.N. 1994. The Dark Side of Object-Oriented Software Development. *Proceedings of the International Conference on Software Maintenance—1994*. Los Alamitos, CA: IEEE Computer Society Press. 438–41.

Lewis H. and S. Henry. 1989. A Methodology for Integrating Maintainability Using Software Metrics. *Proceedings of the International Conference on Software Maintenance—1989*. Los Alamitos, CA: IEEE Computer Society Press. 32-9.

Li W. and S. Henry. 1983. Object-Oriented Metrics that Predict Maintainability. *The Journal of Systems and Software*. 111–22.

Lientz B.P. and E.B. Swanson. 1980. *Software Maintenance Management*. Reading, MA: Addison-Wesley.

Looney C.S. 1993. Concept of Operations for the Common Software Engineering Environment (COSEE). Technical Software Services, Inc., Technical Report.

Looney C.S. 1994a. Functional Requirements Document for the Common Software Engineering Environment (COSEE). Technical Software Services, Inc., Technical Report.

Looney C.S. 1994b. Software Tools Analysis for the NSGAP Common Software Engineering Environment (COSEE). Technical Software Services, Inc., Technical Report.

Looney C.S. 1994c. Detailed Design Document for the NSGAP Common Software Engineering Environment (COSEE). Technical Software Services, Inc., Technical Report.

Mancl D. and W. Havana. 1990. A Study of the Impact of C++ on Software Maintenance. *Proceedings of the International Conference on Software Maintenance—1990*. Los Alamitos, CA: IEEE Computer Society Press. 63–9.

Marciniak J.J. and Donald J. Reifer. *Software Acquisition Management: Managing the Acquisition of Custom Software Systems*. New York, NY,: John Wiley & Sons. 246.

Martin J. and C. McClure. 1983. *Software Maintenance: The Problem and its Solutions*. Englewood Cliffs, NJ: Prentice-Hall.

McCabe T. 1976. A Complexity Measure. *IEEE Transactions of Software Engineering*. SE1(3):312–27.

Moad J. 1990. Maintaining the Competitive Edge. *DATAMATION*. 61–6.

Mosemann II L.K. 1992. Software Management. *CROSSTALK*. 33:6–10.

Muller H.A. et al. 1992. A Reverse Engineering Environment Based on Spatial and Visual Software Development Environments. *Proceedings of the Fifth ACM SIGSOFT Symposium on Software Development Environments (SIGSOFT 1992)*. 17(5):88–98.

Muller H.A., Wong K., and S.R. Tilley 1994. Understanding Software Systems Using Reverse Engineering Technology. *The 62nd Congress of L'Association Canadienne Francaise pour l'Avancement des Sciences Proceedings (ACFAS 1994)*. 181–204.

Munson J.C. and T.M. Khoshgoftaar 1992. The Detection of Fault-Prone Program. *IEEE Transactions on Software Engineering*. 18(5): 423–33.

Munson J.C. and T.M. Khoshgoftaar 1992. Software Measurement for the Space Shuttle HAL/S Maintenance Environment. *Proceedings of the International Conference on Software Maintenance—1992*. Los Alamitos, CA: IEEE Computer Society Press. 387.

Myers G.J. 1979. *The Art of Software Testing*. New York, NY: John Wiley & Sons.

National Bureau of Standards. 1985. *Special Publication 500-13*. Washington, D.C.: National Bureau of Standards.

Nelson L.E. 1994. NSGAP Software Maintenance Process Manual. Technical Software Services, Inc., Technical Report.

Newman J. 1991. Quality and Identity: Goals for Undergraduate Software Engineering. *Proceedings of the First Software Engineering Research Forum*. Pensacola, FL: University of West Florida Press.

NIST. 1991. Reference Model for Frameworks of Software Engineering Environments. *NIST Special Publication 500-21*. Gaithersburg, MD: National Institute of Standards and Technology.

Oman P.W., Hagemeister J., and D. Ash 1991. *A Definition and Taxonomy for Software Maintainability*. University of Idaho. Software Engineering Test Lab Technical Report 91-08 TR.

Oman P.W. 1992. *HP-MAS: A Tool for Software Maintainability Assessment*. University of Idaho. Software Engineering Test Lab Technical Report 92-07 TR.

Oman P. and J. Hagemeister. 1992. Metrics for Assessing Software System Maintainability. *Proceedings of the International Conference on Software Maintenance—1992*. Los Alamitos, CA: IEEE Computer Society Press. 337-44.

Oman P. and J. Hagemeister. 1994. Constructing and Testing of Polynomials Predicting Software Maintainability. *Journal of Systems and Software*. 24(3):251–66.

Osborne W.M. 1989. Building Maintainable Software. *Handbook of Systems Management (Development and Support)*. Boston, MA: Auerbach Publishers. 179.

Osborne W.M. and E.J. Chikofsky. 1990. Fitting Pieces to the Maintenance Puzzle. *IEEE Software*. 10–11.

Parikh G. 1986. *Handbook of Software Maintenance*. New York, NY: John Wiley & Sons.

Park R. et al. 1992. *Software Size Measurement: A Framework for Counting Source Statements*. Pittsburg, PA: Software Engineering Institute, Carnegie Mellon University.

Paulk M.C. et al. 1993. *Capability Maturity Model for Software, Version 1.1*. Pittsburg, PA: Software Engineering Institute, Carnegie Mellon University.

Pearse T. and P. Oman. 1995. Maintainability Measures on Industrial Source Code Maintenance Activities. *Proceedings of the International Conference on Software Maintenance—1995*. Los Alamitos, CA: IEEE Computer Society Press. 295–303.

Pfleeger S.L. and S.A. Bohner. 1990. A Framework for Software Maintenance Metrics. *Proceedings of the International Conference on Software Maintenance—1990*. Los Alamitos, CA: IEEE Computer Society Press. 320–27.

Pigoski T.M. 1990. The Way We Were. *Software Maintenance News*. 8(8):24.

Pigoski T.M. 1990a. The Plan. *Software Maintenance News*. 8(9):14.

Pigoski T.M. 1991. A Review of MIL-HDBK-347. *Software Maintenance News*. 9(5):16–17.

Pigoski T.M. 1991a. Transition. *Software Maintenance News*. 9(10):10.

Pigoski T.M. 1991b. Taking Control. *Software Maintenance News*. 9(5):3.

Pigoski T.M. 1991c. Quality Customer Relations. *Software Maintenance News*. 9(12):23.

Pigoski T.M. 1991d. The Computer Support and Communications Environment. *Software Maintenance News*. 9(3):24.

Pigoski T.M. 1991e. Software Maintenance Metrics. *Software Maintenance News*. 9(8):19.

Pigoski T. M. 1992. A Practical Approach to Software Maintenance Staffing Estimation. *Proceedings of the Second Software Engineering Research Forum—November 1992*. Pensacola, FL: University of West Florida Press. 157–61.

Pigoski T.M. 1993. Maintainable Software: Why You Want It and How to Get It. *Proceedings of the Third Software Engineering Research*

Forum–November 1993. Pensacola, FL: University of West Florida Press. 67–71.

Pigoski T.M. 1994. Software Maintenance. *Encyclopedia of Software Engineering*. New York, NY: John Wiley & Sons.

Pigoski T.M. 1995. *Life Cycle Strategy: Software Support on the Front Line*. Los Altos, CA: Software Maintenance News, Inc.

Pigoski T.M. and C. Cowden. 1992. Software Transition: Experiences and Lessons Learned. *Proceedings of the International Conference on Software Maintenance—1992*. Los Alamitos, CA: IEEE Computer Society Press. 294–98.

Pigoski T.M. and C. S. Looney. 1993. Software Maintenance Training: Transition Experiences. *Proceedings of the International Conference on Software Maintenance—1993*. 314–18.

Pigoski T.M. and J. Sexton. Software Transition: A Case Study. *Proceedings of the International Conference on Software Maintenance—1990*. Los Alamitos, CA: IEEE Computer Society Press. 200–204.

Pressman R.S. 1992. *Software Engineering: A Practitioner's Approach*. New York, NY: McGraw-Hill.

Putnam L.H. and W. Meyers. 1996. *Controlling Software Development: An Executive Briefing*. Los Alamitos, CA: IEEE Computer Society Press.

Rodriguez R.V. 1991. *Proceedings of the First Software Engineering Research Forum*. Pensacola, FL: University of West Florida Press.

Schneberger S.L. 1995. Software Maintenance in Distributed Computer Environments: System Complexity Versus Component Simplicity. *Proceedings of the International Conference on Software Maintenance—1995*. Los Alamitos, CA: IEEE Computer Society Press. 304–13.

Schneberger S.L. 1995. Distributed Computing Environments: Effects on Software Maintenance Difficulty. Ann Arbor, MI: UMI Dissertation Services.

Schneberger S.L. 1996. Distributed Computing Environments: Effects on Software Maintenance Difficulty. Georgia State University, GSU CIS Working Paper, CIS-96-01, January 1996.

Schneidewind N.F. 1987. The State of Software Maintenance. *IEEE Transactions on Software Engineering*. SE-13(3):303–10.

Schneidewind N.F. 1989. Software Maintenance: The Need for Standardization. *Proceedings of the IEEE*. 77(4):618–24.

Schneidewind N.F. 1994. Validating Metrics for Ensuring Flight Software Quality. *IEEE Computer*. 50–7.

Software Engineering Institute (SEI). 1991. *Quarterly Update*. Pittsburg: SEI.

Semich J.W. 1994. Can You Orchestrate Client-Server Computing? *DATAMATION*. 40(15):36.

Sharon D. 1996. Meeting the Challenge of Software Maintenance. Los Alamitos, CA: IEEE Computer Society Press. 13(1):122–25.

Sharpley W.K. 1977. Software Maintenance Planning for Embedded Computer Systems. *Proceedings of the IEEE*. IEEE Los Alamitos, CA: Computer Society Press. 303–10.

Singh R. 1995. An Introduction to International Standard ISO/IEC 12207-Software Life Cycle Processes. Tutorial Presentation. October 22, 1995.

Slonim J. 1994. Challenges and Opportunities of Maintaining Object-Oriented Systems. *Proceedings of the International Conference on Software Maintenance—1994*. Los Alamitos, CA: IEEE Computer Society Press. 440.

Smith S., Bennett K., and C. Boldyreff. 1995. Is Maintenance Ready for Evolutions? *Proceedings of the International Conference on Software Maintenance—1995*. Los Alamitos, CA: IEEE Computer Society Press. 367–72.

Sommerville I. 1989. *Software Engineering*. Wokingham, U.K.: Addison-Wesley.

Stark G.E., Kern L.C., and C.V. Vowell. 1994. A Software Metric Set for Program Maintenance Management. *Journal of Systems and Software*. 239–49.

Software Technology Support Center. 1994. *Process Technologies Method and Tool Report (Volumes I & II)*. Salt Lake City, UT: STSC.

Software Technology Support Center. 1992. *Software Management Guide*. Salt Lake City, UT: STSC.

Swanson E.B. 1976. The Dimensions of Maintenance. *Proceedings of the Second International Conference on Software Engineering*. 492–97.

Swanson E.B. and C.M. Beath. 1989. *Maintaining Information Systems in Organizations*. New York, NY: John Wiley & Sons.

U.S. Government. 1990. *Military Handbook Mission-Critical Computer Resources Software Support (MIL-HDBK-347)*. Washington, D.C.: U.S. Government.

U.S. Government. 1994. *Military Standard 498 Software Development and Documentation (MIL-STD-498)*. Washington, D.C.: U.S. Government.

Vallett J.D. et al. 1994. Building on Experience Factory for Maintenance. *Proceedings of the Software Engineering Workshop*. Software Engineering Laboratory. 35–46.

Vollman T.E. 1990. Transitioning from Development to Maintenance. *Proceedings of the International Conference on Software Maintenance—1990*. Los Alamitos, CA: IEEE Computer Society Press. 189–99.

Vollman T.E. and J. Garbajosa-Sopena. 1996. CASE Tool Support for Software Product Assurance. *Proceedings of the European Space*

Agency Software Product Assurance Symposium. Noordwijk, Netherlands. March 19–21, 1996.

von Mayrhauser T.E. 1990. *Software Engineering—Methods and Management.* San Diego, CA: Academic Press, Inc.

Welker K. and P. Oman. 1995. Software Maintainability Metrics Models in Practice. *CROSSTALK: The Journal of Defense Software Engineering.* 8(11):19–32.

Werner M.C. 1995. Software Transition Plan for TACINTEL II+ Build 1. Technical Software Services, Inc., Technical Report.

White L. and H. Leung. 1992. A Firewall Concept for Both Control-Flow and Data-Flow in Regression Integration Testing. *Proceedings of the International Conference on Software Maintenance—1992.* Los Alamitos, CA: IEEE Computer Society Press. 262–71.

Wilde N. and R. Huitt. 1992. Maintenance Support for Object-Oriented Programs. *IEEE Transactions on Software Engineering Vol.18.* Los Alamitos, CA: IEEE Computer Society Press.

Wiltse J.D. and M.R. McPherson. 1990. Techniques and Tools Drive USAF Software Evaluation. *SIGNAL.* 44(8):49.

Yau S.S. and J.S. Collofello. 1980. Some Stability Measures for Software Maintenance. *IEEE Transactions on Software Engineering.* SE-6(6):545–52.

Yang H. and K. Bennett. 1995. Acquisition of ERA Models from Data Intensive Code. *Proceedings of the International Conference on Software Maintenance—1995.* Los Alamitos, CA: IEEE Computer Society Press. 116—23.

Yang H. and K. Bennett. Extension of A Transformation System for Maintenance-Dealing With Data-Intensive Programs. *Proceedings of the International Conference on Software Maintenance—1994.* Los Alamitos, CA: IEEE Computer Society Press. 334–53.

Zhuo F. et al. 1993. Constructing and Testing Software Maintainability Assessment Models. *Proceedings 1st International Software Metrics Symposium.* Los Alamitos, CA: IEEE Computer Society Press. 61–70.

Zvegintzov N. 1990a. Software Maintenance Exercises for a Software Engineering Project Course. *Software Maintenance News.* 8(4):6.

Zvegintzov N. 1990b. Rising's College Course with Existing Software. *Software Maintenance News.* 8(5):10.

Zvegintzov N. 1991. Real Maintenance Statistics. *Software Maintenance News.* 9(2):6–9.

Zvegintzov N. 1994. *Software Maintenance Technology—Reference Guide—1994 Edition.* Los Altos, CA: Software Management News.

Index

A

academic initiatives, addressing
    maintainability, 287–290
  Lewis and Henry, 287
  Oman, Dr. Paul W., 287–290
access, COSEE, 207, 208
ACT (actual change traffic)
  defined, 261
  planning maintenance, 108
actual change traffic (ACT), *see* ACT
adaptive maintenance category, 15, 16
AFOTECP (Air Force Operational Test
    and Evaluation Center Pamphlet),
    278, 279
Air Force (USAF), addressing
    maintainability, 278–281
  AFOTECP 800–2, 278, 279
  software
    evaluation categories, 281
    supportability, elements of, 279
Air Force Operational Test and
    Evaluation Center Pamphlet
    (AFOTECP), 278, 279
application mapping to functional
    requirements, COSEE, 207, 208

B

back-end, CASE tools, 190
backlogs, maintenance management, 301
  solution to, 301–303
Booch, OOA methodologies, 326
bug fixing, maintenance and, 17–19

C

Capability Maturity Model (CMM),
    maintenance model, 40
CASE (computer-aided software
    engineering) tools, 13
  adaptation of CASE tools, 196–198
  back-end, 190
  defined, 189, 190
  environment, 192
    architecture, 193
    good, 192
    maintenance-specific, 194–198
    properties, 193
  front-end, 190
  future of, 348
  horizontal, 190
  Integrated CASE (ICASE)

environment, 200–202
tools, defined, 190
integration frameworks, 190
lower, 190
SEE (Software Engineering
Environment), defined, 191, 192
STE (software test environment), 191
upper, 190
CCB (Configuration Control Board)
IEEE maintenance model, 43
software maintenance metrics
experiences, 243
CCC (software configuration tool), 209
Centre for Software Maintenance (CSM),
software maintenance resources,
341
changing priorities, maintenance
management, 303
solution to, 303
charter, maintainer, 184
sample, 185–188
CMM (Capability Maturity Model),
maintenance model, 40
CMP (configuration management plan),
59
Coad-Yourdon, OOA methodologies,
326
COCOMO (COnstructive COst MOdel),
planning maintenance, 103
basic model, 108, 109
intermediate model, 109, 110
Code and Fix development model, 38
coding and review techniques, Federal
Government addressing
maintainability 278
Configuration Control Board (CCB), *see*
CCB
configuration management plan (CMP),
59
conflict complicating transition, 119, 120
commercial-off-the-shelf (COTS)
products, 13
common software engineering
environment (COSEE), 200
competitive edge, 7
computer resources life-cycle
management plan (CRLCMP), 96

computer-aided software engineering
(CASE) tools, *see CASE tools*
COnstructive COst MOdel (COCOMO),
see COCOMO
contribution measurement difficulties,
maintenance management, 299,
300
solution to, 300
control items, ISO/IEC, 54
corrective maintenance category, 15, 16
COSEE (common software engineering
environment), 200
access, 207, 208
application mapping to functional
requirements, 207, 208
described, 202
design of, 207
development, lessons learned from, 212
non-technical, 212
technical, 212–214
developing, 203
goals, 209–211
import documentation, 203, 204
maintenance support, 205, 206
PC/X-terminal operations, 209, 210
requirements, 204
framework, 204
functionality, 204, 205
maintenance support, 205, 206
software
distribution, 209, 210
tools, evaluating, 206
tool summary, 206, 207
topology, 207
logical COSEE topology, 208
cost
life-cycle
estimating, 95
factors for consideration, 95
software maintenance, 29
as percentage of software dollars, 271
as percentage of Software Life-cycle
costs, 30
defining appropriate, 36
delayed error correction, penalty of,
272
factors influencing, 35

increasing costs of, 30, 31
maintenance categories, use in cost
    explanations, 34, 35
maintenance effort, 272
planning, importance of in
    maintenance cost reduction, 33
practitioners costs, 31, 32
reducing via better quality systems,
    271, 272
vs. improvements, 271
transition, 130, 134, 135
COTS (commercial-off-the-shelf)
    products, 13
future of, 349
CRLCMP (computer resources life-cycle
    management plan), 96
CSM (Centre for Software Maintenance),
    341
customer, defined, 4

D

DEC (Digital Equipment Corporation),
    VAX/VMS systems, 200
design phase, Code and Fix development
    model, 38
developers performing maintenance,
    21–23
  advantages, 21
  disadvantages, 21, 22
development
  maintenance coincidence and, 46, 47
  methodologies, OOT, 336
  models, 37
    Code and Fix, 38
    Waterfall, 38, 38
  process, 37
  time, OOT, 333
Digital Equipment Corporation (DEC),
    VAX/VMS systems, 200
distributed computing environments,
    198
  client/server, 199
  research results, 198, 199
documentation guidelines, Federal
    Government addressing
    maintainability 277, 278

E

education and training, software
    maintenance, 305
  college/university, 306
  conducting maintenance classes, 313,
    314
    education summary, 319
    exercise group functions, 316
    exercise the maintenance functions,
      317, 318
    grading maintenance classes, 318,
      319
    organizing the team, 313–315
    presentation of papers by students,
      315
    programming functions, 317
    quality assurance functions, 317
    software configuration management
      functions, 316
    teach maintenance concepts, 315
    test functions, 317
  corporate education, 306
  defining comprehensive program, 311
  on-the-job training, 306
  primary goals of, 311
  seminars/tutorials, 306
  Software Maintenance Training Plan,
    319, 320
  solving lack of education problem, 309,
    310
  starting training, 319
    commercial-off-the-shelf products, 321
    general training requirements, 320,
      321
    introduction, 320
    maintenance concepts, process, and
      environment, 321, 322
    objectives, 320
    purpose, 320
    scope, 320
    system-specific applications, 322
  teaching maintenance, 312, 313
  training software professionals,
    307–309
encapsulation, OOT, 324
enhanced modifiability, OOT, 334

enhancement request (ER), 3
  ISO/IEC 12207, 57
"enhancements", perfective changes, 15,
      16, 17
environment
  case, 192
    architecture, 193
    good, 192
    maintenance-specific, 194–198
    properties, 193
  defined, 190, 191
  distributed computing, 198
    client/server, 199
    research results, 198, 199
  resources, maintenance planning, 113,
      114
    defined, 113
    essential components, 113
ER (enhancement request), 3
  ISO/IEC 12207, 57
Evolutionary model, System Life Cycle,
      11, 12, 13
  Operations and Maintenance phase,
      12, 14

F

FCA (functional configuration audits), 72
Federal Government, The, addressing
      maintainability, 277
  coding and review techniques, 278
  documentation guidelines, 277, 278
  source code guidelines, 277
  testing standards and procedures, 278
financial resources, maintenance
      planning, 114–116
FIPS
  maintenance categories, 15, 16
  software maintenance defined, 8
Firesmith, OOA methodologies, 326
"fixes" categorization, E.B. Swanson, 15,
      16
front-end, CASE tools, 190
FSP (full-time support personnel),
      planning maintenance, 109
full-time support personnel (FSP),
      planning maintenance, 109

functional configuration audits (FCA),
      72

H

high powered workstation (HPW), 209
high staff turnover, maintenance
      management, 298, 299
  solution to, 299
horizontal, CASE tools, 190
HPW (high powered workstation), 209

I

ICASE (Integrated CASE)
  environment, 200–202
  tools, defined, 190
ICSM (International Conference on
      Software Maintenance), 306
IEC (International Electrotechnical
      Commission), 47
IEC 12207 System Life Cycle, fitting
      software into, 9, 10
IEEE 1219 (1993)
  addressing maintainability, 284
    relationship between factors and
        subfactors, 285, 286
    standard usage, 284
    subfactors, 285
  maintenance categories, 16, 17
  maintenance model, 41, 42
    acceptance test phase, 45
    analysis phase, 43
    delivery phase, 45, 46
    design phase, 43
    implementation phase, 43, 44
    problems/modification identification,
        classification, prioritization
phase, 42
    system test phase, 44
  maintenance process, 42
  software maintenance defined, 8
IEEE Computer, software maintenance
      resources, 343
IEEE Software, software maintenance
      resources, 343
import documentation, COSEE, 203, 204

maintenance support, 205, 206
Incremental model, System Life Cycle,
    10, 11, 12
    Operations and Maintenance phase, 11,
        12, 13, 14
industry, addressing maintainability, 282
inexperienced people, maintenance
        management, 296
    solution to, 297, 298
information systems (IS) model, 176
Integrated CASE (ICASE), *see ICASE*
integration frameworks, CASE, 190
integration support, maintainer function,
    171
International Conference on Software
        Maintenance (ICSM), 306
    software maintenance resources, 342
international efforts, addressing
        maintainability, 286, 287
International Electrotechnical
        Commission (IEC), 47
International Organization for
        Standardization (ISO), 47
International Standard for Information
        Technology Software, 47
    objectives, 47, 48
Internet, software maintenance
        resources, 343
IS (information systems) model, 176
ISO (International Organization for
        Standardization), 47
ISO/IEC 12207 (1995) life-cycle model,
    49
ISO/IEC 12207 (1995) maintenance
        categories and, 16, 17
ISO/IEC 12207 (1995) maintenance
        process, 51
    activities, 53, 54
    as part of software life-cycle, 51, 52
    control items, 54
    conventions used in, 55
    customer and maintainer agreement
        in, 53
    defined, 51, 52, 53
    goals of, 53
    implementation tasks, 55
    input items, 54, 56

maintenance review and acceptance
        activity, 71, 72
    approval, 72, 73
    archives, 77
    impact analysis, 76, 77
    migration plan, 75
    migration standards, 75
    notification of implementation, 76
    notification of intent, 75
    parallel operations, 75, 76
    review, 72
    software migration activity, 73, 74
maintainer responsibilities in, 53
modification implementation activity,
        62, 63
    development process, 64–71
    items to be modified, 64
    tasks, 63
output items, 54, 56
problem and modification analysis
        activity, 59, 60
    alternate solutions, 61, 62
    analysis task-steps, 61
    approval, 62
    documentation, 62
    modification analysis tasks, 60
    verification, 59–61
process hierarchy, 54
process implementation activity, 55
    maintenance planning, 56, 57
    modification requests, 57, 58
    software configuration management,
        59
software retirement activity, 77, 78
    archives, 80
    notification of intent, 79
    notification of retirement, 79, 80
    parallel operation, 79
    retirement plan, 78
    tasks, 77
structure of, 53
support items, 54
task, 53
terms defined, 54
ISO/IEC 12207 (1995) model
    acquisition process, 48
    defined, 47

development process, 49
maintenance process, 49, 50
operation process, 49, 50
primary processes, 48
secondary processes, 48
supply process, 48, 49
software maintenance defined, 8
system, definition, 8
ISO/IEC 12207 (1995) problem resolution
 process, 57
IT Metrics Strategies (ITMS), 105
ITMS (IT Metrics Strategies), 105

J

Joint Technical Committee 1 (JTC1), 47
Journal of Software Maintenance:
 Research and Practice, 342
Journal of Systems and Software, 343
JTC1 (Joint Technical Committee 1), 47

L

lack of maintenance training,
 maintenance management, 298
large organizations, maintenance and,
 26, 27
Lehman
 concept of maintenance, 3
 Law of Continuing Change, 14
 Law of Increasing Complexity, 14
life-cycle
 cost,
  estimating, need for, 95, 95
  reduction via OOT, 331, 332
  reduction via planning, 89, 90
  software development and, 30
 model, ISO/IEC, 49
lines of code (LOC), 253
LOC (lines of code), 253
logistics organization
 maintenance and, 85, 86
 relationship with maintainer, 84, 85
lower, CASE tools, 190
"lumping" corrections and enhancements,
 problems associated with, 19, 58

M

maintainability, software
 achievability, 275, 276
 as a goal, 275, 276
  specifying as, 283, 284
 definitions of, 273, 274
 described, 271
 determining maintainable system, 274
 developing program for, 282
 factors affecting
  development process, 276
  documentation, 276
  program comprehension, 276
 maintainer, determining, 274, 275
 players in addressing maintainability,
  277
  academic initiatives, 287–290
  Air Force (USAF), 278–281
  Department of Defense (DoD), 278
  Federal Government, The, 277, 278
  IEEE, 284–286
  industry, 282
  international efforts, 286, 287
  U.S. Army, 281
 recommended practices, 290, 291
 unmaintainable software, causes of,
  282, 283
maintainer
 charter, 184
  sample, 185–188
 configuration management task, task
  steps, 59
 defined, 4, 7
 designating maintainer, 92–96
  evaluation organization alternatives,
   92–94
 functions of, 166
  integration support, 171
  management, 167
  miscellaneous, 174, 175
  quality assurance, 173, 174
  software configuration management
   (SCM), 168, 169
  software modification, 167, 168
  technical assistance, 174
  testing, 172, 173

training, 169, 170
user liaison and help desk, 171, 172
involvement in predelivery stage, 85
management, 167
modification request task, task-steps,
    58
practitioners costs, 31, 32
quality assurance (QA) function, 173,
    174
relationship with logistics
    organization, 84, 85
roles and responsibility, 165, 166
separate, performing maintenance,
    23–26
    advantages, 23, 24
    disadvantages, 25, 26
transition, 121–123
maintenance
budgeting, 3
bug fixing and, 17–19
categories
    adaptive, 15
    corrective, 15
    distribution of, 32
    IEEE 1219 (1993), 16, 17
    ISO/IEC 12207 and, 16, 17
    perfective, 15
    preventative, 16, 17
    use of in maintenance cost
        explanations, 34, 35
categorizing types, 17
commencement, 46
concept, 89
    corrective maintenance, 90
    defined, 90
    designating maintainer, 92–96
    full maintenance, 90
    limited corrective maintenance, 90
    limited software configuration
        management, 91
    postdelivery process, tailoring, 91, 92
    software maintenance scope, 90, 91
costs, 29
    as percentage of Software Life-cycle
        costs, 30
    budgeting for, 3
    defining appropriate, 36

factors influencing, 35
increasing costs of, 30, 31
maintenance categories, use in cost
    explanations, 34, 35
maintenance practitioners costs, 31, 32
planning, importance of in
    maintenance cost reduction, 33
defined, 8, 46, 47
    ISO/IEC 12207, 64
developers performing, 21–23
    advantages, 21
    disadvantages, 21, 22
development coincidence and, 46, 47
difficulties associated with, 19, 20
education, *see education and training*
environment resources, planning, 113,
    114
    defined, 113
    essential components, 113
environments, future of, 348
financial resources, planning, 114–116
large organizations and, 26, 27
Lehman's concept of, 3
logistics organization and, 85, 86
"lumping" corrections and
    enhancements, problems
    associated with, 19
metrics, software, *see metrics*
models, 37
    business oriented, 40
    classification of, 40
    CMM, 40
    history of, 39–46
    IEEE, 41–46
    ISO/IEC, 47–50
    organizational-oriented, 40
    process-oriented, 40
    SEI process modeling, 40
    stages, 39
need for, 12–14
organization
    maintenance organization within
        software development, 180
    organization of, 176–182
    separate maintenance organization,
        181
    small maintenance organization, 182

maintenance (*cont.*)
  software development organization,
    179, 180
  successful, 3
  system development organization,
    177–179
  typical systems organization, 176,
    177
  participation, 3
  personnel resources, 101–103
    estimating tools, 103, 104
    experience (using), 104
    parametric models, 103, 104
  plan, 89
    described, 96
    factors to be considered, 96
    metrics, addressing, 99
    practical example of, 97, 98
    supportability, addressing, 98, 99
  planning, 89
    need for, 89, 90
    reducing life-cycle costs via, 89, 90
  process, 37. *See also ISO/IEC 12207*
    (1995) maintenance process
  responsibility for, 20–27
    developers performing maintenance,
      21–23
    separate maintainers performing
      maintenance, 23–26
  review and acceptance activity,
    ISO/IEC, 71–77
  separate maintainers performing
    maintenance, 23–26
    advantages, 23, 24
    disadvantages, 25, 26
  software, 4
    defined, 8
    future of, 347–350. *See also software*
      maintenance
    metrics, *see metrics*
    need for, 12–14
    published information on, 7, 8
    resources, 341–350. *See also*
      resources
  Swanson, E.B., "fixes" categorization, 15
  System Life Cycle and, 8–10

training, *see also education and*
  training; training
  tracking system for, 58
maintenance-specific environment, good,
  194, 195
  analysis and design, 195
  documentation management, 196
  reverse engineering, 196
  software configuration management,
    195, 196
  testing, 196
management, software maintenance, 293
  backlogs, 301
    solution to, 301–303
  changing priorities, 303
    solution to, 303
  contribution measurement difficulties,
    299, 300
    solution to, 300
  high staff turnover, 298, 299
    solution to, 299
  inexperienced people, 296
    solution to, 297, 298
  lack of maintenance training, 298
  low morale 300, 301
    solution to, 301
  maintainer function, 167
  maintenance professional, 293, 294
  no maintenance process, 303, 304
    solution to, 304
  problems in, 294
    top 19 problems in, 295
messages, OOT, 324
methodologies, OOT, 336
methods, OOT, 324
metrics, software maintenance
  addressing in maintenance plan, 99
  analysis of, case study, 252
    analysis of empirical data, 252, 253
    comment lines, 255, 256
    lessons learned, 268–270
    maintenance categories, 266
    productivity measures, 256–266
    quality, 268
    systems size, 253–255
    timeliness, 266–268

approaching, 222
assessing need for, 217, 218
case study, initial period, 238
  background, 238
  data collection, 241, 242
  lessons learned from, 244
  metrics repository, 242
  organization, 238
  personnel, 238
  problems encountered, 239
  report types, 242, 243
  stated goals, 240
  support systems, 238, 238
case study, second period, 246
  evolution of metrics program,
    247–249
  lessons learned, 249–251
  organization, 246
  people, 246
  support systems, 247
implementing, 218–222
maintenance, 228–230
minimum set of, 232, 233
OOT, 336, 337
  class coupling, 338
  class response, 338
  depth of inheritance tree, 337
  lack of method cohesion, 338
  measuring complexity of interactions
    in design, 337
  number of children, 338
  weighted methods per class, 337
possibilities using, 285
practitioners, lessons learned from, 230
  focusing on few characteristics, 230
  relying on simple measuring, 230
program evolution, 237
resources, 231
  miscellaneous, 234
  U.S. Army, 231, 234
SEI recommendations for, 223, 224
  effort, 225, 226
  quality, 228
  schedule, 227
  size, 224, 225
SEI summary, 228

set, 228–230
software, 215, 216
STEP, 234
models, maintenance, 37
  business oriented, 40
  classification of, 40
  CMM, 40
  history of, 39–46
  IEEE, 41–46
  ISO/IEC, 47–50
  organizational-oriented, 40
  process-oriented, 40
  SEI process modeling, 40
  stages, 39
modification implementation activity,
    ISO/IEC 12207, 62, 63
  development process, 64–71
    coding and testing, 64, 67, 68
    software analysis, 64, 65
    software architectural design, 64, 66
    software detailed design, 64, 67
    software installation, 64, 70, 71
    software integration, 64, 68, 69
    software qualification testing, 64, 70
  items to be modified, 64
  tasks, 63
modification request (MR), *see MR*
morale, maintenance management, 300,
    301
  solution to low, 301
MR (modification request), 3
  importance of, 58
  ISO/IEC 12207, 57
  metrics scheduling, 227
  task, task-steps, 58

N

National Institute of Standards and
    Technology (NIST) Reference
    Model for Frameworks of Software
    and Technology, 204
NIST (National Institute of Standards
    and Technology) Reference Model
    for Frameworks of Software and
    Technology, 204

O

object-oriented analysis (OOA), 328
object-oriented database, (OODB), 330,
    331
object-oriented design (OOD), 327, 328
object-oriented programming (OOP), 328
object-oriented technology (OOT), *see*
    OOT
object-oriented testing 329, 330
objects, OOT, 323
OO
    maintainability, 334, 335
    systems, maintenance of, 332
OOA (object-oriented analysis)
    described, 325
    maintainer requirements in, 326
    methodologies to perform, 326
OOD (object-oriented design), 327, 328
OODB (object-oriented database), 330, 331
OOP (object-oriented programming), 328
OOT (object-oriented technology)
    advantages, perceived, 331
    common definitions, 324
    development methodologies, 336
    development time and, 333
    ease of maintainability and, 334
    encapsulation, 324
    enhanced modifiability and, 334
    future of, 347
    implementing approach, 324
    increasing use of, 331–333
    lessons learned, 338, 339
    messages, 324
    methodologies, 336
    methods, 324
    metrics, 336, 337
        class coupling, 338
        class response, 338
        depth of inheritance tree, 337
        lack of method cohesion, 338
        measuring complexity of interactions
            in design, 337
        number of children, 338
        weighted methods per class, 337
    objects, 323
    OO terms, 325–331

planning maintenance, 101
practitioner views of, 333, 334
qualoty and, 334
reuse and, 333
software maintenance, impact on, 323
summary, 339, 340
training, 335, 336
use of, 323, 324
Operations and Maintenance phase
    consumption of software life-cycle
        resources, 31, 32
    described, 13
    Evolutionary model, 12
    Incremental model, 10, 11
    planning, importance of in cost
        reduction, 33
    Waterfall model, 10
organization, maintenance
    maintenance organization within
        software development, 180
    organization of, 176–182
    small maintenance organization, 182
    separate maintenance organization,
        181
    software development organization,
        179, 180
    successful, 3
    system development organization,
        177–179
    typical systems organization, 176, 177
output items, ISO/IEC, 54, 56
outsourcing, future of, 350

P

parametric models, personnel resource
    planning, 103, 104, 108–112
PCA (physical configuration audits), 72
PC/X-terminal operations, COSEE, 209,
    210
perfective maintenance category, 15, 16
personnel resources, organizational
    structure
    distribution of, 182–184
personnel resources, planning
    maintenance, 101–103
    case study, 106–112

estimating tools, 103, 104
experience (using), 104
empirical data, 104, 105
peers, 105
practical experience, 105
personnel resources, planning transition,
130, 133, 134
physical configuration audits (PCA), 72
Pigoski, maintenance responsibility, 21–27
plan
maintenance, 89
described, 96
factors to be considered, 96
metrics, addressing, 99
practical example of, 97, 98
supportability, addressing, 98, 99
transition
described, 123
vs. maintenance plan, 123–125
planning, maintenance, 89
need for, 89, 90
OOT, 101
reducing life-cycle costs via, 89, 90
postdelivery process, tailoring, 91, 92
PR (problem report), 3
ISO/IEC 12207, 57
predelivery maintenance, software, 86
predelivery stage, software maintenance,
81
conflict resolution, 83, 84
influence on maintenance costs, 82
maintainer involvement in, 85
problems of involving maintainer in,
82, 83
preventative maintenance category, 16, 17
problem and modification analysis
activity, 59–62
problem report (PR), 3
ISO/IEC 12207, 57
process
automation, future of, 348
hierarchy, ISO/IEC, 54
implementation activity, ISO/IEC,
55–59
maturity models, 41
program comprehension, 35
programmer's workbench (PWB), 200

prototyping, Spiral model and, 39
PWB (programmer's workbench), 200

Q

QA (quality assurance), maintainer
function, 173, 174
quality
defined, 273
OOT, 334
software, 284
quality assurance (QA), maintainer
function, 173, 174

R

remote software maintenance, future of,
349
requirements phase, Code and Fix
development model, 38
resources, software maintenance
academic, Centre for Software
Maintenance (CSM), 341
conferences and workshops
International Conference on
Software Management (ICSM), 342
U.S. Professional Development
Institute (USPDI), 342
Internet, 343
periodicals
IEEE Computer, 343
IEEE Software, 343
Journal of Systems and Software,
343
Journal of Software Maintenance:
Research and Practice, 342
recent research, 343, 345
reuse, OOT, 333
Rumbaugh (OMT), OOA methodologies,
326

S

Schneidewind, difficulties associated with
maintenance, 19, 20
SCM (software configuration
management), 59

SCMP (software configuration
   management plan), 120
scope, software maintenance, 90
SDF (software development folder), 59
   transition planning, 121
SEE (Software Engineering
   Environment), defined, 191, 192
SEI (Software Engineering Institute)
   metrics summary, 228
   process modeling, 40
   recommendations for metrics, 223, 224
      effort, 225, 226
      quality, 228
      schedule, 227
      size, 224, 225
separate maintainers performing
   maintenance, 23–26
   advantages, 23, 24
   disadvantages, 25, 26
Shlaer-Mellor, OOA methodologies, 326
Siedewitz-Stark, OOA methodologies, 326
software, COSEE
   distribution, 209, 210
   tools, evaluating, 206
software configuration management
   (SCM), 59
software configuration management plan
   (SCMP), 120
   maintainer function, 168, 169
software configuration tool (CCC), 209
software development, life-cycle cost and,
   30
software development folder (SDF), *see*
   SDF
software development methodologies,
   future of, 348, 349
software development transition, 120,
   121
software engineering, software
   maintenance and, 7
Software Engineering Environment
   (SEE), defined, 191, 192
Software Engineering Institute (SEI), *see*
   SEI
software evaluation categories (USAF),
   281
Software life-cycle costs

devoted to maintenance, 31
   ISO/IEC maintenance as part of, 51, 52
   maintenance cost as percentage of, 30
software maintenance, 4, 7
   defined, 8
   education, *see education and training;
      training*
   future of
      COTS products, 349
      maintenance environments, 348
      OOT, 347
      outsourcing, 350
      process automation, 348
      remote software maintenance, 349
      software development methodologies,
         348, 349
      standards, 350
   management, *see management*
   metrics, *see metrics*
   need for, 12–14
   OOT impact on, 323
   postdelivery stage, 81
   predelivery maintenance, 86
   predelivery stage, 81
      conflict resolution, 83, 84
      influence on maintenance costs, 82
      maintainer involvement in, 85
      problems of involving maintainer in,
         82, 83
   professionals, 293, 294
   published information on, 7, 8
   resources, 341–350. *See also resources*
   scope of, 90, 91
   training, *see education and training;
      training*
software metric, described, 215–217
software modification, maintainer
   function, 167, 168
Software Productivity Research (SPR), 105
software quality, 284
software retirement activity, ISO/IEC,
   77–80
software supportability (USAF), 279
software test environment (STE), 191
software transition, *see transition*
SOPs (standard operating procedures),
   141

source code guidelines, Federal
  Government addressing
  maintainability 277
speed of transition, 130, 133
Spiral model, 38, 39
SPR (Software Productivity Research), 105
Stagewise model, 38
standard operating procedures (SOPs),
  141
standards, future of, 350
STE (software test environment), 191
supplier, defined, 4
support items, ISO/IEC, 54, 56
supportability, addressing in
  maintenance plan, 98, 99
Swanson, E.B., "fixes" categorization, 15,
  16
system, ISO/IEC 12207 (1995) definition,
  8
System Life-Cycle
  defined, 8–10
  Evolutionary model, 11, 12, 13, 14
  IEC 12207, fitting software into, 9, 10
  Incremental model, 10, 11, 12, 13, 14
  interpreted, 9
  maintenance and, 8
  preplanned product improvement
    model, 10, 11, 12
  Waterfall model, 10, 11, 13
    drawbacks of, 10

T

technical assistance, maintainer function,
  174
testing, 172, maintainer function, 173
testing phase, Code and Fix development
  model, 38
testing standards and procedures,
  Federal Government addressing
  maintainability, 278
"toaster" model, 204
tool summary, COSEE, 206, 207
topology, COSEE, 207
  logical COSEE topology, 208
tracking system for maintenance, 58
training, *see also education and training*

described, 305
maintainer function, 170
transition, 130, 133
transfer of knowledge, 129, 131, 132
transition, software, 117
  case studies
    maintainer "comfort", 139–146
    transition systems, 157–163
    transition training, 146–153
  checklist for, 127, 128
  communications
    with developer, 129, 132
    with the user, 129, 130, 132
  complications during, 118, 119
  conflict complicating transition, 119, 120
  cost of, 130, 134, 135
  documentation, 129, 132
  experiences, 139
    maintainer "comfort" case study,
      139–146
    transition training case study,
      146–153
  issues involved in 129, 130
  maintainer transition, 121–123
  model and process, 135
    software configuration management
      (SCM), 135, 136
    summary, 138
    transition model, 136, 137, 138
  OOT, 335, 336
  personnel involved in, 130, 133, 134
  plan
    described, 123
    vs. maintenance plan, 123–125
  planning, defined, 118
  smooth, orderly plan, importance of,
    125–127, 148
  software assessment, 150–152
  software development transition, 120,
    121
  speed of, 130, 133
  training, 130, 133, 154, 155
    case study, 146–153
  transfer of knowledge, 129, 131, 132
  transition systems case study, 157–163
  turnover process, 130, 132
turnover process, transition, 130, 132

U

unmaintainable software, causes of, 282, 283
upper, CASE tools, 190
U.S. Army, addressing maintainability, 281
U.S. Professional Development Institute (USPDI), 342
U.S. West, software maintenance and, 26
user, defined, 4
user liaison and help desk, maintainer function, 171, 172
USPDI (U.S. Professional Development Institute), 342

W

Waterfall
    development model, 38, 39
        enhancements to Stagewise model, 38
        problems associated with, 38
        Spiral model and, 38, 39
    System Life Cycle model, 10, 11
        drawbacks of, 10
        Operations and Maintenance phase, 10, 13
Wirfs-Brock, OOA methodologies, 326